FROM BERLIN
TO THE BURDEKIN

FROM BERLIN TO THE BURDEKIN

The German contribution to the development of Australian science, exploration and the arts

Edited by

David Walker and Jürgen Tampke

PRESS

Published by
NEW SOUTH WALES UNIVERSITY PRESS
PO Box 1 Kensington NSW Australia 2033
Phone (02) 398 8900 Fax (02) 398 3408

First published 1991

National Library of Australia
Cataloguing-in-Publication entry:

From Berlin to the Burdekin: the German contribution to the development of Australian science, exploration and the arts.

Bibliography.
Includes index.
ISBN 0 86840 332 6.

1. Germans — Australia — History. 2. Science — Australia — History. 3. Arts — Australia — History. 4. Australia — Discovery and exploration. I. Walker, David (David Robert). II. Tampke, Jürgen.

994.00431

Available in North America through:
International Specialized Book Services
5602 N.E. Hassalo Street
Portland Oregon 97213–3640
United States of America
Printed in Singapore through GlobalCom Pte Ltd

ACKNOWLEDGEMENTS

This book was made possible through the generous financial assistance of the University of New South Wales, Bayer Australia, Dalgety Australia Operations and Deutschtours of Australia.

CONTENTS

Introduction   vii

PART 1 SCIENCE AND EXPLORATION
1. Exploration as escape: Baron Sir Ferdinand von Müller
   Edward Kynaston   3
2. The education of an explorer: Ludwig Leichhardt
   Colin Roderick   22
3. Georg von Neumayer and the Flagstaff Observatory
   R.W. Home   40
4. Amalie Dietrich *Ray Sumner*   54
5. Robert von Lendenfeld: biologist, alpinist and scholar
   David Sandeman   67

PART 2 ENCOUNTERING ABORIGINAL CULTURE
6. Ludwig Becker and Eugène von Guérard: German
   artists and the Aboriginal habitat *Marjorie Tipping*   81
7. In Search of Carl Strehlow: Lutheran Missionary and
   Australian Anthropologist *Walter Veit*   108
8. The study of Australian Aboriginal culture by German
   anthropologists of the Frobenius Institute
   Silke Beinssen-Hesse   135

PART 3 LITERATURE AND IDENTITY
9. Hugo Zöller: a German view of Australian society
   Irmline Veit-Brause   153
10. Imagining an Australian nation: The German community
    of South Australia during the nineteenth century
    Gerhard Fischer   175
11. The 'Vossification' of Ludwig Leichhardt *H. Priessnitz*   196
12. Leichhardt's diaries *Robert Sellick*   218
13. Intercultural encounters: Aborigines and white explorers
    in fiction and non-fiction *Volker Raddatz*   228

Notes   241
Bibliography   257
Index   267
Notes on Contributors   273

INTRODUCTION

The last decade has seen a wave of publications dealing with the role played by Germany and German-speaking people in Australia's modern history. Evidence of rising interest in this field goes back to the 1960s and 1970s[1] but the 1980s saw an avalanche of publications connected in one way or another with the topic Germany and Australia.[2] They all stress—it is commonplace today—the importance of the contribution made by Germans in Australia since white settlement, a contribution which unfortunately fell victim to the anti-Germanism of this century. Indeed a recent book on the topic claims that the Germans, after the Aborigines and the British–Irish, were the third most important contributor to our history.[3]

During the Bicentenary year a number of Australian and German academics from a wide range of fields, other scholars and interested members of the public, attended an interdisciplinary conference held at the University of New South Wales to discuss the German contribution to exploration and the development of science and the arts in Australia. *From Berlin to the Burdekin* offers the reader a selection of the many papers presented.

Edward Kynaston's introductory article on Baron Sir Ferdinand Jakob Heinrich von Müller—distinguished botanist and explorer as well as the author of many works on Australia's flora and fauna—refers to Patrick White's reminder that exploration is a two-way process: explorers not only act upon, but are also acted on (and transformed) by their subjects. In a challenging and daring opening chapter Kynaston argues that it was not simply for health reasons (von Müller's family was suffering from pulmonary tuberculosis) or scientific curiosity that led him to come to Australia: it was essentially exploration as an escape. As with Leichhardt, in von Müller the two way process of exploration eventually merged.

The great explorer himself is analysed in chapter two. Leichhardt, a legend in his own time and an outstanding Australian explorer, was perhaps the most maligned victim of the anti-Germanism that has prevailed for most of this century. Professor Colin Roderick shows how the basis of the explorer's excellent scientific performance goes back to his thorough education before his departure for Australia—an area in which up until now there has been no substantial research. Professor Roderick carefully traces every educational step, from his Gymnasium years at Cottbus, his philological and philosophical studies at Berlin University, his move into the natural sciences at Göttingen and his extensive studies in Paris, all of which illustrate Leichhardt's enormous scientific curiosity.

The three scientists and explorers who conclude Part One are—because their field of interest lay outside that of the 'glamour' sciences, or because their work only recently has been rediscovered, or because of their limited stay in Australia—relatively unknown to the public. Professor Rod Home (Melbourne University) deals with the founder of the Flagstaff Observatory in Melbourne, Georg von Neumayer, who, although a well-known personality in Melbourne during his stay, subsequently fell into oblivion in Australia (while in his homeland he became one of the most highly respected scientists of his age in the field of hydrography, meteorology and terrestrial magnetism.) Home shows the background to the establishment of the Melbourne Flagstaff Observatory which conducted a series of research projects partly for straight economic reasons—an understanding of the winds and currents of major ocean trade routes would result in more efficient shipping—and partly to gather information which fascinated the scientists in his field such as meteorological observations, recording of weather patterns and magnetic surveys. Professor Home's article shows that von Neumayer in his approach was well ahead of his time and has to be ranked as a significant figure in the history of science in nineteenth century Australia.

Ray Sumner deals with a rare phenomenon in nineteenth century Australia and Europe: a woman scientist. By placing some of the previous popular accounts of Amalie Dietrich into proper perspective, Dr Sumner presents the first thoroughly researched account of the fascinating story and work of this outstanding woman who spent nine years in Queensland assembling an enormous collection of Australiana (Aboriginal artifacts, birds, reptiles, insects and plants). Robert Ignaz Lendlmayr von Lendenfeld was born in Graz, Austria, in 1856. A biologist and keen alpinist (he had several first ascents in the Austrian Alps to his credit) von Lendenfeld lived in Australia and New Zealand with his wife for four and a half years (1881–1885), mainly lecturing at technical and agricultural colleges. David Sandeman (Professor of Zoology at the University of New South Wales) has studied the Austrian's time and work in

Australia. His article concentrates in particular on Lendenfeld's role
in the controversy (still newsworthy) over whether Strzelezki was
referring to Australia's highest mountain when he named it Mt
Kosciusko or whether he was measuring the slightly lower peak of
Mt Townsend.

Substantial as the changes in the evaluation of the role played
by German speaking people in Australia are, there has been in
recent decades an even greater change in the interpretation of the
life and lifestyle of the Australian Aborigine. Part Two deals with
German–Aboriginal encounters. Marjorie Tipping argues that
German scientists and artists did not regard the Aboriginal people
as inferior. Much earlier than the British, artists such as the Austrian Eugène von Guérard (who came to Australia to seek gold) and
the Hessian Ludwig Becker (who was forced to leave his homeland
in 1848 for political reasons and who came to an ignominious end
in the Burke and Wills expedition) painted realistic and compas-
sionate pictures of the Aborigines. Professor Walter Veit (Department of German, Monash University) writes about another
German–Australian who has virtually fallen into obscurity:
the missionary and anthropologist Carl Strehlow, father of
T.G.H. Strehlow, a very controversial figure in Australian anthropology. Carl Strehlow lived among the Australian Aborigines for
almost thirty years. He first arrived in Australia in 1892 to take up
duties as Lutheran missionary at the Bethesda station near the
Birdsville track, south of Coopers Creek, from where he was
instructed by the Lutheran church elders to take over the
Hermannsburg mission station (130 km south-west of Alice
Springs) which the previous missionaries had been forced to abandon. An excellent observer and scholar of Aboriginal culture and
customs, Carl Strehlow published the seven volume *Die Aranda und
Lorita-Stämme in Zentral-Australien* between 1907 and 1920. But
the combined impact of two World Wars and the 'scientific' paradigm of social anthropology and empirical field studies that followed in the wake of Baldwin Spencer ensured that the work of the
missionary was pushed into the background. Veit argues persua-
sively that the translation of his works should now be published
urgently to enable Strehlow's outstanding scholarly contribution to
be recognized.

Finally, Silke Beinssen-Hesse deals with more recent German
research into the work of the Froebenius Institut in Frankfurt
(Main), which sent anthropologists to Australia in 1938, and the

findings of their successors after World War Two, who concentrated on Aboriginal society at a time when it was attempting to come to terms with white culture.

Opening part three, 'Literature, society and identity', Associate Professor Irmline Veit-Brause presents a late 19th century view of Australian society: the work of Hugo Zöller, journalist for the *Kölnische Zeitung* and a keen advocate of German colonialism. Zöller, 'a cosmopolitan anglophile German nationalist' (seemingly a contradiction in terms but according to Veit-Brause a not uncommon phenomenon at that time[4] advances an interesting sociological analysis of life and people 'downunder' concentrating in particular on Melbourne and Sydney. Germany's economic interests were often at the heart of Zöller's observation. Writing at a time when Germany was beginning to establish itself as a major power in the South Pacific, the journalist stressed the key role Australia was playing in the region and by doing so anticipated the Australian–German tension which was to prove so fatal in the 20th century. This emergence of Australian–German rivalry is also the topic of Gerhard Fischer's article on the Australian nationalism that was developing among the South Australian German community. With reference to some of their leading citizens, in particular Carl Wilhelm Ludwig Muecke, Fischer shows how the South Australian German community, the largest in Australia, tried to imbue the colony (and the continent) with the spirit of 1848: the establishment of liberal democratic institutions and the formation of a national identity. This did not mean that the German settlers wanted to break colonial connections with the mother country—they too showed loyalty to the British crown but in contrast to the British–Australians, their loyalty to Australia came first. And it was this Australian nationalism of the German community which so greatly antagonized the British–Australians before and during the Great War.

In its last three chapters the book returns again to Ludwig Leichhardt. Horst Priessnitz, Professor of Anglistik at the Bergische Universität, Wuppertal, offers a fascinating analysis of the changing literary interpretation of the great explorer from the over-romanticized hero worship of the Victorian age through Alec Chisholm's 'constitutional psychopath' to his 'reprussianisation' ('Johann Ludwig Ulrich Leichhardt zu Voss') in Randolph Stow's novel *Midnite*. To Priessnitz, Stow's children's novel is the final product of the Vossification of Leichhardt: that he was (and still is) at every stage of his career a personification of the desires and problems of Australian society. Robert Sellick, who together with Marlies Thiers is publishing Leichhardt's diaries, highlights the problems and difficulties facing the biographer and at the same time gives us a foretaste of the fascinating material contained in the diaries. Sellick refers to the tension that is created between the primary impulse of the explorer and the diaries' emphasis on a rejection of the external world which makes the *Tagebücher*, and Leichhardt himself, such a fascinating object of study. Lastly, Volker Raddatz presents a comparative analysis of Patrick White's *Voss* and Leichhardt's '*Journal of an overland expedition*' with particular emphasis on White–Aboriginal encounters. Raddatz does not attempt an historical evaluation of the novel but shows how fiction and non-fiction illustrate cultural affinities and differences.

The chapters presented in *From Berlin to the Burdekin* illustrate the depth and range of the German contribution to the formation of this country. They also suggest the rich potential for research into the German presence over two centuries.

Jürgen Tampke   David Walker
University of New South Wales, Kensington   Deakin University, Geelong

Part 1

Science and Exploration

Exploration as escape:
Baron Sir Ferdinand von Müller

Edward Kynaston

Exploration is a strange business and one we tend to take far too much for granted in Australia. Curiosity is one of the most powerful of human instincts, but having said that, we too often take the motivations of explorers to be of the most singular and simplistic sort.

The era of earth exploration came largely to an end during the last century and a very different era began. With the surface of the earth known, if not always adequately mapped, and the technology for planetary exploration not yet available, it was probably inevitable that an era of outward orientation should begin to be replaced by one of internal orientation.

It seems to me to be a significant coincidence that in the year 1900, when Sigmund Freud published his *Interpretation of Dreams*, the exploration of the continents, with the exception of Antarctica, was complete. It also seems to me a pleasant paradox that the awakening to modern *self*-consciousness should have begun through dreams and the *un*conscious.

Freud, Jung, and Adler accelerated a new and growing awareness of long-neglected areas of the human psyche. Creatures who had been mostly world-aware began slowly to become more self-aware, a still continuing process that may yet be accelerated by the absence of other life forms in our corner of the universe, and the extreme difficulty of human exploration of the outer planets and possible nearby systems in our galaxy. Earth exploration has come to an end. Planetary exploration ended almost before it had begun. It seems that there is nowhere to turn now for further exploration but ourselves.

Australia was the last of the continents to become fully explored. Again, I think, significantly, the last Australian expedition of importance was mounted in the year 1901, when F.S. Drake-Brockman led a successful expedition to the centre of the Kimberleys in Western Australia.

Here in Australia, adjacent as we are to Antarctica, we are probably more aware of the importance of explorers and exploration than people in longer and more densely settled areas of the world. Our explorers are still part of our awareness, still recent enough to provoke our interest and concern, still close enough to seem ordinary human beings to whom we can relate and whose motives we can question.

The motives of explorers have been as various as the people themselves. Like unclimbed mountains the empty spaces on the maps beckoned certain people powerfully. Curiosity, a sense of strange destiny, ambition, evangelism, science, territorial acquisition have all been primary motives of explorers. Profit has been more often a secondary motive than one might think. Economic determinism has proved to be a limited and inadequate explanation.

Leichhardt, that most fascinating of Australian explorers, opened up huge areas of grazing land as a consequence of his expedition to Port Essington. Major Mitchell opened up the rich grazing land of the Western District. For both Leichhardt and Mitchell the opening of the land to settlement was incidental to the serious business of exploration. Profit was almost always more in the thoughts of the stay-at-home moneybags who backed the expeditions than in the minds of the explorers advancing day after tedious day across awesomely unfamiliar territory.

That profit may be a concealed motive is evident enough. Some concealments were odder than others. This was particularly the case in South Africa where, by the time exploration was complete, a Zulu could sum it up neatly in his comment to a white missionary: 'When you came we had the land and you had the Bible, now you have the land and we have the Bible.'

There are other stranger motives, none more curious perhaps than the English Public School ethos and sense of Imperial Destiny in the motivation of the hugely heroic but massively incompetent and misconceived expedition to the South Pole in 1911 of Captain Robert Falcon Scott. In its own bizarre way Scott's expedition seems almost to have been a prefiguring of the ineptitude of the General Staffs and the senseless slaughter of the First World War that was already looming on the horizon in the Agadir crisis of the same year.

In the long years of relative tranquillity that had marked the reigns of Queen Victoria and King Edward the Seventh, society had become flaccid, airless, imprisoning. Young men felt this keenly. They felt the need of more robust activity, a more bracing air, a more challenging way of life. So that when war came in 1914 the poet Rupert Brooke could write, inexplicably as it seems to us now, of turning to it,

'Glad from a world grown old and cold and dreary',

and more grandiloquently,

'Now God be thanked who has matched us with this hour.'

There is no denying that there is something of this heedless do-or-die feeling in Scott and in the members of his expedition. It is a notable undercurrent in the superficially simple motivation, muddying the apparent purity of the hearty, the heroic intention. It is also a useful reminder that the motives, even the motives of the noblest explorers, are not always as simple and straightforward as they would believe or have us believe.

Women explorers have always been thin on the ground and particularly so in Australia. We can boast no Lady Hester Stanhopes, no indefatigable Mary Kingsleys plunging on through steaming heat decorously dressed in layer after layer of constricting Victorian women's clothing. Nor can we count on notable eccentrics and romantics like Sir Richard Burton, invader of sacred forbidden Mecca, explorer of the Nile basin, explorer of the highlands of Brazil and almost everywhere else you care to think of. Burton was a prolific author with a list of books as long as your arm including, beside the many books of his travels, treatises on *Falconry in the Valley of the Indus*, *The Book of the Sword*, *A Complete System of*

Bayonet Exercise, and translations of the erotic masterpieces *The Kama Sutra* and *The Thousand Nights and a Night.*

In examining the motives of explorers it is important to beware of stereotypes. It is also important to recognise the variety and subtlety and complexity of the motives involved. There is, for instance, an element of identity-seeking in most explorers. It seems that some people can only find and confront the unknown within themselves by finding and confronting the unknown beyond themselves. Exploration of the geographical unknown becomes, simultaneously, exploration of the psychological unknown.

At its simplest this may occur as a challenging of feelings of inferiority, or a testing of reaction to acutely recognised and deeply held fears. In the case of a Sir Richard Burton, or a Ludwig Leichhardt for that matter, the motivation becomes enormously complex, elusive and sophisticated. Nothing is plain or obvious. It was no accident that a great creative artist like Patrick White should have sensed the complicated dark depths of Leichhardt, with all their immense possibilities, and based Voss, a giant mystical character, upon him.

Voss is not only about a man, it is about the profoundest nature of a continent. Voss and the continent are almost interchangeable entities, metaphors for one another. As the unknown continent takes in Voss (the pun is intentional), so Voss takes into himself aspects of the ancientness, the mystery of the continent.

It takes a Patrick White, or a Carl Gustav Jung, to remind us that exploration is a two-way process. Explorers not only act upon, but are consequently acted on and transformed by their subjects. Ludwig Leichhardt, despite his antecedents and nationality, was an Australian. The continent claimed him almost as soon as he landed here. His letters of those first days have a rapturous, lyrical quality. There is in them the joy of recognition and of love. There is something supremely, if tragically, appropriate and inevitable in his disappearance, and in the mystery of that disappearance that he left behind him. Leichhardt and Australia remain secret. And what better place to hide secrets than in our brilliant light in which everything is plain and obvious and of course nothing at all is plain and obvious.

Australia has intoxicated very few explorers. More commonly it has dried out and sobered its investigators; except when it has not actually destroyed them, as it did Burke and Wills with their top-heavy expedition and their careless presumption. This continent has always demanded respect, humility, and care. It has responded best to men like the still underestimated Gregory brothers, superb bushmen with a feeling for the land, and unobtrusive masters of the logistics of expeditions in Australian conditions. The Gregory brothers were oddly modest men. Their occupation was surveying, their vocation exploration. Their vocation was their motive, and their motive was their vocation. It was, for once, as simple as that. They were professionals.

Ferdinand Müller's motives for exploration were, on the face of it, simple enough. He was a botanist. He was also something of a geologist, biologist, geographer, forester, agriculturist, chemist, pharmacist, taxonomist. But botany was his subject, and still largely unexplored Australia his delightful treasure house of unknown, undiscovered, beautiful, utilitarian, bizarre botanical specimens. What more simple and natural than that he should become involved in exploration?

A character in Melville's *Moby Dick*, long before psychiatric Mr Laing and his book of psychological knots, remarks that 'the simplest things are the knottiest of all'. Ferdinand Müller was, on closer examination, as complex and contradictory a mass of cordage as anyone could imagine. He was haunted, perhaps obsessed, by the ghost of Ludwig Leichhardt. Müller arrived in Australia in December 1847. Leichhardt set off from western Queensland on his last expedition early in April 1848, four months later. He expected to be away two and a half years. He never re-emerged from the interior.

In 1850, six months before the two and a half years planned by Leichhardt has elapsed, Müller has begun writing to the *Adelaide Deutsche Zeitung*. He proposed an expedition to travel to an area around the boundary of South Australia where he believed Leichhardt's party might still be. His experience of Australian conditions was at this time limited to solitary excursions, on foot, to the Mount Lofty ranges behind Adelaide, the Murray scrubs, and further afield along the Flinders Ranges to the vicinity of Lake Torrens. Müller was being presumptuous to put it mildly. Needless to say no one took much notice.

Müller was still a tyro. He was a good botanist but still an amateur explorer. He worked at a pharmacist's shop in Adelaide's Rundle Street and botanised in his spare time. He was a prodigious walker. He thought nothing of walking hundreds of miles. He preferred to walk. As he walked he observed and learned, absorbing the hard lessons of the bush: how to cope with the heat, flies, stinging ants, mosquitoes, snakes, lizards, spiders, possums, wallabies, kangaroos and a startling variety of birds. Especially the sulphur-crested cockatoos that hung untidily in the trees like washing and almost deafened him with their resentful cries.

He had to learn to appreciate the value of water and the indications of its presence. He had to learn to survive on damper bread and dried or salted meat, and to drink his tea with sugar but without milk. His scientific training made him an excellent navigator through uncharted country even with very simple instruments. Later, almost as an afterthought, as the immensity of the country became a reality to him, he learned to manage horses, how to travel fast and light, how to repair harness and make hobbles. He botanised indefatigably all the time. Excursions and expeditions got him away from other human beings. Botanising gave to his wanderings an extra purpose. He began to be at home in the bush. He was never comfortable or at home among people in large towns and cities.

Müller's health improved. Rough living hardened him, filled out his small frame. And he grew a beard. The disease he had learned to fear never struck him.

Müller had always been preoccupied with health and, inevitably, with its antithesis, disease. In this case the disease was pulmonary tuberculosis, the wasting, the burning up of the lungs, that had been the scourge of Europe for centuries. The reason he and his two sisters were in Australia was tuberculosis, and its seemingly inescapable concomitant, death.

Ferdinand Müller was born in Rostock in northern Germany. His father was a customs officer who had become infected with pulmonary tuberculosis, or consumption as it became known. Consumption was a good name. Müller's childhood was spent watching his father being consumed by the disease, listening to his insistent dry cough, hiding from the great feverish flushes, running in fear from the wild oscillations of mood between rage and euphoria that have always characterised the pulmonary tuberculosis patient. Death was omnipresent in his house.

Müller had one older and two younger sisters. His mother was harassed, overworked, always tired from nursing her husband. It was a sad, difficult childhood, and its painful lessons were not over. Müller was ten in 1835 when his father died. Soon after, he saw for the first time in his mother the unmistakable signs of the tuberculosis that had killed his father. The Müllers moved to the small coastal town of Tönning to be near relatives. Müller's mother weakened, took to her bed, coughed up more and more blood. The years moved at a funereal pace. It must have seemed to the adolescent boy that eternity was something that began to occur long before death.

Tönning had its small compensations. In Eiderstedt, the country around the town, there was the welcome impersonality of grass and sea, sand and sky, and great natural beauty. This was a crucial period for the young Müller. The biggest, hardest lessons of his life so far had been that human relationships were painful and dangerous, and that human beings were essentially untrustworthy: they died. Solitude, nature, were safer and more rewarding. As I have written elsewhere:

> Eiderstedt was his first landscape to explore. He became accustomed to space around him. He learned to enjoy and treasure birds and plants and animals. Alone he felt much safer than among human beings. He absorbed the dunes and meres and sea and beaches and they filled him and shaped him. Death was dark narrow rooms and the corrupting flesh of human beings. Life was light and space and boundless nature all around. As his unconscious attitude to people narrowed so his attitude to the world broadened to the furthest horizons. His interior landscape formed and began to establish itself. It was a landscape without figures.

Muller had found a way of escape. An explorer was born.

The long journey from Eiderstedt and North Germany to the Murray scrubs and the Victoria Desert was more inevitable than it might have appeared. The fit and bronzed and bearded young man tramping happily hundreds of miles through the Australian bush was closer than Müller might have dared hope at that time and in those tragic circumstances.

Müller's mother died in 1840 and he was apprenticed to, and went to live in, a local *Apotheke*, or pharmacist's, in the nearby small town of Husum. He began in earnest to study botany. His other, much harder, lessons were not quite complete. Iwanne, his elder sister, had contracted the tuberculosis that had killed her parents. Müller plunged into his studies, spent all his spare time out doing fieldwork. He seldom went home to Tönning. His sister Iwanne died early in 1843.

Müller was eighteen. His life was a monotony of mourning and death only marginally alleviated by study and fieldwork. Iwanne's death intensified his isolation. He studied doggedly, French, Latin, Greek, mathematics, chemistry, laboratory procedures. Each year he took his examinations at the University of Kiel. He received his degree in pharmacy in 1846, and at once submitted a botanical thesis that he had been working on for several years. The thesis was accepted. He was awarded the degree of doctor of philosophy.

It seemed that the dark shadows that had been cast over his life were beginning to fade. They were replaced by even more ominous ones. Bertha, one of his younger sisters, had begun to show what he believed to be the first signs of tuberculosis. His own health, long under siege from grief, worry, overwork and the strain of preparing his thesis, broke down. He had, in fact, a massive psychosomatic reaction, in the course of which he became hypochondriacal about his own health, especially about his lungs. And who would blame him?

Somehow he managed to pull himself together. At the limit of his defences he turned and fought back. He had seen too much bleeding and blistering and starvation diet, which were the recognised treatments of the day. He determined to take his sisters and leave, escape to a warmer climate where their chances of good health would be better. He thought first of Madeira. But then an old family friend returned from Western Australia and talked to him of the exotic botanical novelty of the continent, of the vastness of the unexplored land.

Australia offered not one, but a series of escapes. First from the damp grey skies of northern Europe. Then the prospect of botanical fieldwork on a scale almost beyond imagining. Finally, and perhaps most appealing of all, Australia offered the ultimate escape: from responsibility for his sister's health, from the fragility of human relationships, from the death that had accompanied him for as long as he could remember. The unknown bush and deserts of Australia appeared infinitely preferable to the too well known darkness of death and emotional deprivation. Müller and his sisters sailed for South Australia.

The Mertenses, his mother's family, solid bourgeois to a man, were scandalised. The move to Australia was a chancy gamble and it was expensive. They were right, of course. It was a gamble. But since Müller was prepared to gamble he was favoured with the good luck he deserved and the gamble paid off handsomely. Running away, escaping, was, paradoxically, probably the only way open to him of trying to meet life head on.

He was never able to succeed wholly. He was too emotionally crippled to become involved in large areas of normal human intercourse and activity. Exploring, preferably alone, was the only activity in which he felt able to be wholly himself; then the tense, studious, withdrawn human being became something very different.

When gold was discovered in Victoria in 1852, Müller was almost at once invited to go to the goldfields as a pharmacist. He travelled to Victoria but only got as far as Melbourne. Having gambled again, he was again rewarded with good luck by being introduced to the Governor, C.J. La Trobe. La Trobe mentioned the meeting in a letter he wrote to a friend. 'There is an honest looking German here, Dr Müller, who as far as I can judge seems to be more of a botanist than any man I have hitherto met with in the colony; and I shall give him every encouragement.'

La Trobe did more than merely encourage. He ensured that Müller was appointed to the newly created post of Government Botanist of the Colony of Victoria.

Crowded gold-rush Melbourne was a very different place from quiet Adelaide. Thousands of people were pouring in from all over the world. While the streets were not exactly paved with gold there was plenty of gold in the streets in the pockets of diggers newly returned from the goldfields.

Melbourne was too much for Müller. He fled once more, accompanied by John Dallachy, a taciturn Scot who was the overseer of Melbourne's Botanical Gardens. It was another escape, from human beings, from the risk of too close human relationships. Only this time he was setting out on an officially sanctioned expedition of his own, and would soon be *on* his own as he preferred. Dallachy was on short leave from the Botanical Gardens. After they had climbed Mount Buffalo in north-east Victoria, the first white men to do so, Dallachy had to return to Melbourne.

Müller rode off by himself, with only a single packhorse, towards a high mountain he had seen to the south-west. He climbed the mountain, which was eventually to be named Mt Buller, and wandered happily off, meandering about the Great Dividing Range until he turned south-east and succeeded in reaching the south-east coast of Victoria. When he returned to Melbourne he had been away two months, had travelled 1500 miles in a state only the size of the British Isles, and carried in his saddlebags almost a thousand plant specimens.

Soon after he got back to Melbourne his sister Clara married

and went to live with her new husband in Mt Gambier. Bertha, his
other sister, went with them. Müller was free at last of his closest
human relationships. That he was grateful to be free is very clearly
demonstrated in his ensuring that all his future contacts with his
sisters were minimal and formal.

Whenever he could possibly manage it Müller got away from
the city crowds and went exploring around Victoria. As soon as his
sisters had departed he was off to the Grampian Mountains to the
west. From the Grampians he struck northward to the Murray River
and then travelled westward. He explored the Bogong Range,
crossed the Snowy Mountains, and followed the Snowy River down
to the coast. He was alone, and perfectly happy, for over three
months, in which he travelled 2500 miles. He brought back to
Melbourne 120 new botanical species.

Müller worked frantically on the specimens he had collected,
on papers and articles and on correspondence with learned societies
around the world. His frenetic activity did not prevent him making
short forays of exploration along the Victorian coastline whenever
he saw an opportunity. Australia suited him perfectly. His health
had improved and his constitution had hardened. He was, in fact,
as tough as an old boot. He was enjoying his success and he could
hardly believe his good health. But inside himself he was still the
same apprehensive old-young Ferdinand Müller. He still feared
that he might contract tuberculosis and was something of a
hypochondriac.

The solitary explorer who had lived contentedly alone in the
roughest conditions for months at a time bought himself a long
woollen muffler to wind around his neck to protect himself from the
chills that might so easily descend to his chest and lungs. Müller's
muffler subsequently followed him everywhere and into old age. He
wore it on every possible and impossible occasion. When he was an
old man he put it on to accompany visitors to the tram near his
house in 100°F Australian summer heat.

Despite his fears he was soon off again, into the Snowy Mountains. High in the hills he became ill with a fever. He lay alone for a
fortnight before he began to recover. There were small snowdrifts in
the hollows. The nights were freezing cold. He might have died but
he didn't. His hypochondria, his fear of tuberculosis and death were
dramatically revived. It took him six weeks to get back to
Melbourne.

Leichhardt still haunted Müller. He was a gaunt ghostly presence in almost every article Müller wrote about Australian exploration. In 1855 Müller was proposing yet another expedition in search of Leichhardt whom he believed to be a prisoner of natives in the interior. He had a strange strong faith in Leichhardt's survival, yet he must have known from his own experience that the chances of Leichhardt's survival were minimal. Again as I have written elsewhere: 'Like most highly rational men Müller was capable of resounding irrationalities. All that was starved in him—feeling, intuition, sentiment, love in the sense of romantic idealism—clung on to Leichhardt as a symbol, perhaps the most important symbol of his life.'

An expedition to north-west Australia was now in the offing. A Dr Thomson was to accompany the expedition as botanist but found himself unable to go. Müller took his place. He was already looking forward to an extended full-scale expedition in remote and unexplored country and the opportunity of finding new species of plants in northern Australia. But underlying this there was, undoubtedly, another motive, which was to travel through country that had been traversed by the man who was his hero, Ludwig Leichhardt.

The North Australian Expedition was led by A.C. Gregory. His second-in-command was his younger brother H.C. Gregory. The Gregorys were superb bushmen, fine organisers and perhaps most important of all, were men with a wide experience of the Australian outback.

The expedition was carried north by ship. It rounded Cape York in tropical waters and entered the Victoria River to the south of where Darwin is today. It was October. The thermometer showed 114°F in the shade. The expedition moved slowly inland. There were the usual difficulties and frustrations that beset large expeditions. Bread from the ship was found to be ruined by sea water, six and a half hundredweight of rice was spoiled. The small canvas boat in which they had intended to travel up the shallower reaches of the river was useless because the varnish used to seal the canvas had melted in the heat.

The Gregorys took it all philosophically. They possessed the most important basic attribute of explorers: unflappability. On 4 January 1856 a large party led by A.C. Gregory began to move south, through low rocky sandstone hills. Müller seems to have had quite enough of human beings by this time. Gregory's diary entry for 4 January reads: 'Started at 7 a.m. and followed up the creek; but

Dr Müller having wandered away into the rocky hills and lost himself, I halted at the first convenient spot, having despatched several of the party to search for him, but it was not until 4 p.m. that the Doctor reached the camp.'

It seems doubtful that Müller was actually lost; he was too good a bushman to let that happen. What seems more likely is that he needed to be by himself after many weeks of close proximity to the other members of the expedition, and made botanising his excuse. This is borne out by his behaviour throughout the remainder of the expedition when he proved himself as tough and competent as anyone else, including the Gregory brothers.

Müller's party reached the source of the Victoria River and penetrated into an area of salt lakes and desert. They returned, uneventfully, to their base on the Victoria River and set off, the whole expedition this time, to explore across northern Australia and then southward through the country backing the east coast.

Müller was in his element. Hard travel had brought out an innate toughness in him. In large landscapes he felt safe and free. In his exploration of them he discovered not only unique botanical specimens but new aspects of his own interior. His hypochondria seems to have vanished; his confidence in himself had grown. At times a sort of intoxication appears to have overtaken him, as if for the first time he felt wholly free from the visions of disease and death that had burdened him for so long. As if for a time, in these glorious moments of escape, he felt safe and secure in his own identity.

For most of his life Muller had doubted his own emotional identity. His greatest need was always to feel safe and sure in a solid reliable world. As a consequence he was, throughout his life, a pot-hunter, a seeker after honours, an over-anxious solicitor of recognition. It was a vulgar pursuit but he was compelled to it in order to prove his reality to himself. Honours were one of his defences against an intrusive and frighteningly lethal world. Ironically, his botanical work more than earned the large number of titles and honours he manoeuvred for and accumulated, among them a German barony and an English knighthood.

That Müller was literally riding high on the North Australia Expedition is proved by the entry from A.C. Gregory's diary for 29 July.

About three miles before we reached the camp, Dr. Muller had fallen some distance behind the party; but as this was a frequent occurrence in collecting botanical specimens it was not observed until we reached the camp, when he was out of sight. After unsaddling the packhorse, I was preparing to send in search of him, when he came up to the camp, the cause of the delay having been that his horse had knocked up. This was unfortunate as the load of one of the packhorses had to be distributed among the others in order to remount the Doctor who requires stronger horses than any other person in the party, having knocked up four since January, while not one of the riding horses has failed, though carrying heavy weights.

Müller's behaviour was uncharacteristic. He was sensitive, gentle and normally considerate and he must have understood the importance of horses to the success of the expedition. Yet he disregarded common sense, behaved badly, and became a source of worry to the expedition leader. It is possible, though rather unlikely, that he wanted to present himself as a hard case. In the end it is impossible to avoid the conclusion that Müller was inflated with his own success, inebriated with the momentary totality of his escape from the sickness that had shaped him secretly and determined the course of his life.

The expedition was a remarkable success, a success that was attributable largely to its leaders. Müller was very lucky to have taken part in a piece of major exploration under such outstanding leadership. The experience had changed him in the sense that he had become more the sort of person he really was. After the months in the north his own solitary travels round the Victorian Alps must have seemed like comfortable Sunday afternoon rambles.

He also learned thoroughly, possibly painfully, the lessons of large-scale exploration. He was never to forget them and subsequent expeditions both inside and outside Australia benefited from his experience. When he returned to Melbourne Müller was appointed Director of the Botanical Gardens in addition to his post as Government Botanist. In his spare time he was expected also to direct and manage a zoological gardens of thirty-three acres. His salary as Government Botanist was £600 a year. After his several new appointments his salary remained exactly £600 a year!

Müller worked indefatigably at all three appointments. He was in touch with correspondents all over the world and was soon writing 2000 letters a year. His correspondence with Sir William Hooker, of Kew Gardens, alone amounted finally to 29,000 letters.

The success of the North Australia Expedition encouraged

ideas of further exploration. Invoking the name of Leichhardt, which was rather like invoking the name of the Holy Ghost, a Dr Wilkie moved a resolution at a meeting of the Victorian Philosophical Institute proposing that newly gold-wealthy Victoria mount an expedition to cross Australia from east to west. Müller was elected a member of the Exploration Committee.

It was decided to ask A.C. Gregory's opinion of the route chosen. Gregory had just been appointed by the New South Wales Government to lead an expedition in search of Leichhardt. He intended to travel westward so the point of the Victorian proposal seemed to be lost. Müller then suggested an expedition northwards. In the meantime the committee awaited Gregory's reply.

Gregory spared the members of the committee nothing. Their proposal was hopelessly impractical, desperately difficult. He said: 'I therefore consider that it is almost hopeless to attempt to traverse this tract of country from east to west, and that the only prospect of success would be to penetrate it in the direction of the shorter diameter (north or south).'

It was almost exactly Müller's conclusion. One tragedy had been forestalled, but another had been set in train. Gregory's and Müller's suggestion led directly to the awful fiasco of the Burke and Wills expedition. If Müller and Gregory had got their way there would have been no catastrophe at Cooper's Creek. Müller made sure that Gregory was invited to lead the expedition. He was unable to go and suggested Major Warburton from South Australia, who was an experienced explorer. Müller strongly supported the Warburton proposal.

The Victorian Exploration Committee, flushed with parish pump patriotism, ignored this sensible suggestion and, rather as if they wanted an office boy or a tea lady, decided to *advertise* for a Victorian to lead the expedition. They got Robert O'Hara Burke, a Superintendent of Police, a man wholly innocent of experience of exploration, and the expedition departed in an Alice-In-Wonderland atmosphere, more circus than serious exploring party. The rest is a tragic and too well known piece of Australian history.

Burke and Wills vanished with their entourage into the interior. Christmas was approaching. Müller felt the need to escape, as he always did, the unavoidable social jollifications. He set off with a party of four to explore the Victorian Baw Baw Ranges about a hundred miles east of Melbourne. It was hot that Christmas in Melbourne, but at 5000 feet the air was pleasantly cool and there were both koalas and wombats. Müller was happy, off botanising by himself for much of the time, and was rewarded by finding a new genus of a native plant, which he named after a distinguished German scientist.

By 1864, after a disastrous tragi-comic personal interlude and several years of intense work, Müller was again in need of escape. Providentially at this moment there came from northern Queensland news of the discovery of traces of Leichhardt's last expedition. Muller was revivified, galvanised into action. His first need was to raise money to back a new expedition. In January 1865 in a letter to the President of the Royal Geographical Society in London, he wrote: 'Within a few days I contemplate lecturing publicly on the subject to endeavour to arouse sympathy for the forsaken travellers, and to call upon the ladies of all Australia to gather the means of sending forth a new search party. What a triumph if the Ladies Expedition should disclose Leichhardt's fate!'

Leichhardt had been missing for seventeen years. Müller was undismayed. There was the possibility of an expedition. A Ladies' Committee was formed. Müller was tireless in his support and advice. He recommended that the Ladies' Committee drum up support from the Princess of Wales, the Empress of France and the Princess Royal of Prussia, and at a more prosaic level from the churches to which they belonged. Queen Victoria sent £100 and the Royal Geographical Society £200. Altogether, the very large sum of £4000 was raised.

Müller's position was slowly changing. Perhaps his need to escape was lessening, as well it might as he got older, as he enjoyed greater success and began to accumulate honours and decorations. At all events, while his obsession with exploration remained as strong as ever, he seems to have been more prepared to participate vicariously, as instigator, adviser, and consultant.

Müller and Dr Wilkie oversaw the fitting-out of the Ladies' Leichhardt Expedition, which set off from country south of the Gulf of Carpentaria. Soon after starting off the leader of the expedition died. There was no one capable of taking over from him and the expedition broke up in dissaray. There was no fuss. It was soon forgotten.

In 1868 there were reports from Perth that the remains of white men had been found near a lake to the east. To Müller this could only mean one thing: Leichhardt! He at once offered to lead an expedition to investigate the reports. The Government of Western Australia accepted his offer. Before the expedition could start Müller withdrew. His place was taken by a young man named John Forrest. No trace was found of Leichhardt's expedition.

Müller by this time was no longer plain Doctor Ferdinand Müller, but Baron Ferdinand von Müller, Commander of the Order of St Michael and St George and in the running for a K. At last he could feel relatively safe and comfortable in the world. In future his escapes by exploration would be entirely vicarious.

Despite his achievements the emotional toll had been heavy. He already felt himself to be an old man. He began to adopt a defensive eccentricity and an old man's mannerisms. He wore his long woollen muffler all the time. Possibly this was a part of the defences against the world that he still maintained. He was just forty-four years old.

In 1872, significantly following a period of great difficulty in his work as Director of the Melbourne Botanical Gardens, Müller tried to revive the idea of an east–west crossing of the continent. He was personally unpopular. Press, public and government were still in a state of shock from the Burke and Wills expedition. No one was interested.

About this time Müller met Ernest Giles, a bushman and experienced explorer who wanted to attempt the east-west crossing. Müller managed, singlehanded, to raise £350 for him. It was a sadly small sum and Giles set off with only two companions. The expedition failed but led to a revival of interest in Australian exploration. Undeterred, Müller raised the money for a second expedition but this again failed.

In a bitter irony, while the Giles expedition was away, John Forrest succeeded in crossing the continent from west to east. By the time Giles returned Forrest was making a successful crossing from east to west almost along the line taken by Giles.

Exploration in Australia was coming to its end. The only unexplored areas remaining were in the north-west of Western Australia. Müller turned his attention to New Guinea. He had the opportunity to go there but was prevented by ill-health.

By 1881 Leichhardt had been missing for thirty years. The *Bulletin Weekly* now offered £1000 reward for information about the fate of Leichhardt's party. The ghost of Leichhardt still haunted Müller. He tried once again to launch an expedition to try to find traces of Leichhardt. The *Bulletin* got involved in a lawsuit with the donor of the £1000 reward. Evidence that had been promised was not forthcoming. Müller's expedition never set out.

Müller then began to press for the exploration of Antarctica. The Geographical Society obliged by setting up an Antarctic Exploration Committee in which he was involved. Years were to pass before anything practical was done, but Müller's was the initial push that set in motion a new impetus to Antarctic exploration.

Müller was now not only a baron but had received the long hoped for addition of a K to his C.M.G. and had become an English knight. In 1887 he received the Copley medal of the Royal Society of which he had long been a member. He found himself in august company: recipients have included Faraday, Lister, and later, Sir Ray Lankester.

The end of Müller's involvement in Australian exploration was not quite yet. Enthused by Müller, Sir Thomas Elder of South Australia put up £10 000 for the exploration of the unexplored areas of Western Australia. It was an extraordinarily generous gesture. Müller and a committee organised the expedition, which was led by David Lindsay and departed in 1891. It was the last large-scale effort of Australian exploration, an unwieldy undertaking that included seventeen men and forty-four camels.

Lindsay and his party were away for eleven months and travelled over 5000 miles. Towards the end disputes and disagreements flared among the participants. Factions formed. The expedition finally broke up in disarray, its work incomplete. Happily there was no loss of life and despite all the difficulties large new areas were explored.

For Müller it was almost the end of vicarious exploration. Only Antarctica remained. Pushed by Müller, a joint Antarctic Exploration Committee of the Association for the Advancement of Science and the Royal Geographical Society raised the money necessary for a first venture south. Eventually the steam whaling ship *Antarctica* explored as far south as the 74th degree of latitude and put a party ashore on South Victoria Land.

The venture was modestly successful. It stimulated the growing interest in the exploration of the Antarctic continent and led directly to the expeditions to the South Pole and the south magnetic pole. Once again Müller's need to escape, if only vicariously, had put him ahead of his contemporaries.

This was the last expedition in which he had any part. He was approaching seventy. He knew that the last and greatest escape was drawing near. Looking back he must have sometimes pondered over and marvelled at his remarkable life that had begun in the long dark shadow of his father's illness and death and culminated in the brilliant midday light of a continent half a world away. All his escaping had led on only to success and world fame.

It has only been possible here to deal briefly and much too superficially with Müller's connection with Australian exploration and the motivation that compelled him, gladly, into the Australian wilderness. It has to be remembered that he was also one of the foremost botanists of his day, the author of forty books, innumerable articles and papers and a staggeringly large correspondence. He spoke and wrote fluently, if inelegantly, in several languages. As well as his barony and his knighthood he received over 160 honours and decorations for his work.

There can be no doubt that Baron Sir Ferdinand von Müller earned his right to be an Australian. Few men have contributed more, single-handed, to the development of this continent. Before almost anyone else he became aware of the need to conserve the delicate Australian ecosystems; almost alone he founded Australian forestry. If Australia has founding fathers he must surely be one of them. And yet Müller has been all but forgotten. He was a success and to orthodox Australian eyes was a somewhat comical, wildly eccentric foreigner even after half a century. The combination of foreignness and unconventionality made it inevitable that he would slip quietly from sight in a country that was as provincial and chauvinistic then as it is now.

It has been suggested that young countries develop individual national myths which become part of the national unconscious. The myths persist even as the country grows and matures. It is difficult today to equate the positive, optimistic image of the pioneer frontiersman of American myth with what happens on the streets of Los Angeles, or Dallas, or New York. Yet the fearless frontiersman image persists, gaining strength as its obvious untruth and irrelevance become increasingly plain.

In Australia the national myth is quite different, more diffuse, characterised by its negative and pessimistic aspects. At the back of Australian consciousness is the image of tragic failure, heroic defeat. It is the image of Burke and Wills, the image of Leichhardt, the image of the heroism and senseless slaughter of Gallipoli. It too has grown and persisted in inverse proportion to its truth and is increasingly difficult to accept in the self-satisfied somnolence of the still Lucky Country.

Leichhardt was much the most fascinating character of all the Australian explorers, but as an explorer he was, ultimately, a tragic failure. Consequently he engages much of our attention. He is investigated, remembered, commemorated, fictionalised, discussed. The remains of his expedition are still sought for, a sort of ever elusive Holy Grail of Australian mythology.

It seems that until we outgrow the primitive mythology of our comparative youth, Ferdinand von Müller, for all his achievements, will stand little chance of the recognition he has earned and deserves.

The Education of an Explorer: Ludwig Leichhardt

Colin Roderick

It was not until late in his Australian education that Leichhardt conceived the idea of leading the party of 1844–45 from the Moreton Bay District to Port Essington. In fact, he had pursued advanced studies up to that point with the aim of doing in Australia what Alexander von Humboldt had done and Hermann Burmeister was to do in South America. He could not have made those advanced studies as efficiently as he did if he had not had a liberal secondary education. Assuming that as a child he had a good elementary education in a private school conducted by the pastor at Zaue, close to his natal hamlet of Trebatsch, I propose to look first at his course of study in the gymnasium, then at his first-year work in the University of Berlin, his two semesters at Göttingen, and at what followed for the next three years at the University of Berlin. After that came further self-directed study in England, then his decisive work for three years in Paris, then field studies in the Auvergne, Italy, and Switzerland. Finally, the studies that he pursued in Sydney, the Hunter valley, and the Moreton Bay district

were of importance; but since these are well covered in Marcel
Aurousseau's edition of Leichhardt's letters, given in both German
and English, everyone can explore it there.

His studies came to a climax when on the ninth day of April
1844 he sat down and in his neat Gothic hand recorded in his
diary, but of course in German:

> In the Russell brothers I believe I have found two such men as I
> would want for an expedition. They are superlative bushmen, excel-
> lent marksmen, active, genial, and tolerant with each other. We have
> discussed a plan from every angle, and I hope to put it into practice as
> soon as possible. The expedition comprises the two Russells, the
> Fiver, two blackboys, and my humble self.

Although Leichhardt's ancestry was Saxon and Slavonic, his
native village came under Prussian administration when he was two
years old, so that from childhood he lived in an environment
organised in accordance with Prussian polity. By then the rebuild-
ing of Prussia after Jena and Auerstadt was well under way.

To understand Leichhardt's rebellion against the Prussian
system, it is necessary to remind ourselves that every aspect of
Prussian life was then regimented towards a regeneration of the
national spirit. Fichte's *Reden an die deutsche Nation* had inspired
Wilhelm von Humboldt to reorganise the educational system as an
instrument in that regeneration. Humboldt founded the University
of Berlin, swept away the clerical-dominated schools, and established gymnasia along the lines of the French lycées but with even
tighter control. The gymnasia were conducted under royal preroga-
tive and were largely staffed by men with university training. Essentially the gymnasium prepared the youth for university studies in the
four standard faculties: philosophy, law, theology, and medicine: in
fact, his leaving certificate carried the heading, *Universitäts-Reife*,
implying that he was fit for university study without any further
matriculation examination. Although many ex-soldiers became elementary school teachers, the gymnasium also prepared youths for
that employment. The course in Leichhardt's time lasted from a
minimum of seven to a maximum of nine years, and during that
time lynx-eyed teachers kept a close watch on each youth, noting his
social conduct as much as his scholastic progress, from the leaving
certificate that he would receive on taking his *Arbitur* or final examinations would assess his personality as well as his scholarship. It
was no printed cut-and-dried affair giving academic results and a

curt Good, Bad, or Indifferent for conduct and industry. It was a
personal document arrived at after discussion among the boy's
teachers. It was also precious because it exempted its owner from
the normal two years of military training and by some kind of
ministerial oxymoron substituted one year of compulsory service as
a volunteer and not a conscript: perhaps it was a subtle way of
recruiting officer material.

At the age of eleven Leichhardt entered the Friedrich Wilhelm
Gymnasium at Cottbus, where he lived with an elder sister and her
husband, Carl Schmalfuss, who was the gymnasium's drawing
master.

By the time Leichhardt came at the age of eighteen to take his
Abitur after the seven-year minimum his teachers had summed him
up. Their estimate of his personality—which opens his treasured
document—was an index of the characteristics he was to display as
man and explorer. They remarked on the ease with which he comprehended the subjects of study. He had a retentive memory and a
capacity for independent judgement. He was inclined to be
solitary—a loner, as we say—but was not anti-social and got on
well with his fellows. He had on only one occasion shown something of his rebelliousness. The subjects he studied gave him a
sound humanistic foundation. His results, like every other student's,
were given, not with a mathematical mark or points to be fed into a
computer, but in descriptive human detail.

In Latin his compositions were rather laborious, but through
the benefit of his reading they were on the whole good; translation
and exposition exhibited spirit and talent. In Greek he was in composition and interpretation conspicuously good; in elucidation of
Herodotus and Homer his accomplishment was excellent. Not only
at that point, but later, in his choice of quotations in his diaries and
in his attitude to life, Leichhardt's preference for the free spirit of
Greece rather than the legal precision of Rome was manifest. In
German he strove for thoroughness and was receptive to German
poetry, something that stayed with him all his life. Three years later,
a letter to John Nicholson, the brother of his later friend William
Nicholson, so far unpublished but which we may as well look at
briefly now, revealed that he was still a thoughtful reader of German
poetry. At the end of it he writes:

> Here I add that I am now beginning to understand and grasp Schiller:
> his 'Knabe an der Quelle' ['Der Jüngling am Bache'—'The Boy by the

Brook']; his 'Sehnsucht' ['Longing']; 'Der Pilger' ['The Pilgrim']; 'Die Ideale des Lebens' ['Die Ideale'—'The Ideal']. And as I recapitulated them today, I almost had to gnash my teeth with regret that I hadn't realised that the prime poem was directed not to the beloved but to the great unknown, the future.

He wrote 'erste', and if you check the poems mentioned, it would seem that he used 'erste' in the literary distributive sense. This letter is one of six in Leichhardt's diaries that do not appear in Aurousseau's edition of Leichhardt's letters; it is also significant for the light it sheds on his relationship with the Nicholson brothers and on his temporary switch at Göttingen from philology to natural history as evidenced in the certificate of studies reproduced opposite it on the sheet. As for the Schiller poems that he refers to in casual terms, the evidence is that he knew them by heart, for in 1848 in his last letter written in the Queensland bush to Schmalfuss he quoted the last four lines of 'Sehnsucht' almost perfectly, writing only 'hoffen' for 'glauben' in the first line.

At Cottbus he was rather backward in French. One has only to read his letters to his Parisian landlady to agree with his French master. He was competent in Hebrew, necessary if he were to enter the faculty of theology. He was not so strong in the pure sciences. He was tolerably good in mathematics, in physics good only in spots, and in natural history merely good. As for the social sciences, in geography and political history he was excellent in comprehension, judgements, and presentation. In philosophy he had mastered the fundamentals of logic and psychology, rhetoric, and poetics. In religion—the gymnasia were Lutheran—he displayed what was described as a 'participatory' outlook, which took him over the religious test.

To all of this the rector and registrar appended signatures and seals and released him with avuncular blessings as fit to enter the faculty of philosophy. So on 6 November 1831 the Dean of the faculty at Berlin admitted that most excellent young man—*virum iuvenem praenobilissimum Ludovicum Leichhardt*—as of right to be taught in it.

The course that he undertook was in the humanities, with the emphasis on philology, which he began with Sanskrit and comparative philology under Franz Bopp, one of the great names in linguistic research. The effectiveness of Bopp's method emerges from the copious notes made in his diary at home during his first vacation on

the relationship between his mother's Slavonic-influenced dialect
and High German.

For this diary—the sine qua non of Leichhardt research—the
man to be thanked was his teacher of philosophy, Professor
Benecke. Benecke inspired him to begin keeping it as a means of
reaching an understanding of himself and of man's place in the
universe. Benecke imbued the youth with Kant's transcendental
idealism and with Fichte's development of it. Philosophy was a
passion in the German universities of the day, a passion encouraged
because as a substitute for politics it induced the students to let off
harmless steam. By the time he was twenty Leichhardt had come to
conclusions in philosophy that never changed. What he arrived at
was a conscious submission of his ego to Fichte's Absolute Ego, the
Infinite Will, towards which he demanded freedom to strive.

This was a concept approximated by Schopenhauer, who at
that very time was vainly trying as a *Privat Dozent* (private university
lecturer) at Berlin to get students to listen to him. Leichhardt saw
that life could not be lived in a philosophical vacuum. Benecke
convinced him that life as one must live it can never reach Fichte's
Ideal. For Leichhardt the Ideal had to be spiritual, not corporeal.
The carnal life, he concluded, was part of a continuum that did not
cease with the dissolution of the mortal element. The body housed
an immortal principle; if that was to strive after fulfilment through
union with the Ideal, the individual's relations with the corporeal
world must be pure. So, he reasoned, not only human beings, but
also the world of natural objects bore upon the development of the
self. To know one's self one must also seek an understanding of
natural phenomena. Pursuit of the Ideal was imperative; but in this
sublunar world attainment of the Ideal was not feasible. Essential to
harmonious reconciliation of the Real and the Ideal was quiet
resignation to the Infinite Will.

In this philosophical belief the significant events of
Leichhardt's life had their roots. But much educational experience
lay ahead of him before circumstances drew him into those events.

In his second semester he came up against the feuding between
the followers of Fichte and the devotees of Hegel. Benecke was no
Hegelian. Nor was Leichhardt's next professor, the Norwegian
Henrik Steffens, who had a new message that provided Leichhardt
with a *vade mecum*. Steffens was also a student of natural science,
and the core of his philosophy was that individualisation—not
in the later Jungian sense, but in the sense of specialised

development—was the leading principle of life, as well in the world of Nature as in the mind of man. The higher the intelligence the greater the individualisation.

Most students, however attracted to this doctrine, took it as just another theory and went on along the course laid out for them. Not so Leichhardt. He looked to philosophy for a guide and rule to practical living. His thoughts ran deep, and Steffens' illustrations of his theory from geology—taken from Lyell—struck him forcefully. He listened intently and took himself off to tell his diary of the pleasure Steffens' discourses gave him: it was a pity he got lost when Steffens went to zoology to illustrate his psychological theories. Nevertheless, this search for proofs in the plant and animal kingdoms was new and exciting. One wonders if the older Leichhardt, after ten years of study of natural science, ever went back to read the words he wrote as a 19-year-old student: 'Professor Steffens gives me complete satisfaction.'

At that time Leichhardt had no idea that his life was to be spent in the world of Nature. But the reactions chronicled in his diary make it clear that it would not have needed many men like Steffens to enlist him as an apostle.

The lectures of one other professor appealed to Leichhardt. This was Karl Lachmann, an ex-soldier who had been professor of classics at Göttingen for seven years before Leichhardt heard him. His exposition of such works as the *Agamemnon* led Leichhardt to read more in Greek tragedy; *Oedipus Rex* made a deep impression on him. Lachmann had the knack of using the Greek classics to throw light on modern life, and throughout Leichhardt's diaries one finds quotations from the Sanskrit, Greek, Latin, German, French, and English classics as epigrams. The Greeks appealed strongly to him. 'Perhaps,' he diarised, 'they help me to understand the spirit of opposition that stirs in me.' Those familiar with Goethe—another of Leichhardt's exemplars—may trace this self-analysis to his *Geist der stets verneint.*

During this semester he attended some of the medical lectures of Johannes Müller. They impressed him so much that he recorded the details of those on sex and reproduction. Nevertheless, they did not induce him to study medicine—that was to come later—for in 1832 his attitude was that medicine was a fine study but that as a profession it was not for him.

Then came what was to be a crucial year. To fill his *Wanderjahr* he hit on Göttingen, the university founded by George II of England

and in Leichhardt's time closely linked with Great Britain. To continue his studies in the humanities he entered the faculty of philosophy on 28 October 1833, confident that Johann Friedrich Herbart
would fill the gaps in his moral philosophy.

Herbart was the man of the hour in Kantian philosophy, but in
putting Herbart on a pedestal, Leichhardt had no idea that his
influence would be crucial to his future career. Herbart also lectured
on forestry and forest management; but Leichhardt enrolled only for
his course in moral philosophy or 'Practical Philosophy', as one
sees it denominated on his *Anmeldungsbogen* (enrolment form).

Herbart was far from being the only teacher to influence
Leichhardt at Göttingen. All four of his first semester professors
were Olympian figures. Their repute endures to this day. He attended Carl Ottfried Müller's lectures on ancient mythologies and
religions and from his course gained a picture of society in pre-
Christian times. Privy Councillor Jakob Grimm, the discoverer of
Grimm's Law, lectured on the history of German grammar. His
fourth professor, Georg Heinrich Ewald, was a towering figure in
Oriental studies. With him Leichhardt pursued comparative studies
in Persian and Sanskrit.

Despite these exemplars, and moved by poverty so sore that he
avoided going to church at Christmas because he hadn't a *Heller*
(cent) to put in the plate, he became a prey to doubt. Was he
becoming a mere theoretical man? Should he be undertaking a more
practical line of study?

His indecision was dispelled by Herbart. Leichhardt recorded
the conversation that diverted him into his first studies in natural
science under the date of 6 March 1834. Herbart had taken a liking
to the grave student and on that day was chatting with him in the
garden before beginning a lecture. In Leichhardt's words, Herbart's
comments 'shook him to the core . . . worked on him like a doctor's
physic'. Herbart, who had developed a system of expressing his
philosophical tenets in algebraic form, told him that the great
philologists were also great in mathematics and physics (which
makes Herbart sound like a prophet of latter-day linguistic techniques). Herbart convinced Leichhardt that he must acquire a
broader general knowledge.

Leichhardt was shattered. He had abandoned mathematics and
physics; but his resolve marked the man he was to become: 'I must
and shall put that right.'

A week later came the turning-point: he casually attended—

German has a special word for it: *hospitiren*—a lecture in natural science by the venerable Blumenbach, as bright a star as any in the Göttingen constellation.

Johann Friedrich Blumenbach, privy councillor, principal professor of medicine, and senior professor of the university since 1816, had been a full professor for fifty-eight years when Leichhardt first heard him and was to retire in 1837 after sixty-one years in the chair. This extraordinary man was a member of seventy-five scientific societies, including the Royal Society of London. He lectured mainly in physiology and comparative anatomy. These had led him into physical anthropology, and he it was who first divided the human race into distinct families, of which he enumerated five: Caucasian, Mongolian, Malayan, Negroid, and American Indian. His contemporaries hailed him as the founder of the science of anthropology.

Leichhardt devoted more space in his diary to Blumenbach than to any other professor he met: 'a remarkable ancient monument: a stooped old man once obviously hefty and still with a big strong face; large faded eyes; abstracted manner; a researcher into Nature for two generations.'

To Leichhardt Blumenbach came as an inspiration. But he was still unsure of the course he should follow. Was it to be philosophy? Or a practical body of knowledge? Should he take Herbart's advice? Should he follow natural science? He had only a week to decide. He confided his decision to his diary: 'I am happy with my decision. Yes! I bow to Nature's call. My study will be of her. I will study botany with Bartling and natural history with Blumenbach. I will hear Weber in physics, and Herbart's metaphysics will round out the others. If only I had met Herbart three years ago!'

So he delivered himself to fate.

This brief summary of what actually occurred is confirmed by his *Anmeldungsbogen* (enrolment form). It disposes of the myth that it was the English student John Nicholson, a former Oxford medical student who had come to Göttingen for further study, who diverted Leichhardt into natural history. The reverse actually occurred. Nicholson switched from medicine to philosophy and had in fact left Göttingen to go back to Bristol to perfect his German before Leichhardt's talk with Herbart and his casual attendance at Blumenbach's lecture. Leichhardt's acquaintance with John Nicholson was brief, and correspondence between them shows no

sign of influence except of Leichhardt on Nicholson. The unpublished letter shows plainly that philosophy and religion formed their
topic of common interest. Note particularly the sentence beginning
'*Religion und Philosophie müssen harmonieren*: 'Religion and philosophy must harmonise, for where they deviate the fault is in philosophy: the divine is the most certain and the most secure, and it will
be a fine thing if human inquiry reaches the same conclusion.' This
explodes John F. Mann's opinion that Leichhardt was an irreligious
man.

Behold Leichhardt then, in the hands of Blumenbach, Bartling,
Weber, and Herbart. Of the four Bartling is today forgotten. He was
an extraordinary professor in the faculty of philosophy: the course of
lectures that Leichhardt took with him was designated *Spezielle
Botanik* (Special Botany): it was an introduction to systematic
botany.

Bartling's course is of historic interest to Australian students of
Leichhardt as his first course in botany, and, although this has not
been recognised, to the University of Göttingen as the only known
first-hand record of any course at Göttingen surviving from the
1830s. The course began on 28 April 1834 and with one lecture a
week ran to 29 August. Leichhardt used to make his notes in the
lecture room, take them to the library, where he read the books to
which Bartling referred the students, then, under the date of the
lecture, make a fair record in his neat hand in a bound notebook
that has survived to this day. This beautiful manuscript volume of
188 pages, now in the Mitchell Library, Sydney, is in fact the only
known record of a full course of lectures given by any German
professor in the decade 1830–39. It was the forerunner of studies in
the organic sciences that Leichhardt was to pursue in Paris before
he followed his star to the Australian bush.

Of the other professors he heard, Blumenbach and Weber
stayed with him. Weber's influence was pervasive: his lectures in
electromagnetism were to prove useful to Leichhardt in his investigations into the climatology of New Holland, as most of Australia
was still called.

With the end of the semester came a change in Leichhardt's
career, induced by his father's financial distress. Over this
Leichhardt worried until he felt that he must abandon natural
science and undertake studies that would enable him to begin earning as early as possible in the practical world of commerce or the
public service. He consulted Herbart, who set out the subjects cov-

ered in the field of finance and public administration and the range of opportunities they offered. Leichhardt should go back to Berlin. The prospect of losing contact with Herbart, Bartling and Blumenbach was not a pleasant one, but as the semester drew to a close Leichhardt had to make a decision. He decided on what he called 'the practical life', and he arranged at once to study political economy and public administration in his old faculty. Providence, he convinced himself, had so decreed.

There he pinned his faith on studies leading, with some that he had already done, to a practical profession. For the winter semester of 1834–35 he enrolled, from Herbart's list, for mathematics, anatomy, finance (*Cameralwissenschaft*), national economy, physical geography, and chemistry. The last two he was advised to postpone to the next semester. He was to have read mathematics with Ohm; but in the event Ohm decided to stay at Nuremberg, and Leichhardt took his mathematics with Milton. He was persuaded also to take zoology with the celebrated Lichtenstein instead of anatomy, apparently because of class numbers. That he was hard up appears from the date when he paid his fees, without which his lecturers were not asked to comment on his attendance or estimate his performance. Although the semester ended in March 1834, his zoology fees were not paid until eight months later. None of his professors was eminent, with the exception of Lichtenstein, and Leichhardt found them uninspiring.

Although anxious to begin earning he was determined not to sacrifice his talents in a narrowing occupation. His diary reveals that during this year he aimed as much at the enrichment of his mind as at preparing himself for a vocation. With the theological controversy aroused by Tholuck and Strauss he was quite familiar. He did not presume to live a religious life of his own devising. On the contrary he came during this year to the conclusion from which he never wavered, namely, that the life and ministry of Christ constituted more than a historical event: it was the way and the truth. This he confided to his diary, and that belief, simple to all appearances, but profound in its influence on his character and his career, gave him the confidence to undertake hazards that would have deterred a man less certain of being an instrument of the Infinite Will.

On 29 April 1835 Leichhardt recorded the arrival of a student at Berlin who was to influence his studies in the following year, but not in the summer semester of 1835. This was William Nicholson,

John's younger brother. William, who was three years younger than Leichhardt, had at the age of eighteen completed the winter semester of 1834–35 at Göttingen 'with laudable industry' in chemistry and anatomical dissection and left on 24 March 1835 to pursue his doctorate in medicine at Berlin.

William had no immediate influence on Leichhardt's studies, nor Leichhardt on his. William, then living in Unterwasserstrasse, went on with his medical courses. Leichhardt, at 20 Old Leipzig Street, enrolled in April 1835 for a fearsome array of eight courses in the faculty of philosophy, all bearing on public administration. He was then twenty-two.

On the legal side he took the Prussian pandects and law of inheritance with Dirksen, constitutional law with Eduard Gans, and the law relating to loans and investments. To these he added demography and the geography of Prussia, and mindful of Herbart's admonitions, chemistry with the eminent Eilhardt Mitscherlich, whose specialty was the chemistry of metals and applied science with Heinrich Gustav Magnus, whose excursions to factories in the city opened Leichhardt's eyes to its growing importance. On the rural side he took agricultural science; and, more significantly for his work in Australia, physical anthropology with Hermann Burmeister. He was to build on Burmeister's lectures in Paris. And his diary contains a great deal of systematic anthropological work which has lain neglected since 1844.

His courses during 1835 kept his nose to the grindstone every day from 7 a.m. to 5 p.m. Some of the classes were large by any standard; for example, in constitutional law there were more than 140 students. Somehow he found the money to pay his fees, even though all but Dirksen's were not paid until June. His professors' comments on his attendance and progress were uniformly favourable. Dirksen even favoured him with two lines: he had worked 'with most notable diligence and undivided attention'. For all of them he was '*ausgezeichnet fleissig*' ('extraordinarily industrious').

Towards the end of the semester friendship began to develop between Leichhardt and William Nicholson. In September, while William was in Norway for the summer vacation, Leichhardt hired rooms for him at Number 2, Hof der Katholischen Kirche. William had intended sharing the rooms with a student named Wood, but Wood had to abandon his studies early in 1836. Leichhardt meanwhile had gone home, for without money he could neither live in Berlin nor pay his fees. For half of the winter semester of 1835–36 he was at home, and in his depression he was tempted to throw his diary into the fire. What restrained him was the knowledge that it was a faithful record of the development of a young man's personality, with all its doubts and fears, its hopes and setbacks.

A few days later an invitation came from William to take Wood's place. Leichhardt joined him at the end of February, too late to enrol for the winter semester of 1835–36, even though William was prepared to pay the fees. As a substitute he began to read William's textbooks in medicine and its auxiliary sciences.

This abstention from the programme he had come to Berlin to follow was the turning-point in Leichhardt's life. Had he had the money to enable him to continue with it, the probability is that Australia would never have heard of Leichhardt and Prussia would have had one more anonymous public servant. But reading William's textbooks and hearing the substance of his lectures renewed his interest in natural science. Occasionally he paid casual visits to lectures with William, but being penniless and with no prospect of help from his father, he had by 14 March 1836 made no decision about his future studies. William made the decision for him. In his diary Leichhardt wrote in December 1837 of the twist his fortunes took: 'When I linked up with William I was a student of public finance and administration and had the firm objective of remaining such. ... That medicine became my field of study was due to my unfortunate circumstances at the time. My aunt died without leaving me a *Heller,* and William said: "Be a medical student, and we can continue together."' So, on 26 April 1836, the dean and the professors admitted 'the most illustrious— *ornatissimum*—Ludovicum Leichhardt' to the faculty of medicine. William paid his fees, shared his textbooks, and lodged him gratis. To William Nicholson, then, the knowledge of medicine that Leichhardt acquired and the extension of his studies in natural science were directly due. Since Leichhardt has in Australia more than once been dubbed a 'bogus scientist' and a 'failed medical student' we might dwell for a moment on that medical training and its results, even though it means jumping forward chronologically in this account of his education.

For his first semester in medicine—the summer semester of 1836—Leichhardt first enrolled in three of the auxiliary medical sciences: mineralogy, molluscs and zoophytes, and infusoria; but by changing from mineralogy to comparative anatomy he was able to make use of William's textbooks: anatomy he studied with Johannes

Müller. That he profited from the course in molluscs and zoophytes appears from his Mediterranean researches in 1841 and from his Australian identifications. His course on infusoria was with the leading microbiologist of the day, Christian Gottfried Ehrenburg, who had an international reputation as a zoologist. According to his record, only Müller certified that he had followed the course with great diligence. Wiegemann and Ehrenburg made no comment, probably because of after-events.

On 12 November 1836 Leichhardt enrolled for the winter semester for work normally taken by the student in the final semester before writing his dissertation. It would appear that he did this because he could accompany William and discuss the results with him. The first course was at the eye clinic in the Charité, the second at the surgical clinic there. Both were practical surgical courses, and Leichhardt must have given the impression that he intended to work for the German medical degree. But at Berlin he went no further in medicine, for William completed his course in March and left with his doctorate. Leichhardt hankered after completing the degree, but he had no money: as he wrote, 'Alas! William went, and I went with him.'

At the time it seemed that his medical studies would end there; but, as we shall see, he did much more work in the discipline in London and in Paris.

When he came to New South Wales people referred to him as a doctor, even though he specifically disclaimed the title and declined medical practice—except in bush emergencies. At Durandur, in the upper Brisbane valley, for example, he diagnosed as a hydrocele what the ex-government surgeon designated a hernia, and when the child's condition became acute operated on it successfully with a sharpened stock knife. And there can be little doubt but that his treatment saved the lives of Roper and Calvert after they had been gravely wounded in the attack on the camp during which Gilbert was fatally speared.

So, in May 1837, after getting a postponement of his year of military training and permits from his father and the ministry to travel to England, Leichhardt took up residence with the Nicholson family at Bristol. Then came geological excursions in the Mendip Hills and excursions to Brixham, where William and he dissected a range of marine life given them by the fishermen.

In October they were back in London, where they first contemplated going to Australia to undertake pioneering work in natural science. That meant extended study in London and after that in Paris, where the Museum of Natural History in the Jardin des Plantes was the Mecca of European students in natural science. In London for the next eight months they worked in natural history on collections in the museums of the Zoological Society, the British Museum, and the Royal College of Surgeons. As a travelling medical student, with bona fides established by his travel permit and his *Anmeldungsbogen*, Leichhardt was admitted to the two principal teaching hospitals, St Guy's and St Bartholomew's. He studied in the anatomical museum at St Bartholomew's and accompanied one of the visiting surgeons there, making copious notes on the cases he observed.

At the end of June 1838 the two crossed to France and by mid-July had presented themselves at the Jardin des Plantes and begun the courses that were to give Leichhardt unrivalled preparation for his career in Australia. Without the knowledge that he acquired during the next two and a half years, he would not have possessed the armament that enabled him to make his Australian journeys.

Moreover, everything he wanted to know was free. The lectures he heard, the practical work he did, and the excursions he made, cost nothing. His teachers were world leaders in their disciplines, and their lectures, whether at the Museum of Natural History, the School of Mines, the medical clinics or the Sorbonne were all of university standard.

Had earlier writers read Leichhardt's detailed record of these lectures and investigated his studies in Paris, depreciation of him as a bogus scientist, with all the damage to his reputation as it has done, would long ago have been dismissed as frivolous chatter.

Who, then, were some of his teachers in Paris in 1838 to 1841? In brief, they were the great names in the history of French science.

First, Adrien Laurent Henri de Jussieu, known throughout the world for his textbook, *Botany*. In botany Leichhardt worked also with Adolphe Brongniart, who in 1843 commissioned him to collect impressions of fossil plants from the Hunter valley and a range of Australian timbers for the museum. With Adolphe's father, Alexandre, who was not only professor of mineralogy at the Museum but also director of the porcelain factory at Sèvres, Leichhardt studied mineralogy and geology. 'I was too busy in London with comparative anatomy to make much use of the fine

museum of the Geological Society,' he wrote. 'Here I began regular
excursions linked with an ever-increasing and more serious study of
geology.' He became a competent geologist. For the whole of 1840
he worked hard at it, going systematically through the collections.
At the Museum he heard the lectures of Pierre-Louis Cordier, who
kept in touch with him after he came to New South Wales, and to
whom in 1844 he sent his *Observations on the Geology of Australia.*
At the Sorbonne he attended Constant Prévost's lectures in struc-
tural geology and palaeontology, and found that Prévost agreed with
Lyell's theory on volcanic cones. During subsequent fieldwork in
the Auvergne Leichhardt's observations led him to agree absolutely
with Prévost and Lyell, and his conclusions in 1844 on the volcanic
cones of Peak Range, Queensland, were to rest on these studies.

To improve his knowledge of mineralogy he attended François
Beudant's lectures at the Sorbonne. At the School of Mines he
heard Elie de Beaumont and Dufrénoy, the two leading practical
geologists of the time and the men jointly responsible for the first
geological map of France. That Leichhardt was not a passive recipient of certain of Dufrénoy's theories is proved by his rejection of
them after his observations in the environs of Naples.

In Paris Leichhardt was determined to become an all-round
naturalist. The entomologist Jean-Victor Audouin impressed on him
something commonplace today, but then neglected, namely, the
basic importance of making one's own systematic collection of insects. Audouin made a special study of insects harmful to the vine,
and Leichhardt's interest in oenology made him an attentive
listener, especially since Audouin was a gifted lecturer. Indeed,
when Leichhardt came to give his lectures in botany in the Sydney
School of Arts in 1842, he adopted Audouin's technique of
coloured visual representation.

Leichhardt's studies in natural science comprehended much
more. In comparative anatomy and anthropology he heard Pierre
Flourens, in chemistry Joseph Louis Gay-Lussac and Michel Eugène
Chevreul, in meteorology Antoine-César Becquerel, in zoology
Valenciennes, and in ornithology Isidore Saint-Hilaire. None of
these he ever forgot. He thought Becquerel a dry old stick and was
reminded of him by a lean, grizzled Aboriginal that he met later near
Port Stephens. Valenciennes impressed him hugely. But Chevreul
was the amazing one. He had been director of the Gobelins tapestry
works before taking a chair in chemistry at the Museum of Natural
History at the age of forty-four. He became its director, resigning

that post at the age of ninety-three, but remaining as professor of organic chemistry until his death ten years later—possibly the only professor in the Western world ever to pass the age of a hundred in his chair.

Of Leichhardt's medical studies in Paris something should also be said, for during the autumn months he and William spent time between lectures walking the hospitals and attending the clinics attached to them. Foremost of these was La Charité, which was only half an hour's walk from their lodgings. The St Louis, which took in sufferers from skin diseases, was also convenient. L'Hôpital de la Pitié was even closer—only seven minutes away; and at the clinic there, as well as at the school of medicine at the Sorbonne, they attended lectures and demonstrations. Another hospital nearby was l'Hôtel-Dieu; there Leichhardt interested himself in ophthalmology, no doubt because he was having trouble with flickering spots in his vision.

Of the medical figures whose lectures and demonstrations they attended, those that impressed Leichhardt most were Biett, who gave practical lectures at La Pitié, and Alfred-Armand Velpeau at La Charité. In another unpublished letter to a Göttinger *Studiengenosse* (Hallmann) Leichhardt described these and others. Hallmann had switched to medicine and was doing his course at Brussels. To him Leichhardt wrote of these two and of what Hallmann might expect in Paris.

His letter, copied into his diary of 1840, reveals Leichhardt's familiarity with the medical round in Paris. For example in paragraph 2 of page 1 he gives Hallmann the semester timetable; in paragraph 3 he describes the hospitals he visits: 'If you live with us or choose rooms in the neighbourhood you will have La Pitié quite handy (seven minutes away). L'Hôtel-Dieu, the clinic, and the School of Medicine likewise are not far away.' In fact Leichhardt and William were living in a pension on the corner of what is now the rue Monge and the rue des Ecoles that leads directly to l'Ecol de Médecine, still in use, but not for medical studies. '. . . You could hardly find a better locality unless you select some other hospital to visit.' 'At the Charity,' he wrote and went on, 'is Bouchand.' Then he mentions 'Velpeau, the leading surgeon at la Charité, must be visited because of his splendid lectures.' He then contrasts Velpeau's views on disorders of the eye with those of the Berlin ophthalmologist he had heard. Paragraph 4 draws attention to the strictly scientific basis of French medicine. This he follows, on page

2, with information on other ophthalmologists and describes Biett and his lectures, concluding with information on the museums and with a warning that Hallmann would find the going hard if he didn't master French.

Velpeau's lectures attracted Leichhardt so much that he began toying with the idea of resuming a medical course. He might well have done so had he and William not by then arrived at a plan to go to New Holland to investigate its nondescript natural history. 'If it please God,' Leichhardt wrote to an old fellow student, 'we will fulfil our chosen vocation of interpreting Nature under the more friendly skies of Australia.'

That meant more fieldwork, and this the pair now undertook with an extended study tour of the Auvergne, Italy, and Switzerland. They intended to study vulcanology also in Sicily; but family responsibilities—and perhaps a realisation of the physical stress of their projected work in Australia—forced William to abandon the enterprise. He wanted Leichhardt to finish his medical studies in Britain and settle into practice there. But Leichhardt had made up his mind. He was still only twenty-six, and if all went well, he would, like Humboldt, have a lifetime to work over his discoveries in New Holland. Of William's defection he had no complaint to make, but for himself there was only one course, and in his diary he set it down: '*Folge jeder seinem Triebe*' ('Let every man follow his bent').

Nevertheless, William agreed to do the projected European tour with him. Every hour of it deepened Leichhardt's preparation for the work he was to do in New Holland. From Captain Jammes of the 52nd Light Horse at Clermont, an amateur geologist, he had his first lessons on living off the land. In Naples his knowledge of marine biology and vulcanology deepened. Switzerland yielded further geological experience.

In 1841, on the eve of leaving London for Sydney, he summed up his years of study in his diary:

> My preparatory studies must now be considered as finished. I have followed Herbart's philosophical scheme with deep inward resolve to become an all-round naturalist. I have heard abundant argument against it and am now convinced that I should devote myself to one thing. But the scheme comprehends that, and in no way does it contradict the general thrust of my work. What that one thing is to be will depend on the circumstances in which I find myself and on the final purpose.

No one reflecting on the decade of Leichhardt's studies could deny that they were an unrivalled preparation for the work he was to undertake in the colonial society in which he was soon to find himself. That he was cut out to explore a new world is evident from his next sentence, written on 26 August 1841:

> I see very clearly that Nature holds equal interest in many directions for the zealous investigator. Only a novice would dispute that, whether he be botanist, mineralogist, or zoologist. . . . I will never forget that in all my studies, the last course I had followed always led me on to a new one.

His reflections were a striking forecast of the experiences that were to lead him to fill in half the map of north-eastern Australia. He could not have had the faintest expectation of 'the one thing' that awaited him. What he did have was a conviction that something worthwhile would come his way.

CHAPTER 3

Georg von Neumayer and the Flagstaff Observatory, Melbourne

R.W. Home

A number of German and other central European scientists were prominent in Australian scientific circles in the 1840s, 50s and 60s—more, indeed, than at any other time in Australia's history. Among them were such well-known figures as Paul de Strzelecki, Ludwig Leichhardt, Ferdinand Mueller, Wilhelm Blandowski, Ludwig Becker and Gerard Krefft, as well as the man whose work provides the focus for this chapter, Georg Balthasar Neumayer.

Reasons for Germany, in particular, being so well represented at this time are not hard to find. Relations between Britain and Germany were particularly close following the marriage of Queen Victoria to Prince Albert of Saxe-Coburg, and German scholars and scientists found a ready welcome among their British confreres. Substantial numbers of Germans of all classes were migrating to Australia during this period. It is not surprising that there were scientifically literate people among them, especially as the German system of higher education was producing many more scientists than the national economy could absorb, so that many were forced to seek posts outside Germany. Moreover, the level of scientific training provided by the German universities was far in advance of anything available anywhere else in the world (except perhaps at the Ecole Polytechnique in Paris). In sharp contrast to most of their British-born fellow immigrants who took up scientific pursuits, the majority of the Germans arriving in Australia who subsequently became known for their scientific work came already trained for careers as professional scientists.

Georg Neumayer was among the most highly respected of them all at the time of his return to Europe in 1864 after seven and a half years in Victoria. Subsequently, however, his name has fallen more or less into oblivion, at least in Australia. There, when he is remembered at all, it is as the founder and director of the Flagstaff Observatory that he set up on Flagstaff Hill in Melbourne and that was later, in 1863, merged into the new Melbourne Observatory established in the Domain, next to the Botanic Gardens where another influential German-born scientist, Ferdinand Mueller, reigned supreme. In his native country Neumayer's name remains better known, because after his return from Australia he rose to become one of the most highly respected German scientists of his generation as founder of the German Naval Observatory and a major contributor to the sciences of hydrography, meteorology and terrestrial magnetism. His election in 1899 to the elite band of Foreign Members of the Royal Society of London and his ennobling as von Neumayer by the King of Bavaria testified to the standing he eventually attained. The fields to which he contributed are not 'glamour' sciences, however, and even in Germany his name can hardly be said any longer to be well known. My intention in this chapter is to draw attention to the significance for Australian science of his Australian sojourn and, I hope, to render his visit comprehensible by setting it in its scientific and also, to some extent, its sociopolitical context. I shall also provide some straightforward biographical details and a brief narrative of the events leading up to the establishment of the Flagstaff Observatory, these being of some interest in themselves and several of them not having previously been securely established.

Neumayer certainly falls into the category of those who came to Australia already scientifically trained. Born at Kirchheimbolanden[1] in the Bavarian Palatinate in 1826, he studied at the Polytechnische Schule (the precursor of the Technische Hochschule) in Munich, 1845–47, and then at the more specialised Ingenieurschule there before successfully sitting the *Staatsexamen* in engineering towards the end of 1849. He then worked for several months at the Bogenhausen Observatory outside Munich under the supervision of the noted physicist and astronomer Johann von Lamont, who encouraged him to continue his studies. At the same time he also worked as assistant to Professor Karl Joseph Reindl at the Physics Institute at the University of Munich. During this period he concentrated particularly on terrestrial magnetism and electricity, subjects on which Lamont was a world authority and then at the height of his powers.

In an autobiographical fragment that Neumayer dictated late in his life,[2] he describes how, as a youth, he was greatly influenced by the argument advanced by Friedrich List in his book *Das nationale System der politischen Oekonomie*, concerning the importance of sea power to national prosperity, and how this was confirmed in his mind by the manifest impotence of the German people in the struggle with Denmark over Schleswig-Holstein in 1848. He tells us that he resolved there and then to devote himself to helping to build up German naval power. His subsequent studies were intended to fit him better for that task. Then, in search of practical experience of seamanship and navigation, and to prove to himself that he had the physical and moral strength required for the task that lay ahead, in August 1850 he went to Rotterdam and bought himself a berth as a trainee on a 300-ton barque out of Hamburg, the *Luise*, bound for Brazil via Newcastle-upon-Tyne. Returning to Hamburg in April 1851, he sought out Christian Carl Rümker, principal astronomer at Governor Thomas Brisbane's Parramatta Observatory in Sydney in the 1820s and subsequently for many years director of Hamburg's navigation school and observatory and, at the time, the dominant figure in navigational science in Germany. Neumayer evidently created a very favourable impression on Rümker and acquired thereby a patron who was able to assist him considerably later on. For the time being, Rümker admitted him to the navigation school and to his house. After some weeks of study, Neumayer sat the *Schifferexamen* and obtained his mate's certificate.

Afterwards, Rümker arranged introductions in Vienna and Trieste, headquarters of the newly established Austrian fleet, but Neumayer, convinced that he needed to acquire further experience at sea, declined the position he was offered as an instructor in the officers' school at Trieste and returned to Germany. For some months he lectured at Rümker's school in Hamburg (this presumably being the basis of the courtesy title of 'Professor' that he was later often granted in Australia), and then he signed on as a crewman on the *Reiherstieg*, a vessel belonging to the famous Hamburg shipping firm of J.C. Godeffroy and Son, for a voyage to Australia.

In Australia, the *Reiherstieg* traded along the coast between Moreton Bay in what is now Queensland and St Vincent's Gulf in South Australia. Throughout the voyage, Neumayer noted the wind and ocean currents, and the elements of the Earth's magnetic field. Once in Australia, most of the crew deserted, attracted by the lure of gold. Eventually Neumayer was paid off and he, too, made his way to the goldfields where he worked for a time as a digger on the Bendigo field. While there he established an informal navigation school for German seamen working on the field, imparting knowledge that they would find useful when they resumed their former calling. He made enough money on the goldfield to finance a journey from Melbourne to Adelaide and then up the River Murray for some considerable distance. He was an inveterate collector of information about the country through which he was passing, and his experiences supplied the basis for a series of lectures on Australia that he presented for the benefit of would-be emigrants in many of the principal German cities after his return to Europe in 1854.[3]

Back in Europe, Neumayer also sought support for the project he had conceived of establishing a meteorological and magnetic observatory in Melbourne. Aware of how little geophysical research was being done in the southern hemisphere and of how much more needed to be done if the main questions concerning the Earth's magnetic field were to be answered satisfactorily, he had evidently concluded that Victoria's gold-induced wealth offered the prospect of his finding there the financial support that such work required. Rümker provided him with an introduction to the aged patriarch of exploration science, Alexander von Humboldt, while it was probably Lamont who brought him to the attention of the chemist Justus von Liebig, then at the height of his power as adviser to the scientifically inclined King Maximilian II of Bavaria. Thanks to Liebig's intervention, the King made available the substantial sum of 3232 guilden—about 400 English pounds—to support Neumayer's project. This Neumayer spent on a splendid set of magnetic and meteorological instruments of the latest design, many of which had been developed by his mentor Lamont. During the summer of 1855, Neumayer tested his instruments by undertaking a magnetic

survey of his home province, the Bavarian Palatinate. In the following spring, he also surveyed Hamburg and part of Schleswig-
Holstein. With the help of the shipping magnate Godeffroy, he
obtained a commission from the City of Hamburg to investigate the
application, 'in the first instance to the voyage to and from the
Australian colonies', of the hydrographical principles that had been
announced by the famous American hydrographer, Mathew
Fontaine Maury. Godeffroy also provided him with free passage to
Melbourne on one of the company's ships, the *La Rochelle*. En
route, the navigation of the ship was entrusted to him so that he
could try out Maury's principles; once in Melbourne, he was able to
continue his shipboard magnetic and meteorological observations
for six weeks while the ship lay in harbour while simultaneously
making the same observations on shore, thus firmly connecting the
data he was later to collect in Victoria with those previously obtained in Europe.[4]

Before leaving Europe, Neumayer also attended the 1856 meeting of the British Association for the Advancement of Science
armed with letters of recommendation to Edward Sabine and
Michael Faraday, the leading British magnetic investigators of the
period, and to a leading patron of early Victorian science, Dr John
Lee of Hartwell House. Immediately upon arrival in Melbourne in
January 1857, Neumayer began lobbying for local support for his
venture. The details of the long drawn out campaign that he had to
wage before his efforts were eventually crowned with success are
described in a fascinating document that survives in Germany, that
is shortly to be published elsewhere.[5] Neumayer was inclined to
blame the opposition he unexpectedly encountered chiefly on the
university professors William Parkinson Wilson and Frederick
McCoy. Unknown to him, however, the principal source of his
difficulties was Robert Brough Smyth, the *bête noire* of many a
scientific enterprise in colonial Victoria, to whose control of the
colony's meteorological service Neumayer posed a distinct threat.[6]

Neumayer in time developed a great deal of public support for
his venture, and the local press sprang to his defence when the
government denied him financial support. So, too, did the German
community, which undertook an appeal to raise the funds he required. Within a few days, the remarkable sum of £500 had been
collected. In addition, a petition signed by the assembled captains of
all the ships then in the port of Melbourne, urging that Neumayer's
work be supported, was presented to the Government, strengthen-

ing backing he had already received from the Chamber of Commerce. Even the Governor took a hand by pointedly inviting Neumayer to dinner immediately after the unfavourable vote in Parliament. The Government quickly caved in. On 20 August, Neumayer was invited to discuss his plans with the Chief Secretary, who assured him that 'he would never have opposed a motion in favour of my research projects if he had known as much about the matter as he did now'. 'He excused himself,' Neumayer tells us, 'by saying that the men of science who were experts on such matters had all been opposed to my ideas. He had now come to the conclusion that they had been motivated by petty jealousy'. Within a few days, the question was resubmitted to Parliament and the necessary funds agreed. By the beginning of the following year, the observatory was established on its site on Flagstaff Hill and Neumayer had commenced systematic recording.[7]

For the remainder of Neumayer's stay in Victoria, it was relatively plain sailing. On 1 March 1859, control of the colony's chain of meteorological recording stations was transferred from Brough Smyth to Neumayer,[8] and from then on his work focused on four separate programmes of investigation:

1   collecting and analysing the logs of all ships entering the port of Melbourne for information about prevailing winds and ocean currents;

2   coordinating the colony's chain of meteorological recording stations, and maintaining systematic observations at the Flagstaff Observatory;

3   maintaining a system of hourly recording of the elements of the Earth's magnetic field—declination, inclination (or dip) and horizontal intensity; and

4   carrying out a magnetic survey of the entire colony.

This last obviously required Neumayer to be away from the Observatory for extended periods. In his absence the work was carried on by some very competent assistants whom he recruited and trained. The best known of these was the young W.J. Wills, who in due course took leave from the Observatory to go with Burke on their ill-fated exploring expedition.

Throughout his time in Victoria, Neumayer presented papers regularly to the Royal Society of Victoria describing aspects of his work. Four of these were subsequently published in the Society's *Proceedings*. He also came to play an active role in the Society's affairs, being vice president at the time of his return to Germany. At his departure, the Society bestowed life membership upon him, an honour it has guarded jealously and granted only extremely rarely.[9]

Neumayer was also active in Melbourne's German immigrant society. News of his doings appeared regularly in the local German-language newspapers, and also the texts of the lectures he presented from time to time at meetings of Melbourne's Deutscher Verein. It was in one of these that he unveiled plans that he continued to push for years afterwards, for an ambitious programme of Antarctic research. When Neumayer was leaving for Europe, the Deutscher Verein presented him with a large album of photographic portraits of his Melbourne friends and acquaintances. This precious record of colonial society in the early 1860s survives today in the Neumayer-Archiv at Bad Dürkheim, in Germany.

Neumayer was not content merely to publish papers in the *Proceedings* of the Royal Society of Victoria. Two large volumes of observatory data were published by the Victorian government printer before his departure, and two more volumes, one discussing the observatory's magnetic data, the other setting out the results of the magnetic survey of the colony, were published later, in English, in Germany, under the supervision of the Royal Society of London.[10] Papers on particular aspects of the work continued to appear occasionally for another thirty years and more.

What, though, was the point of all this work? This is not the place to go into too many technical details, but something needs to be said about it in a general way.

First, it should be emphasized how squarely Neumayer's approach lay within a scientific tradition that emerged during the first part of the nineteenth century and that is associated particularly with the name of Alexander von Humboldt.[11] Humboldtian science was the very antithesis of narrowly restricted laboratory investigation. Quite the contrary, it took the whole Earth as its subject and sought to understand it as a single, interconnected physical system. Not, however, that the Humboldtian scientist rested content with vague generalisations. Instead, he sought to advance understanding wherever possible by means of precise, quantitative measurements. Major advances were made at this time in fields such as meteorology, oceanography and terrestrial magnetism by scientists inspired by Humboldt's vision who approached these subjects from a large-scale or even global perspective rather than the traditional local one.

The hydrographer Maury, whose writings exerted a profound influence on Neumayer, worked very much within the Humboldtian framework. By standardising and sifting large numbers of ships' logs, he revolutionised understanding of winds and currents on the major ocean trading routes. Neumayer claimed to have introduced Maury's methods to Rümker's school in Hamburg. Now he sought to bring the same approach to bear on a study of the waters around the Australian coast. Efficient shipping was, of course, of vital importance to the remote and widely separated Australian colonies, as well as to the profits of the shipowners. The successes Maury had achieved elsewhere were well known. Little wonder, then, that Godeffroy, busily developing extensive trading interests in the Pacific, supported Neumayer's initiative. Little wonder, either, that Neumayer was able to muster such strong support from Melbourne's maritime and commercial interests. He promised them, and the colony, substantial and immediate benefits. The backing he received from them for this aspect of his research programme was crucial to the further development of his plans, enabling him to overwhelm the opposition he faced initially from entrenched interests in Melbourne's scientific establishment, and later to gain access (compulsorily, if necessary) to the ships' logs he needed. Large numbers of ships' captains, especially those engaged in the coastal trade, agreed to use the standardised method of reporting that he developed, and also the standardised instruments that he issued from the Observatory. In due course he was able to publish practical recommendations on the planning of routes for voyages to and from Australia.[12]

The science of meteorology also made dramatic advances in the first half of the nineteenth century with the growing recognition that such well-established wind patterns as the trade winds and their variations with the seasons could be accounted for in terms of large-scale movements of air arising from temperature differences between the equatorial and polar regions of the globe. The leading figure here was the German physicist Heinrich Wilhelm Dove, and part of Neumayer's work in Melbourne was specifically directed towards confirming some of Dove's conclusions.[13]

For the most part, however, Neumayer's efforts in this field were directed simply to establishing a system of accurate recording of the weather at the various stations that came under his control, in order to generate a better knowledge of local weather patterns. Again, this was something that promised immediate benefits to the local communities concerned. Neumayer worked hard to recruit dependable observers in more localities and to furnish them with reliable measuring instruments. During his extensive travels around the colony in connection with the magnetic survey, Neumayer always carried with him meteorological instruments that had been standardised against those at the Flagstaff Observatory; and he used these to verify, in their turn, the instruments being used in the country recording stations.

Neumayer's activities in this regard came just too early to take advantage of the telegraph network that was beginning to stretch out across south-eastern Australia. It was a decade after he returned to Europe before a system was established in each of the colonies of simultaneous meteorological recording at stations linked by telegraph to a central station in the capital, thus permitting the construction of the first Australian synoptic weather charts of the kind familiar to us today, that also began to be generated in Europe at about this time.[14] Neumayer did seek, with limited success, to have the meteorological recording entrusted wherever possible to those responsible for managing the local telegraph station. His report makes it clear, however, that he did not at all foresee the direction in which the systematic use of the telegraph was soon to take the discipline:

> With the sanction of the General Superintendent of Electric Telegraphs (Mr. McGowan) I endeavoured to have the meteorological instruments entrusted to and the registrations kept by the managing gentlemen of some of the telegraph stations. This plan met, however, with some unexpected difficulty, and I was but partly successful in carrying it into effect; but I am still of opinion that this will be the only mode to insure regularity in observation and registration, and rapidity of communication in cases of particular interest, where corresponding observations are required.[15]

Mid-nineteenth-century developments in the study of terrestrial magnetism were perhaps even more spectacular—their prosecution was certainly more spectacularly expensive—than anything discussed so far. From one point of view, this was a more 'pure' research topic than either hydrography or meteorology, since a major early inspiration for it was the desire to test the highly abstract mathematical theory of the Earth's magnetic field developed in the 1830s by the great German mathematician Carl Friedrich Gauss. Yet this investigation, too, was closely linked to practical ends because of its intimate relationship with the ocean-going navigator's principal tool, the magnetic compass.

Not only had Gauss developed a theory of the Earth's magnetic field, he had also, together with his Göttingen colleague Wilhelm Weber, developed vastly improved instruments for measuring the field including, crucially, the first reliable instruments for measuring the horizontal intensity of the field. Combined with the variables that had traditionally been measured, the angles of declination and dip, this sufficed to fix the absolute intensity and direction of the field at each point. Gauss and Weber had then distributed sets of these instruments to observatories throughout central and eastern Europe that had agreed to cooperate in what came to be known as the Göttingischer Magnetische Verein.

The idea of coordinated observations at widely distributed localities had then been picked up by the British. Extensive lobbying by leading members of the British Association for the Advancement of Science and the Royal Society of London had led to the British government committing an enormous sum—over £100 000—to a worldwide 'magnetic crusade' intended to enhance understanding of the Earth's field and its variations. The high point of the crusade was a scientific exploring expedition to the Antarctic under Captain James Clark Ross during the years 1840–42, which succeeded in mapping the field over vast reaches of previously unmapped territory.[16]

Equally important in achieving the objectives of the crusade was a chain of fixed observatories established at different points throughout the Empire: Toronto, St Helena, several stations in India, Singapore, Hobart. These were devoted to systematic recording of the field, intended to advance knowledge not of the general shape of the field, as was Ross' expedition, but its manner of variation over time, in the hope of finding long-term regularities.

These hopes were not disappointed. By comparing the data from Toronto and Hobart, Edward Sabine, directing the project from his base at the Woolwich Arsenal, identified an eleven-year cycle in the field that he was able to link with the then recently identified eleven-year cycle in sunspot activity on the Sun. Other daily and seasonal variations were linked directly with the Sun's position in the sky. By the early 1850s, however, the initial aims set for the crusade had been met and the programme was wound down.

Admiralty funding of the Hobart Observatory ceased in April 1853, and though the work continued for a further eighteen months at local expense, the Observatory closed altogether at the end of 1854.[17]

Neumayer tells us that as a young man he was particularly excited by reports of Ross' expedition. Later, as we have seen, he studied for a time under Lamont, who was the leading German authority in this field in the generation after Gauss and who had developed instruments considerably more sensitive than those of Gauss and Weber. These were therefore able to register more minute variations in the field and thus held out the prospect of bringing to light still further regularities besides those identified as a result of the British efforts. Moreover, despite the achievements of the British, the 'great questions' (as Neumayer called them) concerning the Earth's magnetism remained unanswered, namely 'the locality of the magnetic force and the cause of the horary and annual variations of the needle'. It was on these that he hoped to shed further light through the operation of the Flagstaff Observatory. What is more, Neumayer had specific ideas that he wished to pursue, namely the by then widely recognised but not at all understood connection between seemingly irregular variations in the magnetic field and the appearance of aurorae; and a belief that he held in common with many other geophysicists at this period, that some of the other variations were linked with meteorological changes, especially in the patterns of the winds.[18]

The observations Neumayer recorded during his time in Melbourne did not lead directly to any significant advances along either of these lines of inquiry. His labours should not, however, on that account be simply dismissed as a waste of time. In this kind of work, long runs of observations are required before one can be sure that hoped-for regularities are *not* there. A fairer question is whether it was reasonable to pursue the particular regularities Neumayer was after; and in the context of the time, there can be no doubt that they were reasonable questions to investigate. Moreover, the systematic recording he initiated at Melbourne has been continued to this day (through two changes of location). It constitutes one of the longest series recorded anywhere in the world, and provides important data that continue to be exploited on the longer-term variations in the field.[19]

Neumayer also undertook a magnetic survey of Victoria. In his submission to the colonial government for support for this project,

Neumayer asserted that recent work in Europe with instruments of the sensitivity of those he possessed had proved 'that there exists a relation between the productiveness of a tract of land and the values of the magnetic constants' and 'between the same quantities and some geological formations, for instance the Coal-beds as I have shown in the Palatine'. 'These facts are true beyond doubt,' he said: 'The old countries have given us the opportunity of making such observations, let the new ones reap the advantage. By a magnetic map of a country we can draw a conclusion as to its probable value for agricultural and mining purposes.' Finally, 'It is more than probable that there exists a relation of terrestrial Magnetism and the great tracts of auriferous land in Australia, and such a map would enable us to point out new spots of the above mentioned interest without making trials on an expensive scale'.[20]

Neumayer's hopes here were not fulfilled either. From his journals of his travels on the survey, however, there can be no doubting the sincerity of his belief that magnetic surveying could contribute directly to the colonial economy in the way he suggested.[21] Once again, the 20th century has seen his hopes fulfilled as ever more sensitive magnetometers have yielded rich rewards in the hands of exploration geophysicists. Local variations in the field that Neumayer's instruments could not detect, or at least could not detect with enough certainty, taken at many more points much closer together than it was feasible for Neumayer ever to contemplate, today provide the vital clue that leads the miner to a new ore deposit. In this respect, Neumayer was simply ahead of his time. In the meantime, the determinations recorded on his map of Victoria were used as reference points by surveyors for many years thereafter.

Neumayer was more than just ahead of his time. He was the first professionally trained physicist to work in Australia, and he brought with him new standards of precision and sophistication in physical inquiry. As has been indicated, the kind of physics he brought with him was not laboratory-style investigation but the Humboldtian, field-based, observational and world-encompassing style, entirely of a piece with that which motivated many of the great naturalist-explorers such as Ludwig Leichhardt.

The alternative, laboratory-based style of physical research first emerged in a systematic way in some of the German universities in the 1830s but only became generally established, even there, after

the 1850s. It was brought to Australia in the 1880s by Richard
Threlfall, first professor of physics at the University of Sydney.[22]
Before this, Neumayer's work provided a lead for precision work of
a more geophysical orientation. This was carried on at the
Melbourne Observatory after Neumayer's departure by people
whom he had trained or inspired.

Precision work is an art, one that Neumayer had learned at first
hand from Lamont and perhaps to some extent from Rümker; and
he was able to pass on the knowledge involved to men such as Wills
and also Charles Mörlin, who subsequently successfully operated
the Melbourne Observatory's magnetic instruments for many years.
The need for such direct, hands-on training, and the problems that
can arise in its absence, are made all too plain by the sorry story of
the Great Melbourne Telescope, one of the largest telescopes in the
world when it was installed a few years after Neumayer's departure
under the superintendence of the self-taught director of the
Melbourne Observatory, R.L.J. Ellery, but which never lived up to
the high hopes held for it.

In summary, then, Neumayer emerges as a very significant
figure in the history of science in nineteenth-century Australia, despite his having spent only a few years in the country and his work
having led to no spectacular scientific outcomes. He brought about
a substantial improvement in the level of work being done in the
physical sciences and established a base for further such work in the
future. The various colonial observatories were perhaps the leading
institutions of late-nineteenth-century Australian scientific life.
There is a striking improvement in the quality of their work that
coincides exactly with Neumayer's presence; and I for one am prepared to attribute much of it to his influence.[23]

Part of Neumayer's success in Australia was undoubtedly due
to his very attractive personality. Except for the letters of the irasci-
ble Brough Smyth, every document I have seen bears testimony to
Neumayer's ability to charm those with whom he had to deal. To be
sure, his success in marshalling support for his cause shows that he
was also a good politician; but, in addition, people just seem to have
liked him and to have liked helping him. The tributes paid him at
the time of his departure from Melbourne were heartfelt and parallel
the love and esteem accorded him in his native province when he
retired there in his declining years. It is too easy for us to forget that
success in building scientific institutions depends not only on the
scientific importance of the work proposed but still more upon the

non-scientific, personal qualities of the institution-builders. Neumayer's achievement brings the point very forcefully to our attention.

CHAPTER 4

Amalie Dietrich

Ray Sumner

The German naturalist-collector Amalie Dietrich made a singular contribution to Australian science in the latter part of the nineteenth century. She spent almost ten arduous and often lonely years in colonial Queensland acquiring, preparing and assembling comprehensive collections of plants, birds, reptiles, insects and Aboriginal artefacts, all carefully packed for shipment to the Museum Godeffroy in Hamburg. The fact that such an extensive and scientific collection was undertaken by a woman would have been remarkable even in Europe; and it certainly sets her apart in the history of colonial science. In general, those few women in Europe who demonstrated an interest in aspects of natural history at that period were middle-class wives, whose comfortable circumstances and good education allowed them to pursue an unusual pastime. Their status was strictly amateur, their collections usually decorative rather than scientifically classified or arranged. 'Real' scientists were men.

The German city with which Amalie Dietrich was most closely connected was not Berlin but Hamburg where her specimens were studied, curated and displayed, and where she lived the last eighteen years of her life. She possibly visited Berlin only twice in her lifetime; but that city played an important role in Amalie's life as the destination of a trip made in 1851 by her husband Wilhelm Dietrich. The story was recounted as follows by their daughter Charitas.[1]

Soon after the death of Amalie's mother, Cordel Nelle, in 1850, Amalie found herself unable to manage the demands imposed by housekeeping, motherhood and the labours of collecting and preparing scientific specimens with her husband. They decided to engage a housemaid, an orphan named Pauline (Paula) Wallfahrt. The girl was young and attractive—'an unusually beautiful appearance ... Her pretty fresh face with its fine nose and large blue smiling eyes was surrounded like a halo by an abundance of red-blond hair'.[2]

The two women had difficulties from the start. Amalie was a poor housekeeper, unused to giving orders, small and unassuming; Paula was capable and condescending. She managed the housework easily but deprecated Amalie's scientific work and treated collecting and preparation of specimens as a frivolity. Matters came to a head when Paula struck the child Charitas who fell against a box and injured herself. Amalie dismissed the girl immediately.

Sometime later Wilhelm declared that he must travel to Berlin in order to collect in person the outstanding payment for a herbarium they had sold. While Amalie continued to work diligently at home in Siebenlehn, the child discovered in her father's coat pocket a letter to Wilhelm from Paula, revealing that he had gone to a *rendezvous* with her. This deception led Amalie Dietrich to undertake her first long trip, to her brother Karl in Bucharest. Her passport for the trip was issued in Siebenlehn on 25 October 1851.

Amalie Dietrich made a number of trips in Europe. These have been insufficiently researched, but the following summary gives an indication of the extent of her journeying.

Amalie Nelle was born in the Saxon town of Sienbenlehn in 1821 and lived there for twenty-five years with her parents until in 1846 she and her new husband Wilhelm Dietrich made a honeymoon trip to Thüringen to meet his relatives.[3] They then spent five or six years in Siebenlehn collecting specimens of plants, insects and rocks from the surrounding countryside and forest.

In 1851, Amalie took her daughter via Dresden, Prague, Vienna and Pest to Bucharest. After a short time there Amalie was employed by a miller's family in Siebenburgen (Transylvania) near

Kronstadt. During this period she made a three-day collecting foray into the Carpathian mountains.[4] In late 1852 Amalie and Charitas returned to Wilhelm Dietrich in Siebenlehn.[5]

Some while later, possibly in 1855, Amalie and Wilhelm made a journey on foot through Thuringia, Hesse, Westfalia to Cologne, selling their collections and taking seventeen weeks for the trip.[6] Around 1856 they purchased a large dog and a cart to transport their collections, and set out on a four-month journey through Lusatia, Bohemia, Silesia to Cracow.[7] One summer Amalie went alone on foot, carrying a large basket for her collections, and spent eleven weeks gathering specimens in the Salzburg Alps.[8] On another occasion Wilhelm, accompanied by his assistant Donath, travelled to Poland to sell collections.[9] Amalie later took the dog-cart on a trip to Magdeburg and Berlin.[10] Finally in the summer of 1861, Wilhelm sent Amalie, again with the dog-cart, on a long trip to sell through Germany, Holland and Belgium and to bring back algae and seaweed for their collections. The planned route led through Bremen, Arnhem, Maastricht, Liege, Brussels, Louvain, Malines, Antwerp, Rotterdam, the Haag, Leiden, Haarlem, Amsterdam, Krefeld, Kassel, Göttingen, Thüringen. Amalie became ill in Holland and spent four weeks in the hospital at Haarlem. She was away from Sienbenlehn some four months. On her return she discovered that Wilhelm, assuming she had perished, had abandoned their daughter and taken a post as tutor to the children of Graf Schönfeld in nearby Herzogswalde.[11]

In 1862 Amalie travelled by train to Hamburg where she was engaged by Johann Cäsar VI Godeffroy (1813–85) to collect in Australia for ten years. She returned to Siebenlehn to farewell her father.[12]

Amalie Dietrich set sail from Hamburg on the Godeffroy clipper *La Rochelle* on 15 May 1863, bound for Moreton Bay. She arrived in the Colony of Queensland on 7 August 1863. During the next nine years Amalie collected at Brisbane, Gladstone, Rockhampton, Mackay, Lake Elphinstone and Bowen.[13] In all these locations she worked on the fringes of the small and recent settlements, collecting apparently on daytrips into 'the bush'. The natural world she found was so bountiful of specimens, many so new to European science, that she had no need to venture farther afield.[14] Before her return to Germany, Amalie visited Sydney and also collected, briefly, at Tonga. She returned to Hamburg on 8 March 1873.

Amalie Dietrich was not an explorer in the conventional sense. She did, eventually, travel round the world, and she did live and work in remote and primitive places. But she discovered no new mountains or rivers; there are no landscape features named in her honour, no towns. Her Australian experience is not comparable in geographic extent with that of her compatriots such as Ludwig Leichhardt or Baron von Mueller.

Her travels were, however, unusual for a woman at that time, even more unusual for a middle-aged woman travelling alone, and remarkable for a person of her social origins. In the realm of science Amalie Dietrich achieved a position of real significance as one of Australia's foremost naturalist collectors.

Amalie's singular achievements seem attributable to two closely related factors: the influence on her life of several notable role models and her undiminished love of science.

Wilhelm Dietrich (1811–66) was of course Amalie's chief model (*Vorbild*) as a naturalist. After having to give up his medical studies when his father died, Wilhelm subsequently trained and worked as an *Apotheker* for many years. He came to Siebenlehn in 1835. Not long before meeting Amalie he had decided to give up his employment and earn an independent living as a naturalist.[15]

It was Wilhelm Dietrich who first opened Amalie's eyes to the beauty and fascination of the world of plants and insects. He taught her the importance of acute observation: 'People have eyes but they do not see . . . Can you imagine anything more charming than this tree stump?' he asked, pointing out to Amalie moss, grass, tiny flowers, shimmering beetles, agaric and a fine spiderweb.[16] Amalie learned from Wilhelm how to collect and preserve plants. He taught her the Linnean system of classification and nomenclature. She showed immense enthusiasm and great talent for such scientific work, her energy and zeal frequently earning his praise. For several years Amalie absorbed Wilhelm's instruction in both fact and technique. He introduced her to the collection and preparation of insect specimens, requiring painstaking care with the delicate items.[17]

When he designated himself a *Naturforscher* (naturalist), Wilhelm Dietrich used the term with its original meaning of encompassing all three of the natural kingdoms: animal, vegetable and mineral.[18] By the mid-nineteenth century however the number of known species had increased so greatly that biology, botany and geology had become separate fields of scientific specialisation. The Dietrichs seem to have concentrated on plants and insects, with

some minerals. Their specimens were meticulously collected, prepared and identified and carefully assembled into sets for sale
throughout Saxony and even further afield. This was the family's
chief source of income and their life was penurious, but they perse-
vered as naturalists.

We have an unsatisfactory picture of Wilhelm Dietrich from his
daughter, whose attitude towards him was obviously ambivalent but
predominantly bitter. He married Amalie in 1846, being then thirty-
five years old and Amalie twenty-five.[19] In Charitas Bischoff's
biography of her mother, *Amalie Dietrich. Ein Leben*, he is described
as tall and slender, pale, elegantly dressed; but he spends all their
income on books, does no physical work himself while placing great
demands on Amalie, and perhaps worst of all, frequently declares
he wanted a son not a daughter.[20] Dietrich is portrayed as basically
a cold and unfeeling man, whose greatest crime was infidelity.

In Bischoff's second book *Bilder aus meinem Leben* the characters of both Wilhelm and Amalie are rounded out and softened.[21]
Here Wilhelm is no longer shown as a lazy, ineffective and improv-
ident bookworm. Instead we find that he was usually silent, always
busy and serious, speaking mainly about work, trips and collecting.
Wilhelm was in fact a well-respected naturalist in Saxony. Professors brought their classes to hear his talks; school principals came
with student-teachers; Professors Willkomm and Rheum (i.e.
Reum) came each year from Tharandt to visit and inspect the
collections; the mining students came from Freiberg, and Wilhelm
also had private pupils.[22]

Wilhelm is also said to have been the first teacher of science to
(the later) Dr Karl Müller (1818–99) of Halle and to have awakened his interest in the study of mosses for which Müller became
famous.[23] We are now shown Wilhelm Dietrich as a man respected
and admired for his learning, his chief failing being that he was a
perfectionist who would not accept untidy work from his daughter.

There is no known portrait of Wilhelm Dietrich. Only a few of
his business letters survive, in small neat handwriting, carefully laid
out and using elegant language.[24]

Amalie Dietrich was also strongly influenced by her mother. In
fact the two had an unusually strong bond. Amalie was the Nelle's
youngest child and a late child, born when her mother was forty-two
years old. Amalie lived in her parents' house until her marriage;
soon afterwards they sold their house and lived with Amalie and
Wilhelm until the mother died. Amalie's mother, like many country

women of the time, had a reputation as a skilled herbalist, and the
young Amalie had often accompanied her mother to collect
medicinal plants which were dried and made into infusions, salves
and poultices. But for Wilhelm, this may have remained Amalie's
sole knowledge of botany.

It has been suggested that a second female role model for
Amalie was Maria Sibylla Merian (1647–1717), who studied and
depicted in minute detail the plants and insects of Surinam.[25] The
daughter of a noted engraver, Merian had originally studied miniature painting. In 1679 she began publishing volumes on European
insects, illustrated with her own engravings. In 1685 Merian left her
husband and moved to Holland where she became interested
in tropical insects. Taking one daughter, Merian spent two
years (1699–1701) collecting and painting insects and flowers
in Surinam (later Guinea). The *Metamorphosis insectorum
Surinamensium* was published in Amsterdam in 1705.[26]

In her youth Amalie Dietrich was an avid reader. Her daughter
tells us that Amalie plagued her mother with questions concerning
foreign places she read about in bible stories; later Amalie borrowed
from a local lending library many books, ranging from mediaeval
romances and moral tales to travel accounts.[27] There is no indication however that she knew of Merian's life or work.

There were of course some women who made significant contributions to scientific research in the nineteenth century. Outstanding examples such as Mary Anning's palaeontological work or
Mrs A.W. Griffiths' dedication to algology come to mind.[28] Like
Amalie Dietrich these women were meticulous field naturalists who
published nothing under their own names.

There were even some nineteenth-century women who travelled
extensively and alone. Two artists come immediately to mind. The
indefatigable traveller and apparently tireless painter Marianne
North (1830–90) scoured the globe from 1865 to 1885, painstakingly recording in oils plants and flowers in their natural habitat.
Her museum of paintings at Kew displays over 800 of her works,
arranged by her.[29] Much closer to home we had Marian Ellis
Rowan (1847–1922) who also travelled alone through remote
north Queensland painting rare flowers from nature. In her fifties
she also visited North America and England.[30] Both were women of
great resolve, tenacity and endurance, but their achievements lie in
the realm of botanical illustration (and autobiographical writing)
rather than natural history. For similar reasons it is not proposed to

discuss here the work of other Australian women whose names have been linked with Amalie Dietrich: Georgina Molloy, Louisa Meredith, Elizabeth Gould, Louisa Atkinson.[31]

Although their achievements in illustration and even in collecting are notable, the range and importance of Amalie Dietrich's scientific work make such comparisons inappropriate.

There was however a significant and previously unrecognised role model for Amalie Dietrich—the Viennese traveller and author Ida Pfeiffer (1797–1858). Ida was the third child and only daughter in a family of seven children of a wealthy merchant, Reyer. In 1820 she married Dr Pfeiffer who was considerably older than she. They had two sons. In 1842, at the age of forty-five, Ida Pfeiffer was a Viennese widow of modest means. She embarked on a series of journeys, unaccompanied, to remote and exotic lands, which she then recounted in a number of well-received books. Ida Pfeiffer visited the Holy Land (1842), Iceland (1845), and made two trips around the world (1846–48 and 1851–54).[32]

She collected natural history specimens on her travels which were donated to the British Museum and to the Königliches-kaiserliches Hof-Naturalien-Kabinett in Vienna. Ida Pfeiffer was elected to honorary membership of geographical societies in London, Paris and Berlin, and received a gold medal (for Science and Art) from the King of Prussia.[33]

Ida Pfeiffer's travel narratives were read by the great German geographer Alexander von Humboldt. In volume 4 of his *Kosmos* he gives a description of the eruption of the volcano Cotopaxi in early April, 1854, which had been witnessed by 'the excellent, brave world traveller Mrs. Ida Pfeiffer'. Humboldt is said to have praised elsewhere the 'indomitable force of character which she displayed everywhere she was called, or better was driven, by invincible passion to explore nature and the customs of various races of people'.[34]

Ida Pfeiffer recorded that the motivation for her extraordinary, extensive and adventurous journeys was 'not vanity but inborn love of travel and unbounded desire for knowledge . . . I am driven to see the world . . . Travel was the dream of my youth, the remembrance of things seen is now the solace of my old age'.[35]

Only the merest hint of the undoubtedly significant influence of Ida Pfeiffer's life for Amalie Dietrich is given by Bischoff when she remarks in her second book that as a child she had to read books aloud to her parents in the evenings while they worked. These were mainly travel narratives and she particularly recalled the remarkable experiences of Ida Pfeiffer.[36]

The parallels between these two women's lives are obvious— both brought up with no sisters, both married to older men, both beginning extensive travels at middle age (Pfeiffer forty-five, Dietrich forty-two). Their portraits also show a similar seriousness, even severity. Ida Pfeiffer had intended to travel to Australia at the start of her second journey round the world but this plan was altered when she heard of exorbitant prices here arising from the great gold discoveries. The inspirational example of Ida Pfeiffer was possibly the most significant influence on Amalie Dietrich's life. But it was not a passion for travel which brought Amalie to Australia. Amalie Dietrich's life was characterised above all by a passion for knowledge of the natural world.

Even after Wilhelm Dietrich had abandoned Amalie she would not give up the work she had grown to love. Her thoughts at this time of uncertainty and deepest depression, as portrayed by her daughter, were 'She could display nothing tangible but had her inner life not been greatly improved?'[37]

With specimens from their earlier years Amalie continued to eke out an existence for Charitas and herself until in Hamburg she met the wealthy industrialist Heinrich Adolf Meyer (1822–99), an enthusiastic collector who later received an honorary doctorate from the University of Kiel for his services to science, particularly marine biology.[38]

Meyer introduced Amalie to her future employer Johann Cäsar VI Godeffroy, head of the shipping and trading firm J.C. Godeffroy & Sohn, who was just then setting up the Museum Godeffroy, an institution which would draw on his vast South Sea 'empire' and serve as both a respected public museum of science and ethnology and a source of further income through the sale of specimens.

Before Amalie went to Australia as Godeffroy's naturalist, she received further training necessary for her task: the use of weapons, the evisceration of animals, their preservation in alcohol, and the preparation of bird skins.[39] She had a contract to spend ten years in Australia collecting for the Museum Godeffroy. She was the only woman Godeffroy ever employed as a naturalist.

Amalie was the antithesis of the conventional scientific figure: a woman, a competent and dedicated field naturalist, and a person of working-class origins. She received no formal education beyond the village school (200 pupils in two rooms, with two teachers and an

assistant); her parents would not have believed in higher education
for girls, even if they had been able to afford it. Amalie is a rare
demonstration that hard work, ability and ambition could overcome
class origins, education, age and even sex. In the mid-nineteenth
century serious and professional science was still an exclusively
male preserve; furthermore it was the province of wealthy men.

The study of natural history was growing however into a truly
popular middle-class pursuit. By the 1890s various branches of
'nature study' were enthusiastically embraced by women, clergy-
men, even a few working-class people. The socially acceptable version of such 'science' was a pleasant group outing for a day out of
doors, sketching from nature or collecting pretty flowers or colourful
insects or gathering seashells. These 'specimens' could then be
arranged into an artistic display for parlour or boudoir.

None of this affected Amalie Dietrich, for whom the serious
pursuit of natural history created a link with a world beyond her
class origins, the world of scientific scholarship. Her main cus-
tomers were *Apotheker* and professors and their students, and her
encounters with men such as Professors Heinrich Moritz Willkomm
(1821–95), Christian August Friedrich Garke (1819–99), Johannes
Leunis (1802–73), Karl Müller (1818–99) and above all
H.G.L. Reichenbach (1798–1879) were a source of inspiration
to her.

Letters in the Bischoff family archive from Dr Karl August
Friedrich Wilhelm Müller show that he knew and admired Amalie
for some 40 years. Müller was a former *Apotheker* who became a
respected bryologist and co-founder of the journal *Natur*. Amalie
had stayed with his family several times over the years when she
travelled about in Germany selling her collections. Müller later identified the mosses Amalie collected in Australia and named four new
species in her honour. In her old age Amalie sent him a personal
present of a large packet of Australian plants.[40]

Heinrich Gottlieb Ludwig Reichenbach was a particularly
important and influential acquaintance of Amalie Dietrich.
Dr Reichenbach came to Dresden in 1820 as both Inspector of the
Royal Naturalist Cabinet and Professor of the Academy. Here he
became a close friend of King Friedrich August II. Reichenbach
taught, laid out the Botanic Gardens and transformed the Curiosity
Cabinet into a scientific museum. In 1833 he was president of the
Dresden Botanical Society 'Flora' and in 1834 founded the natural
history society 'Isis', serving as its president for twenty-five years.

Reichenbach's dual expertise as botanist and zoologist, and even more specifically his love of 'organic nature', made him a person for all naturalists to admire and emulate. He stressed the importance of field studies, often remarking that observation of the living world was essential to an understanding of nature, while regretting the growing trend to dissect nature and examine the tiniest particles through a microscope.[41]

Amalie Dietrich was keenly aware of the growing nineteenth-century division between the field naturalist and the closet naturalist: the former were keen observers of living organisms in their natural environments, usually amateurs, and often with broad interests and knowledge; the latter, in the museum, laboratory or 'closet', studied dissected dead organisms. These people were 'scientists', usually holding professional positions, and they were occupied, sometimes obsessed, with the description, naming and classification of species. Their interests were so specialised that many devoted their life's work to the study of a single class, or even a single order.

Such a confined view was as incomprehensible to Amalie as it was to the older Reichenbach. Amalie's confidence in her fieldwork showed clearly in two ornithological examples. She did not hesitate to correct a published scientific description of the jabiru by his son Heinrich Gustav Reichenbach. She knew from minute observation the variations in iris colour and leg colour between young and mature jabirus. Amalie also challenged the published description by another German scientist of one of her own specimens. Her field observations showed clearly that he had made an incorrect identification[42].

The importance to Amalie of links with scientists in her homeland echoes in the jubilant words of her first letter from Rockhampton: 'In all regions new and unknown things! And all these wonders of nature, . . . all, all serve to bind me with my old homeland. Invisible threads run from here to there; from me to the learned men who work on these items. Thus I am acknowledged. Do not think that I am insensible or indifferent to this.'[43]

As a young woman Amalie is said to have related to her mother a dream in which she saw tall palm trees, colourful birds, distant mountains, sailing ships and black men, and where she wandered freely and happily in the glowing sun.[44] Amalie was well past her youth when J.C. VI Godeffroy sent her to Australia. Unlike her fellow voyagers she had no desire to start a new life here. She looked forward to a time, ten years hence, when she would return to her daughter, Charitas, the 15-year-old girl she had left in Hamburg.

Godeffroy was not to be disappointed by his seemingly rash choice. In Australia Amalie had the opportunity to prove her worth, and she did it even beyond Godeffroy's expectations. Amalie in return was profoundly grateful to him for this scientific opportunity, for the salary which afforded an excellent and expensive education for her daughter, for her own freedom from want (all materials were supplied, transport arranged), and above all for his trust and confidence. In the first letter, from Brisbane, Amalie writes: 'A proud happy feeling filled me at the thought of being employed by such a business house.'[45] But even more clearly she writes lyrically in the first Rockhampton letter of her freedom, boundless enthusiasm, and joy in the rich collections she can now make: 'I have no fear that I could disappoint the expectations the Godeffroys have of me. . . . I feel as if Godeffroy had given me the whole great continent as a present.'[46]

Amalie Dietrich's love of science shows most clearly in the size and significance of her Australian collections. The Amalie Dietrich collections covered almost the whole range of natural history and abounded in species new to science. Her beautiful collection of Australian flora included all plant forms from trees and shrubs, to ferns and grasses, and even tiny mosses, fungi and algae. Amalie Dietrich's birds represent probably the largest collection of Australian avifauna ever made by a single person. Her entomological collection contained several hundred beetles and a large selection of Australian butterflies, but more importantly, she was the first to make a significant collection of Australian spiders; these were the basis for what is still the major reference work on Australian *Arachnida*.[47] Marsupials, fish, sea-slugs and corals were also collected, and her outstanding herpetological collection included some of Australia's deadliest snakes.[48] She also collected numerous ethnographic articles, now valuable relics of an almost lost traditional aboriginal culture.

What a challenge Australia was to Amalie Dietrich. The wonders of nature were open to her, and through her, to European science. Wherever she looked, everything was new, from the huge ferns, which she pressed so carefully, to the many varieties of 'evergreen' eucalyptus, the birds and splendid butterflies, the glorious reef fish, and the almost unbelievable marsupials. Free at last from financial problems, she could rent a house, order supplies, engage assistants, and devote her whole attention and energy to her collections. She had a horse and cart to carry her goods and collections, and a small boat to make excursions to offshore islands. She entered into the scientific life of the small communities where she lived, donated specimens to local Schools of Arts, sharing her knowledge and experience with the few other local enthusiasts, people whose names are also important in Australian history.

Despite such work, Amalie Dietrich is virtually unknown in Australia today. While the names of Ludwig Leichhardt and Carl Lumholtz are familiar as other foreign naturalist-explorers in Northern Australia, Amalie Dietrich is a stranger. The reasons for this are not difficult to discern. She was always an unusual figure, an outsider, in Germany as in Australia. Her dedication to natural history necessitated long excursions alone, followed by the intensive labour of preparation, drying, preserving, labelling and packing the specimens. She had little time for social gatherings or pleasant pastimes. Just as she had not fitted into the conventional pattern of behaviour of other women in Germany, she was an outsider in the Australian frontier towns. A remote and solitary figure, she obviously had little contact with most residents of the embryonic ports on the Queensland coast. In addition, her poor grasp of English led her to seek out mainly German contacts, reinforcing her separation from the majority of settlers.

This then was Amalie Dietrich in Australia. She laboured for almost ten years on the Queensland frontier. She worked there in obscurity despite the remarkable and even bizarre aspects of her occupation; just as quietly she departed; her impact on colonial society was apparently negligible. Her contemporary acquaintances in Australia died, and their children, in the great wave of anti-German feeling which swept this country from 1890 to the Great War and beyond, suppressed all trace of their origins. By the next generation, all record or recollection of Amalie Dietrich was gone.

Amalie Dietrich's impact on European science was, however, a different matter. Museum Godeffroy correspondence reveals how contemporary European scientists eagerly awaited each of Amalie's consignments of specimens from the field in Australia. From the Museum Godeffroy in Hamburg collections were sent to specialists in Berlin, Copenhagen, London, and elsewhere. Amalie's Australian timber collection won a gold medal in Hamburg. She was elected to membership of the world's oldest and greatest entomological society in Stettin. Numerous scientists praised Amalie's work. Several even named new species of plants, insects and other animals in her honour.

Amalie Dietrich played a unique role in Australian scientific history and in the continuing development of Australian–German relations.

CHAPTER 5

Robert von Lendenfeld: biologist, alpinist and scholar

David Sandeman

Robert Ignaz Lendlmayr Reichsritter und Edler von Lendenfeld was born on 10 February 1858 in Graz, Austria, to Johann and Ellen von Lendenfeld. Robert's mother came from a Quaker family in Godalming, England. His father died when Robert was twelve years old. He went to school in Graz, studying languages, and followed school with a stint in the army reserve as a lieutenant. After being part of the occupational force in the artillery at Herzegowina (Jugoslavia) he returned to Graz and studied the natural sciences, in particular zoology and geology, at the University in Graz, obtaining his D.Phil. for a thesis on the flight of dragonflies. He was already an alpinist of some reputation and led a number of first ascents of peaks in the Austrian Alps including the north-east flank of the Grohmannspitze. During his holidays he often worked in the marine station at Trieste. In 1881 he married Anna Skala from Graz and in the same year left for Australia with his young wife to study the little-known invertebrate marine fauna of that land. For four and a half years he lectured in Sydney (Technical College), Melbourne and Christchurch (Agricultural College), and under contract to the Sydney Museum carried out a study on the systematics of the Australian sponges, hydroids and medusans. He travelled widely, visiting the Australian and New Zealand alps where he and his wife were the first to ascend the Hochstetterdom.

In 1885 he returned to Graz and in 1886 began work with Ray Lankester at University College, London and the British Museum. In 1887 he returned home to a position at the University of Innsbruck where he continued with his work on sponges. He was appointed professor in 1895 at the German University in Prague. Now an internationally recognised authority on sponges, he was called upon to work on the material brought back from the expeditions of the research ships *Valdivia*, *Challenger* and *Albatross*. A measure of his stature can be gained from the knowledge that he collaborated on equal terms with the great Alexander Agassiz on descriptions of the material from the American Albatross expeditions. In 1913 he was elected to rector of the German University in Prague and died in that year. He and his wife had nine children, two of whom died. One of these, Albina, died in Melbourne. A small lake high in the Snowy Mountains still bears her name, although few would know the origin of the name.

Robert von Lendenfeld was refreshingly normal and almost modern in his ambition and self-confidence as an exuberant young academic visiting Australia partly out of fascination for his subject, partly out of the adventure of it all and probably partly because like today, any overseas experience would do no harm in furthering his career in the academic world. He was not driven to Australia for financial reasons or to seek escape from a miserable life in Europe as a member of a persecuted minority. In fact his descendants tell of a certain disapproval in the family of his jaunt with his young wife to such a distant land. There is no evidence that he ever wished to settle in Australia. This means that we can perhaps expect a slightly different viewpoint from von Lendenfeld in comparison with that expressed by German settlers who had to face the problems of a divided loyalty between their new land and their birthplace, and the criticism that they were displacing English settlers in their own colony. It is also possible that as an Austrian, von Lendenfeld was to a certain extent immune from the criticisms levelled at the German people in the years after the unification of Germany.

Von Lendenfeld came to Australia to look and above all to undertake some serious science. That he achieved this is clear from his numerous publications. That his postdoctoral stay in Australia was good for his career is obvious from his biography. His interest in Australia was not entirely scientific, however, because on returning home in 1887 he was moved enough by his Australian adventure to write a popular book about his travels and experiences in the Antipodes.[1] This book was written in German although we know he was quite able to write it in English had he so wished. The book was therefore for the home market—he wanted to tell his own people about the wonders of the new continent. He probably had no wish ever to return to Australia (and indeed never did) and so writes frankly about the conditions he found, sparing no one in his criticisms. This is valuable as it mirrors not only the thoughts of the colonists he met but also the attitudes of a certain body of European academics at that time.

Von Lendenfeld provides us with a short sketch of Sydney and Melbourne in the mid-1880s in the following words:

> ... each with a population of about 300,000 inhabitants, they are not like European towns with the same number of citizens. Drainage, telephones, steam trams, theatre, university and library are excellent when compared with conditions in English capital cities, but the theatre and university are bad by German standards.

His account of the people is even more revealing and gives an excellent idea of the social prejudices of the dominant, English, colonists:

> ... although in my experience, it is not possible to find companions of similar taste, the social life of the greater majority of the English business people is very pleasant. Hand in hand with the most complete public freedom, there is an intense private intolerance of religious and national relationships, but these are naturally not perceived by the pious English majority. For an Englishman who honestly pursues his business and goes obediently to church on Sundays, Australia is in the truest sense of the word, a happy land. For the Scottish presbyterian, who everywhere receives deference, if not respect, it is also a happy land. For the Irish Catholic, and of these there are more than half a million, Australia is, in its social aspects, no longer a happy land. The Germans are distinctly not welcomed by the British, and some of them certainly wish for a German State colony where they would be the masters and not, as in Australia, the servants. The same applies to the French and the Italians. There are many Germans in Australia, almost exclusively from north Germany. Bavarians and Austrians are seldom found, and then not in the best circumstances; for them the conditions in Australia are clearly unsuitable.

In spite of this rather damning account of the English colonists, it is obvious that von Lendenfeld himself was quite well received. As a highly qualified academic he was financed by the New South Wales Government to carry out some curious missions. He tells for example, of a lecture tour he undertook to the north of New South Wales that was sponsored by the government in Sydney. The subject of his lectures to the colonists, 'the origin of the land on which they lived and was the source of their riches', was received with mixed reactions. In some towns the entire population turned out to hear him, and in others it was difficult to round up more than a dozen. The lectures were held in the schoolroom and the local minister of religion undertook the arrangements. Von Lendenfeld praised the tolerance and education of the Catholic ministers of the time, but clearly ran foul of the Presbyterian clergy, and indeed on one occasion was required to slip quickly out of the lecture hall and spend the night in a hayrick. Considering that he was lecturing on evolution to fundamentalist religious people, it is perhaps no surprise. It is interesting though that the central colonial Government in Sydney was far-sighted enough to support and encourage men like von Lendenfeld to go out to the colonists in the distant small towns and villages and lecture to them on geology and biology.

As a biologist and alpinist, von Lendenfeld was far more interested in the geology, plants and animals in Australia than in the people. A great deal of his book is therefore devoted to careful descriptions of his encounters with the various animals and their habits. Accounts of hunts for kangaroo and dingos give us an accurate picture of the attempt to eradicate these animals. Von Lendenfeld matter-of-factly points out that the kangaroos eat a great deal of the grass that would otherwise be used more profitably to fatten sheep, and that the dingo was a source of hydatids and also caused problems for the sheep farmers. Nevertheless he betrays a certain sympathy for the kangaroos in his statement that the large kangaroo had virtually disappeared from the more populated regions as a result of the 'war of destruction against this beautiful animal'.

Von Lendenfeld quite often used some particular aspect of the geology or biology of Australia as a way of introducing some of the controversies of the day. In his chapter on the forest and its influence on the climate, he points to the importance of forested mountain slopes in the prevention of rapid run-off after rain, at the same time referring to the lack of grass cover on the flat lands where eucalypts grew. The arguments of the day though were apparently not so related to soil erosion but to the possibility that cutting down the trees would lead to an even drier climate than already existed. The counter claim, put, as von Lendenfeld tells us, by the sheep farmers and squatters, was that the climatic changes would be so small as not to be noticed and would anyway be worth the enormous advantage to be gained from clearing the forest. Von Lendenfeld was inclined to favour the view of the pastoralists, at least as far as the flat lands were concerned, because he had seen that where the eucalypt had been cleared by the squatters, 'as far as the law allowed . . . the previously naked ground was covered with a variety of grasses and . . . places where before one could run only 100 sheep, 1000 sheep now thrive'.

His one essay on the Aboriginal people is similarly more an aside following the description of the bogong moths he encountered on a trip to Mount Bogong in Victoria. He does not quote the source of his information about the Aborigines, and does not describe any first-hand encounters with them. Some of the stories he tells are apocryphal and one can only assume that he has written what he heard from the white colonists with whom he came into contact. In itself this is interesting as it gives a rather sad picture of the attitudes of many of the people at that time. He reports that the Aborigines of the mountains and southern parts of Australia were smaller and less enterprising than those of the north. He points out that they were slow and did not make themselves useful to the white man in any way, indeed that they resisted white civilisation and were 'slowly vanishing before its advance'. A telling passage sums up the confidence and arrogance of the new settlers in Australia:

> The philanthropist will read with regret that the indigenous people of Australia are being exterminated with powder and steel and with introduced sickness and rum. Others ask what these people have achieved, having lived for many hundreds of years in the riches of Australia. They have not cultivated one square kilometer of land, nor won a single treasure from the mountains. And look what we have done in a hundred years? Australia delivers gold and wool to half the world. Cereals, sugar, wine and coal are produced in sufficient quantities for the needs of several million inhabitants.

Bold words indeed, and ones for us now to ponder.

We get another glimpse of the racial intolerance of the times in his chapter on a journey through the Kiewa valley in Victoria. It would appear that at that time a significant number of Chinese had

settled and cultivated the land along the Mitta-mitta river. His discovery of their presence there prompted him to digress on their
social position in Australia at the time. They were apparently not
well liked basically because of their propensity to work extraordinarily hard and live very frugally. He regales the reader with
rumours of them never bringing their own wives but instead using
opium to seduce those of the settlers to a fate worse than death. To
top it off, having made their fortunes in Australia, the Chinese
would return to their own land and live like kings. But perhaps the
hardest of all to bear was the fact that the Chinese were known to
regard themselves as being superior to the white colonists! On a
grimmer note, he tells that this view of the Chinese people was the
main reason for much of the violence and dislike directed at them.

In his travels von Lendenfeld met a variety of the settlers including a group of homesick Forty-Eighters in an inn in Victoria, a
Scottish pastoralist who was also his guide in the Snowy Mountains, professional dingo and kangaroo hunters, Irish farmers,
mounted policemen and coachmen. We must assume that when
resident in Sydney or Melbourne he was well known to government
officials and to other German intellectuals. He refers for example to
'his friend' Baron von Mueller. Von Lendenfeld also undertook an
expedition with Stirling, a well-known Australian geologist and surveyor, to look for the evidence of glaciation near Mount Bogong.
These associations were probably responsible for his receiving con-
tracts from colonial government departments anxious to exploit the
knowledge that he and other Europeans had.

It was probably von Lendenfeld's interest and reputation as an
alpinist that secured him the task of firmly establishing which of the
peaks in the Snowy Mountains was indeed the highest. Although
this story is told in a popular way in his book, in which he also
illustrated the peaks he was referring to, von Lendenfeld published
a more authoritative account of the task he was asked to carry out
and the results of his findings are published in the Petermann's
Mitteilungen.[2] A similar account can be found in government reports of the Department of Mines entitled 'Report on the Results of
the Examination of the Central part of the Australian Alps' (1885).[3]
Among his contributions to the history of Australia, this one report
may possibly be of the most general interest, but it has apparently
been ignored. The following is pieced together from his paper in
Petermann's *Mitteilungen* and several chapters in his book
Australische Reise.

Graf Strzelezki ascended the Snowy Mountain range from the Murray valley and named a peak after a Polish patriot, Kosciusko. In his diary Strzelezki is reported to have written: 'the particular configuration of this eminence struck me so forcibly by the similarity it bears to a tumulus erected over the tomb of the patriot Kosciusko that, although in a foreign country, on foreign ground, but among a free people who appreciate freedom and its votaries, I could not refrain from giving it the name Kosciusko.'[4] The altitude given by Strezelezki for this peak was 1980 metres. The next person of note to visit the region was the surveyor Townsend who photographed the main ridge of today's Kosciusko but labelled it Ramshead and commented that it was 'one of the highest of the snowy range'.

To the north of today's Mt Kosciusko lies the peak of today's Mt Townsend. It is clear from von Lendenfeld's account, and from a comparison of his sketch of this peak with a photograph taken from the same standpoint in 1985 (figure 1), and his map (figure 2), that today's Mt Townsend was known to von Lendenfeld as Mueller's Peak. He was led to it by James Spencer, a pastoralist who had settled in the Snowy Mountain area in the 1840s and was also von Mueller's guide. The peak was named by Spencer and the local mountain men after von Mueller, as they had a very high respect for that man, probably because he was also an experienced bushman. It was also popularly thought to be the highest peak. Von Lendenfeld explored the history of the naming of this mountain. It was not drawn onto Townsend's map. On the maps of Selwyn and Wallace, published by the Government of New South Wales, it was labelled Kosciusko! It also bore this name on the official triangulation map of Victoria, but was labelled Ramshead on another official publication from Victoria.[5] The local acceptance of this nomenclature is corroborated in Ziegler's comment, 'There are many oldtimers who refer to [today's] Mt Townsend as Mt Kosciusko . . .'.[6] Von Lendenfeld's solution was to accept the local name of Mueller's Peak and transfer the name Kosciusko to the entire mountain range. He also gives the following altitude measurements noted by the different people who climbed his Mueller's peak:

Strezlezki—boiling point 1980m
Mueller—boiling point 2100m
Clarke—aneroid 2197m
Neumayer—aneroid 2197m

Figure 1 Von Lendenfeld's sketch of what he called Mueller's Peak from the east made in January 1885 and a photograph taken by the author in March 1985 of today's Mt Townsend, also from the east. Von Lendenfeld's drawing shows a small lake in the foreground and snow still lying on the slopes of the peak. In March 1985 all that remained of the 'lake' was a marsh, and no snow lay on the slopes. The overall shape and rocky composition of the peaks in the two pictures are very similar but the most persuasive feature that leads to the conclusion that the two pictures are of the same peak is the large boulder projecting out of the northern slope.

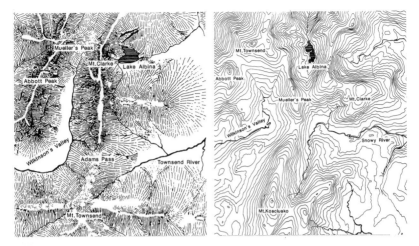

Figure 2 Von Lendenfeld's sketch map (left) compared with a modern contour map (right) of the area between today's Mt Townsend and today's Mt Kosciusko. The main geographical features drawn by von Lendenfeld fit well with present-day maps so that Wilkinson's valley and the two ridges on each side running north to today's Mt Townsend are easily recognisable. Von Lendenfeld's Mt Townsend has become Mt Kosciusko and his Mueller's Peak has become Mt Townsend. Abbott Peak and Lake Albina remain the same, but Mt Clarke has moved from west of Lake Albina to south east of it. Von Lendenfeld's Townsend River has become the Snowy River.

Black—triangulation 2215m
Lendenfeld—aneroid 2196m

We can be fairly sure that all (except Strzelezki) were scaling the same peak because they were guided there by Spencer. Also the Victorian surveyor, Black, built a stone pyramid on the summit, selecting it as the highest point and marking its position clearly on his maps. Thus at the time of von Lendenfeld's visit it was generally accepted that the Muller's Peak (or Mt Kosciusko) of the time was the highest mountain in Australia. Von Lendenfeld's account of his own amazement (and doubtless pleasure) at finding that his theodolite showed even higher ground to the south is entertaining. He was fortunately moved enough to make a careful drawing of this as he had of the peak he was standing on. The coordinates he gives, his description, the altitude he gives (2241 m) and a comparison between his picture and a photograph taken in 1985 of today's Mt Kosciusko from where he was standing in 1885 (figure 3), leave little doubt that he had discovered the true high point of Australia (figure 2). At the suggestion of the then chief surveyor of the New South Wales Government, von Lendenfeld called the newly established highest point of Australia Mt Townsend! The measurements of the altitudes by the surveyors of the time could not be as accurate then as now. Nevertheless, none recorded an altitude for today's Mt Townsend of more than 2215 m (today's measurements record it to lie 2209 m above sea level). Von Lendenfeld's measurements showed the summit of today's Kosciusko to lie 26 m above that of where he was standing. In fact the difference between today's Townsend and today's Kosciusko is 19 m. In spite of the 7 m error, the evidence is fairly strong in favour of von Lendenfeld's claim, and also for his interpretation of the correct naming of the mountains.

Figure 3 Von Lendenfeld's sketch of the view south from the summit of his Muellers Peak and a photograph taken by the author of the view south from the summit of today's Mt Townsend. The profiles of the ridges and peaks match perfectly. Von Lendenfeld was looking at today's Mt Kosciusko, and named it Mt Townsend.

Some of the names that he gave to peaks and valleys have remained where he put them (figure 2). Abbott Peak still lies to the south-west of today's Mt Townsend. Wilkinson's valley still lies to the west of today's Mt Kosciusko and Lake Albina is in place to the north of today's Townsend. Mueller's Peak has been shifted to a smaller eminence to the south-east of today's Mt Townsend, however, and Mt Clarke is now to the south-east of Lake Albina instead of west of it.

The reasons for the changes of the names are perhaps to be found in the papers and maps of the surveyors and cartographers who came after von Lendenfeld. It must be admitted that von Lendenfeld's sketch map is not entirely correct (he shows Lake Albina emptying to the east instead of to the north), but the positions of the main peaks and valleys are accurately and unmistakably depicted. It is therefore a little sad that neither his achievement of establishing the highest point of Australia, nor the name he gave this summit have been acknowledged despite the publication of both in an international journal, and in the official reports of the Government of New South Wales. Perhaps there is a case to be made for setting the record straight by reversing the names of Mt Kosciusko and Mt Townsend. The patriot Kosciusko would at last be remembered by the stately peak that resembles the tumulus over his tomb; Townsend would be remembered as the first to survey the main ridge, and von Lendenfeld would, in the ensuing publicity that such a change would provoke, be remembered as the one who was probably the first to determine which mountain was the highest.

Very recently, an article by Klaus and Teichmann on the naming of Mt Kosciusko and Mt Townsend appeared in the *Journal of the Australian Historical Society*.[7] These authors carefully examined not only von Lendenfeld's account but the report of Count Strzelecki to the Governor of New South Wales and the field notes of James Macarthur. The evidence they produce convincingly corroborates the thesis advanced above, namely that the present-day names of the two peaks are reversed.

Part 2
Encountering Aboriginal Culture

Ludwig Becker and Eugène von Guérard: German artists and the Aboriginal habitat

Marjorie Tipping

B y the end of the eighteenth century the expansionist policies of the more powerful European nations were disastrous for the original inhabitants of occupied countries. No one conceded that what these people lacked, because of their centuries of isolation, might have been, for them, an advantage.

From the time of William Dampier, the first Englishman to write about the native inhabitants of Australia, the British regarded Aborigines as persons of low intelligence and the most degraded outcasts of any society. Captain James Cook assumed that the natives of New South Wales were the most primitive of all races because of their apparent lack of organisation and technology.

In the course of influencing the colonisation of New South Wales, the Royal Society in England, and Sir Joseph Banks in particular, had a passion to explore, sketch and collect specimens relating to the natural sciences. But the British scientists placed less stress on the study of human beings than their European colleagues. The science of anthropology had not yet evolved although Banks himself was well aware of developments on the Continent. But the British took it for granted that European civilisation, especially their own, was distinctly superior to that of any indigenous people.

This supposition, conveniently perpetuated until recent years, was actually challenged as early as 1802 by the French commander, Nicolas Baudin.[1] Other Europeans, particularly German migrants with scientific as well as artistic training, held different opinions. Although their conclusions had some exposure, they had little influence on the Anglo-Saxon establishment that predominated in the colonies. During the course of wandering around a considerable part of the continent which earlier explorers had regarded as *terra nullius*, the Germans gave little indication that they considered the natives inferior to Europeans. Nor did they romanticise the image of the noble savage.

The German interest had originated in the studies of Alexander von Humboldt. During his journey to South America in 1799 he had taken skulls and skeletons from the cavern of Aturuipe near the Mission of Esmeralda on the Orinoco. In Göttingen Johann Friedrich Blumenbach used the skull of one of these extinct Atures Indians for his work on comparative anatomy, *Collectionis Suae Craniorium Diversarum Gentium* (1790–1828). Following on the work of Carolus Linnaeus, who first classified all living things, Blumenbach recognised that these and other skulls he had collected represented five different divisions of the human race. He classified them according to their cranial characteristics.

There were glimmerings of interest in other parts of Europe where reason had begun to question creationist beliefs. Jean Baptiste Lamarck had first used the term 'biology' in France. It was the French who first perceived the need to appoint a person especially trained in observing not only the manners and customs of native populations but also their physical strength and intelligence.

The Institut National organised Baudin's scientific expedition to Australia. Accompanying the expedition was François Péron, a zoologist with a particular interest in the study of man. To date, no English scientist had received instructions such as those issued to Péron. He claimed to be the first person who carried the dynamometer, recently invented by Edmé de Regnier, beyond the seas, employing it amidst the 'hordes of the Southern Hemisphere'.[2] He made his first experiments in Van Diemen's Land, describing the physique of the inhabitants in detail and concluding that 'the inhabitant of these regions unites all the characters of man in an unsocial state, and is, in every sense of the word, *the child of nature*'.[3] The results of his experiments showed that the physical strength of man was not diminished by civilisation, nor was it a natural consequence of a savage state.

These conclusions suggest that the real reason behind such a scientific expedition organised by Britain's archenemy was to test the strength of the native opposition in the event of occupation. After all, they had recently suffered humiliation when Toussant L'Ouverture and his confrères had strongly resisted them at Saint Domingue.

But the French artists accompanying this and other French expeditions romanticised the natives and their world. For them, the ideal of the noble savage continued to live on, whereas the artists of the occupational forces, often ex-convicts, came to view them as caricatures of the human race. With few exceptions, written records were scathing and derisive.

Humboldt was the inspiration for the more adventurous, especially the scientists of Western Europe, whose energy and enthusiasm might take them far afield. His aim to understand the whole world and all it contained (as epitomised in *Views of Nature* and later in *Cosmos*, appearing in 1845) grew out of the Enlightenment. He extended his study of nature, of plant and animal life, to that of man and civilisation as a whole. The sciences would provide a factual statement, as opposed to the romantic view of nature expressed by contemporary artists.

In such an environment lived the two men who are the subject of this chapter. Renunciation of the old world and search for identity in the new were common reasons for many Europeans to emigrate to Australia after the 1848 revolutions—they became known as the 'Forty-Eighters'. But for the Viennese-born Eugène von Guérard, of German parentage, and Ludwig Becker, from Darmstadt, the final decisions to break their ties with Europe differed in origin.[4] They both stemmed from similar backgrounds, had noble connections, and had travelled extensively in Europe. Guérard was a fine landscape painter who sought adventure and riches on the goldfields. Becker, a naturalist as well as an artist, arrived before the gold rush for political reasons. His formal studies appear to have been confined to the art of lithography; he took classes at Frankfurt and worked closely with the distinguished zoologist Johann Jakob Kaup, whose work he illustrated.

Guérard's education had been much more formal. His artist father had taken him to study in Rome, where he was in contact

Figure 1 Eugène von Guérard: portrait by Julie Vieusseux c 1860. Oil. *Private collection*

with the Nazarenes. These were a group of German expatriate artists working in the deserted monastery of Sant' Isidoro in Rome. Their aim was the regeneration of German art through studying the earlier religious art of Dürer, Perugino and Raphael. They were a strong influence on the English Pre-Raphaelites. But Guérard felt their restrictions too confining. While in Rome he came under the influence of the artist Joseph Anton Koch, whom he knew later while studying at the Kunstakademie in Dusseldorf. But the sentimentality which emanated from the Dusseldorf school was not entirely to his liking and he followed the pattern set by the scientists: to go far afield and explore. He viewed the work of great artists in museums throughout Germany, admiring in particular the work of Caspar David Friedrich, and absorbing some of the precepts of the Biedermeier style which would influence his portrayal of Australian Aborigines.

Dusseldorf, however, had left the mark of intellectualism on Guérard, for it was there that he was able to continue in a wider sense a study of the German philosophy that he had first encountered in Rome. He found that he could relate to Kant's dictum that 'Nature adorns eternity with ever-changing appearances' and that the meanest and the noblest of her creatures were just as rich and as inexhaustible.

Not only Kant but Goethe must have had some effect on Guérard's intellectual background. Goethe believed that the artist should not be constricted by Nature but that Nature should be the medium to remove him from the limited vision of contemporary living to eternity. He believed that although man might be master of his own fate, he would always return to the path to which Nature had once directed him. Likewise Schiller believed that Nature gave one inventive faculty, set one 'naked and helpless on the shore of this great ocean—the world; swim those who can—the heavy may go down to the bottom'.

Although his early training did not extend to university, Becker was a man of many attainments and interests, which later earned him the honorary title of 'Doctor' among his colleagues. There are several parallels with Ludwig Leichhardt. Both had been members of a large family following the Lutheran faith. The fathers of both had held minor public office. The sons had studied a wide range of subjects at gymnasia. They had both enjoyed the company of patrons during their wanderings in Europe. While Leichhardt's companion and mentor was the Englishman William Nicholson, Becker had made a significant journey along the Rhine with one of Humboldt's protégés, Louis Agassiz. The latter was already a noted marine zoologist and professor of natural history at Neuchâtel. Soon afterwards Agassiz began his brilliant career as professor of natural history at Harvard University.

Becker's eclecticism undoubtedly caused some petty jealousy among those professionally engaged to follow their own pursuits while he, like Leichhardt, preferred to pursue knowledge for its own sake. His later history in Australia parallels much of Leichhardt's career. Cold-shouldered by most of those in authority, Becker would make independent studies and forays into the Victorian countryside, collecting geological and zoological specimens, shells, native necklaces and artefacts, and anything that came his way. Ultimately he would become the artist and naturalist with the foolhardy Great Exploring Expedition led by Robert O'Hara Burke and, like Leichhardt, Becker would die in one of the loneliest parts of the continent he had set out to explore.

Although largely self-taught and in tune with Agassiz in believing that if you study nature in books you will not be able to find her out of doors, Becker typified the universal man in the tradition of Humboldt and Goethe. It was desirable to be both a scientist and an artist to comprehend the great universal truths that were both aesthetic and scientific. But Becker got caught up also with the political ideas of 1848 which conflicted with the more romantic ideas of his earlier years and those with which Guérard had come to terms. The latter had been in contact with one of Becker's brothers, August, already a noted artist. August's later romantic paintings of the Scottish Highlands would grace the palace of the British royal family, where another brother, Ernst Becker, was secretary to the Prince Consort. The similarity in painting styles of August Becker and Guérard, as well as those of several artists who later went to America, demonstrates the immense influence the Dusseldorf school wielded at that time.

In the meantime, Becker had lost a position he held as artist at the court of the Grand Duke Ludwig III of Hesse-Darmstadt. The extent of his revolutionary activity during 1848 is somewhat obscure, but apparently it was enough to make him *persona non grata* in Hesse-Darmstadt and other German states. He left hurriedly for England. Agassiz had probably advised him to explore the Scottish Highlands and suggested that he deliver papers on their findings during the Rhine journey to the British Association for the Advancement of Science at Edinburgh.[5]

But like Guérard, Becker found that England was to be the starting place for journeys to a newer world. He planned to follow in Humboldt's footsteps in South America. When he embarked in 1850, two years before Guérard, he alighted at Pernambuco and spent several weeks in Brazil. But he decided to sail on in the *Hannah* to Tasmania, where he spent just over one year. There he received the attention given to a celebrity from the Governor, Sir William Denison, and other notables, and joined the Royal Society of Tasmania. With his usual curiosity, he collected numerous natural specimens. During his excursions around the island, he paid his way 'by taking likenesses', as Lady Denison wrote, adding that he was 'one of those universal geniuses who can do anything . . .'.[6] His likenesses included an important series of Aboriginal portraits, quite unlike the manner in which English artists had been portraying the natives. They are sympathetic, if sad, representations of those who were among the last of their race.[7] He also became acquainted with William Buckley, the 'Wild White Man', an ex-convict who had escaped from custody in 1803 and had lived for thirty-three years with the natives of Port Phillip. He painted a fine portrait of Buckley.[8]

As soon as he arrived in Geelong, Guérard headed for the Ballarat goldfields at much the same time as Becker left for the mainland and hurried to the Bendigo field. Becker joined Georg Neumayer, the Bavarian meteorologist, and helped to take observations for him. There he had a little contact with Aborigines and acknowledged their common sense in smearing their bodies with oil to protect themselves, especially their eyes, from the small and irritating flies and the glare of the sun's rays.[9] Neither Becker nor Guérard sketched many scenes on the goldfields which portrayed Aborigines, simply because few of them remained in the busy canvas towns. Guérard met some on the road to the diggings and Becker, in one of his more literary outbursts, mourned their passing, as well as that of the natural forest which gave way to a scene of destruction and desecration. In an engraving he pictured the shades of those who had come to haunt the scene in the shape of charred trees, and among them he imagined the figure of a lubra in mourning for what had passed away.[10]

Guérard found that those who had frequented the towns and learnt the vices of the European were different in character from

Figure 2 Johnny, artist, at Kangatong, Victoria by Eugène von Guérard 1855. Pencil. *Courtesy Mitchell Library*

those in the country, but he treated them all as human beings and not caricatures of a subservient race, as S. T. Gill and others had done. He spotted a miserable group in Geelong 'clad in the most ridiculous European wearing apparel and nearly all in a drunken condition. It is sad to see how the poor creatures are demoralised by the white man's apparel.'[11] However, in Melbourne he found a different type of native, members of the Yarra Yarra tribe, whom he painted as warriors, confidently climbing a hill above the River Yarra, defiant and fine of physique, as if life for them was as purposeful as those in command of their destiny. He met also some who were in mourning and depicted them with compassion as sorrowing persons who had lost a loved one.[12]

Both Guérard and Becker had settled in Melbourne by 1854, after about a year on the goldfields. It was a time when Becker, commissioned to paint a portrait of the Mayor of Melbourne, John Hodgson, mused that his subject had been long enough in the colony to see 'the wild bush retreat before the civilising influences of successive settlers, who converted its wastes into pastures teeming with flocks and herds, and transformed swamp, hill and dale from primeval loneliness into flourishing suburbs and hives, busy with life, enterprise and industry'.[13]

They had found a burgeoning city fast becoming wealthy in the train of mineral wealth and the influx of many immigrants who had subsequently arrived with money and education. All were eager to remain in the Antipodes and contribute to the growth of a pleasant society. Within a short time, while Becker and Guérard were trying to establish themselves, the various institutions that would provide some intellectual stimulus came into being: a University, Public Library, Philosophical Institute, and Society of Fine Arts. Germans, who were the largest of the ethnic groups, were prominent participants in the associated activities, as well as forming their own *Turnverein*.

In 1854 Becker had worked assiduously towards the organisation of the Victorian Exhibition of Produce, Industry and Art, expecting to be sent to Paris as curator of this exhibition. He was neither sent nor compensated for expenses, although in order to work on the exhibition he had refused a lucrative offer from Captain Francis Cadell to navigate the River Murray by steamer.

However, he appears to have made a journey to the Murray some time in 1854, visiting the station Kulkyne on the Victorian

side of the border which a friend, Dr Richard Youl, ran in partner-
ship with Robert Roe Orr. He met the young native Tilki, (also
known as Jemmy), a member of the Tati Tati tribe, and made an
excellent likeness of him, as well as one of Billy, a native of Port
Fairy. Billy had a 'fine manly baritone' and was then one of Dr
Youl's servants.[14] Becker exhibited Aboriginal portraits in the 1854
exhibition, which might have been these or some of the Tasmanian
portraits, together with sketches of Melbourne and Bendigo and a
necklace made of seeds worn by the 'chief' of the Tati Tati tribe. He
also exhibited some miniature portraits of Aborigines in the new
Exhibition Building in December 1856 which the *Herald* critic
thought 'highly meritorious and deserve to be shown where they
could better be seen and appreciated'.[15] In an exhibition the following year he showed a number of Tasmanian necklaces.

It is rare in this country to have an account of Australian
history from the Aboriginal point of view. In Becker's text accompanying the portrait of Tilki, we have a segment preserved relating
to the clash between Major Thomas Mitchell's party and the Aborigines in May 1836, when at least seven natives were killed. While
drawing Tilki's profile, Becker observed that the thumb of his left
hand was in a crippled state. He asked the cause and Tilki informed
him that 'I was a child and on my mother's back, when she, with
other black women, searched for mussel-fish on the Murray near
Mount Dispersion. There some men belonging to Mitchell's exploring expedition fired into us, and a musket ball carried off part of my
thumb, which never grew afterwards so well as the one I have left
here on my right hand'.[16]

Events such as these and the decline in Aboriginal numbers in
Tasmania had coerced a conscience-stricken Britain into a belated
realisation that all was not well in the colonies, and an anxiety that
extinction of the mainland Aborigines seemed inevitable. There was
little scientific knowledge of a people the English had despised as
primitive and of little intelligence. They did not quite fit into
Blumenbach's classification. Britain, in trying to make amends, had
set up an Aborigines' Protection Society to 'assist in protecting the
defenceless and promoting the advancement of uncivilized tribes'.[17]
Included in the proposals for legislation was the formation of an
Aboriginal police force to protect Aborigines from the aggressions of
their own people as well as injuries from the colonists. In Australia
there had been several committees meeting between 1838 and 1858

Figure 3 Aborigines in New South Wales. Actual location Victoria. By Eugène von Guérard c 1855. Water colour. *Courtesy Mitchell Library*

inquiring into the condition of the Aborigines, but few recommendations were ever made and fewer acted upon.

As a result of the British recommendations, the Aboriginal
Police Corps did eventuate and had an interesting but brief history.
Becker's Billy had been a member and some of William Strutt's
best portraits were of the fine and handsome young men chosen for
the Corps—all suitably dressed in uniform.[18]

But during these years some had viewed the natives objectively,
including Ludwig Leichhardt. They were, he thought, 'a fine race of
men . . . I am far more pleased in seeing the naked body of the
blackfellow than that of the white man'. By contrast, he noted that
he had seen few well-made men in the public baths in Paris and that
the black bodies were 'as perfect as those of the Caucasian race,
and the artist would find an inexhaustible source of observation and
study among the black tribes'.[19]

In 1858 the Victorian Parliament appointed a select committee
of the Legislative Council to enquire into the physical condition of
the Aborigines. The questions submitted to those who gave evidence (squatters, members of Parliament, missionaries, magistrates
and other government officials) were those which the British Association for the Advancement of Science had approved in 1839.
This Association had in turn based its report on the queries suggested by the Ethnographical Society of Paris. During the final days
Becker, one of the few qualified to make any scientific analysis, gave
evidence before the committee. He displayed his portraits of Billy
and Tilki and provided explanatory notes on their physique. He also
showed three skulls. One was of King John, a youthful 'chief' of the
Adelaide tribe. The second was that of a very old man from the Port
Phillip district. The third had been a member of the Warrnambool
tribe. He gave detailed descriptions of the crania and teeth measurements, and deduced that all three skulls had one thing in common:
the form of the upper half of the cranium, when viewed from behind
or in front, had a pyramidal shape which appeared to be a typical
characteristic.[20] Interestingly Thomas Huxley, inspecting the crania
of aboriginal Scotsmen, concluded that in their general appearance
the Tasmanians and Australians came nearest to the long ancient
skulls of Europe such as these Scottish indigenes.

Other conclusions Becker drew were that the height of the
Aborigines ranged between five feet five inches and five feet ten
inches; that generally the arms and legs were leaner than in the
negro race; the muscles and sinews were strong; and the want of fat

was not always a sign of want of strength. Their prevailing complexion was chocolate brown, their hair jet-black and, when combed and oiled, fell in beautiful ringlets down the cheek and neck. Beards were black, strong and curly, and their eyes a deep brown-black, the white being of a light yellowish hue. Becker noticed a peculiar odour, but thought it was not for want of cleanliness. He felt that it was as if phosphorus were set free during the process of perspiration and believed it was this odour which enabled horses to alert exploring expeditions to the proximity of Aborigines.[21] Leichhardt and the English explorer A.C. Gregory had both remarked on occasions when horses showed their uneasiness.

Becker agreed that many Aborigines were intemperate and blamed the publicans; that many stole, impelled by necessity; and concluded that they were not below the average intelligence of all the other uneducated masses of nations, whether belonging to the black, coloured or white races of man.[22]

Portrait painting was not to be the lucrative business the artists might have hoped. Only a few dignitaries engaged Becker as an artist and Guérard's only known portraits were of an ad hoc nature. One was a fine full-length figure of a gold-digger, well painted but very stiffly executed. There were a few delightfully spontaneous watercolour sketches of persons on the goldfields, and some Aboriginal portraits. The invention of the camera and its early introduction to Australian society almost put an end to portrait painting. The would-be colonial gentry, flush with golden money, denied a living to artists skilled in portraiture. John Pascoe Fawkner had tried to launch William Strutt by encouraging members of Parliament to perpetuate themselves on canvas, but almost all preferred the new-fangled invention. Apart from John Hodgson, Becker managed to get Sir William Stawell, Peter Lalor, Andrew Clarke, Dr John Macadam and Charles Gavan Duffy to sit for him (or to take their likenesses from photographs). As lithographs, he published the first four persons in his album *Men of Victoria.*

Meanwhile, Guérard had been making regular trips into the countryside and had ventured as far as Tasmania and South Australia. While in Adelaide he made a number of sketches of Aboriginal life, visiting a winter encampment on the banks of the Torrens near the present Botanic Park. The original sketches show only a few pencil strokes for the figures, but a finished drawing of the subject in the collection of the National Gallery of Victoria indicates that the beautifully drawn Aborigines were from divisions of the

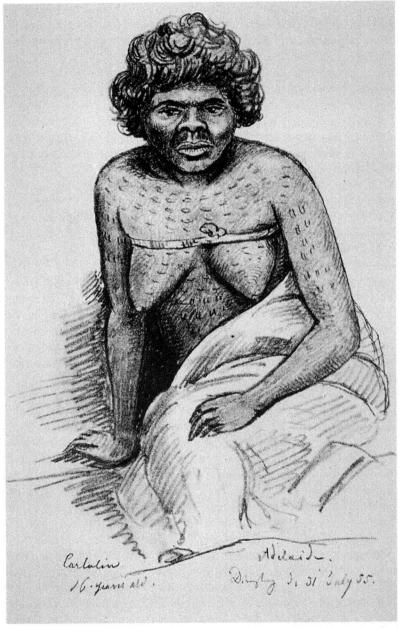

Figure 4 Caroline, the beauty of the tribe, Adelaide by Eugène von Guérard 1855. Pencil. *Courtesy Mitchell Library*

tribes from Lake Bonney and Lake Victoria, about 320 kilometres from Adelaide. Together with several fine portraits taken during this visit, they present an excellent study of the human condition as it applies to Aborigines.[23]

Guérard was about to return to Europe because his work was gaining little recognition when Sir Henry Barkly, Governor of Victoria, saw some of his finished drawings. He commissioned him to make a series of drawings of the Victorian countryside. Guérard retraced his steps across the Western District, as well as journeying in other directions. He visited families whose affluence stemmed from their valuable sheep runs. They were ready to provide him with financial security because their newly built mansions had empty walls on which they might hang paintings of their property or the local scenery. One family in particular, the Dawsons of Kangatong near Port Fairy, had cultivated a friendship with the local Aborigines. The daughter, Isabella, even spoke the local dialect. James Dawson commissioned Guérard to paint the crater, Tower Hill, as he feared that in time its natural beauty, much cherished by the Aborigines, would be despoiled. His judgement was wise. In recent years the Victorian Fisheries and Wildlife Department has taken over Tower Hill and has been restoring it from a barren sheep run to its former glory with the aid of Guérard's meticulously painted canvas and the fine chromolithograph he had made at the same time.

Chromolithography was a new technique and Guérard published twenty-four scenes in a magnificent album, *Australian Landscapes*, covering his tours in four states: Victoria, Tasmania, South Australia and New South Wales. He was not entirely happy with the result and there were imperfections in some of the plates, but they were the first in a technique previously unknown in Australia.[24] The work of others who also used the process, such as Nicholas Chevalier, did not reproduce as well.

There were other techniques by which artists could earn a little money and Becker and Guérard, as well as Chevalier and William Strutt, had numerous woodcuts and lithographs published in the illustrated newspapers which mushroomed during the 1850s. As itinerant artists visiting far beyond the confines of Melbourne, they had opportunities to introduce townsfolk to the bush and sometimes to the inhabitants of the bush. Becker himself transferred some sketches to the stone by his own hand, for he had acquired considerable skill during his studies in Frankfurt. He engraved some of

Chevalier's work, including an excellent portrait of Simon, the son of Barak ('King Billy'). Simon had brought Becker the egg of a lyrebird and acquainted him with the bird's habits and habitat. Becker corresponded on the subject with the French ornithologist Jules Verreaux as well as with John Gould and his old friend Kaup. He later reported on the nest egg and young of the *Menura superba* to the Philosophical Institute in Melbourne. He also published articles in several English and German journals.

Guérard was a more passive member of the fledgling societies that emerged in the Melbourne of the fifties than was Becker who, unlike Guérard, had no family and perhaps had more time to give to social and intellectual activities. Becker was a founding member of the two Fine Arts Societies which flourished for a time, organised festivities in honour of the centenaries of the births of Humboldt and Schiller for the *Turnverein*, and regularly contributed scientific papers to the Philosophical Institute on a wide range of subjects. His observations were full of the exuberance with which he confronted every discovery in the new world. For one whose native language was not English, he had fast learnt to be more lucid in expression in an Anglo-Saxon society than many English-born. He engraved illustrations for fellow members of the Institute which were published in the Transactions, but more importantly he was the illustrator of many of Ferdinand von Mueller's specimens in *Fragmenta Phytographiae Australiae*, Frederick McCoy's memoirs of the Museum in *Prodromus of the Zoology of Victoria* and Sir William Hooker's *Journal of Botany and Kew Gardens Miscellany*.

The Germans contributed more to the Institute than most other members and far beyond the proportion of their numbers. They were an industrious group. Apart from Becker, who carried a great part of the workload in the early years, there were Mueller, William Blandowski, Georg Neumayer and Gerard Krefft, all of whom had arrived in Australia during the early fifties. Not only had they been fired by the example of Humboldt and other compatriots, but also by the encouragement of the English botanist William Hooker and the zoologist Richard Owen. Their keenness to establish a museum of natural history was evident from the fact that they spent much time collecting specimens of the native flora and fauna.

Becker appears to have accompanied Blandowski, the museum's first curator, and the zoologist Krefft to the lower Murray and Darling Rivers in 1856. The Government had sent them to make a collection of items which included Aboriginal artefacts. During their

Figure 5 Ludwig Becker, self portrait 1855. Pencil. *Private collection*

stay at Kulkyne they witnessed fifty or sixty Aborigines 'making young men' in an initiation ceremony, which Blandowski later described in a paper prepared for the Philosophical Society of New South Wales, 'On the manners and customs of the Aborigines of the Lower Murray and Darling'.[25] Blandowski's controversial preliminary report, 'Recent discoveries in natural history on the Lower Murray', created a furore when he named new species of fish after fellow members of the Institute: *Brosmius bleasdalii* (the Reverend John Bleasdale), 'a slimy, slippery fish, lives in the mud'; *Cernua eadesii* (Dr Richard Eades), recognized by its 'low forehead, big belly, and sharp spine'; *Kurrina macadamia* (Dr John Macadam, honorary secretary of the Institute), 'lives principally on little crawfishes—takes its abode in the hollows of the banks of the billabongs, there watching for its prey'.[26]

Naturally enough, these sentiments were abhorrent to Blandowski's colleagues and the Institute. Undoubtedly there were petty jealousies and misunderstandings in the tight little society. The Germans had been well accepted in a colony ruled from afar by a Queen with German origins. But they became more vulnerable as newcomers from Britain, mostly with lesser qualifications but politically and socially more ambitious, eased their way into positions of power. During the fifties reputations were made and unmade. The more ruthlessly ambitious even denigrated their erstwhile friends as well as foreigners.

Becker and others had, perhaps unwisely, opposed McCoy who, while palaeontolgist to the Geological Survey of Victoria, had transferred the natural history specimens to the newly established University of Melbourne, including the Aboriginal skulls which Becker had sold, together with 751 specimens (328 species) to McCoy. Wits of the day had an opportunity to poke fun at the schism in the scientific world. A Melbourne *Punch* cartoon showed McCoy leading the march to the University, while a dismayed German resembling Becker protested to no avail. Mr Punch wrote of:

> Blandowski's pickled 'possums,
> And Mueller's leaves and blossoms,
> Bugs, butterflies, and beetles stuck on pins,
> pins, pins;
>
> Light and heavy, great and small,
> He abstracted one and all—

May we never have to answer for such sins,
sins, sins.

There were six foot kangaroos,
Native bears and cockatoos,
That would make a taxidermist jump for joy,
joy, joy;

And if you want to know
Who took them, you should go
And should seek for information from McCoy,
coy, coy.[27]

In the course of time most of the German scientists became disillusioned and were victimised. Blandowski hastened back to Germany with at least 4000 sketches and specimens which actually belonged to the Museum, collected while he was a Museum employee. They were lost for about 130 years, having disappeared during World Wars I and II. I was able to trace and see some of his booty at Humboldt University, in East Berlin: some 300 items, as well as Australian animals which Becker had stuffed.[28] I heard that the rest of the collection might be in Cracow or Poznan, where many collections were removed during both World Wars.

Neumayer also experienced prejudice and returned to Germany. Krefft, a zoologist of international repute, was later dismissed from the Australian Museum in Sydney. Mueller was dismissed as director of the Botanic Gardens in Melbourne that he had made world-famous. Leichhardt's fate is still unknown.

Yet it had been the scholarly Germans who were most dedicated to the serious purpose for which the Philosophical Institute was originally founded. In some respects it was becoming little more than a club for dilettantes set on a programme for self-glorification, hence the genesis of the Great Exploring Expedition.

It was the encouragement of his friend Mueller, whom he had accompanied on several expeditions to the Baw Baws and as far as Omeo, that helped shape Becker's vision of the bush in Australia and the creatures who inhabited it. It was Mueller who recommended his appointment as artist, naturalist and geologist to the expedition. As it eventuated, Becker was the only serious member of the Institute (or Royal Society as it had become) to join the party, although Neumayer accompanied them for the early part of the journey. If, during the tedious trek north, Becker became frustrated with the poverty of animal and bird life (birds were the subject of

Figure 6 Corroboree. Wood engraving. *News Letter of Australasia* XII June 1857

only three sketches and he must have become bored with the gecko), he did at least produce some of the finest portraits of the Aboriginal people, and showed something of their tribal life. He also incorporated them in several of the topographical sketches which, when magnified, suggest fine landscapes of a part of the continent not previously seen by European explorers. These are romantic in style, the Aborigines appearing small in stature and part of nature's great universe. The portraits are more realistic, finely executed in spite of incredible difficulties. He was able to capture individual likenesses as if in a time warp. They are real people and, like Guérard, he portrayed them with dignity.[29]

Becker's expectations of what his role might be during the expedition met with an overwhelming shock. The maniacal leader cast aside the roles that the scientists had been engaged to play, while he himself forged ahead in a 'death or glory' manner to satisfy his own ambitions and those of the armchair members of the Royal Society of Victoria. Neumayer made observations on some of the Aborigines Becker had sketched, including a group at Spewah: they 'were some of the finest and tallest I have yet seen of that race, and the good condition, in which they apparently were, was probably to some extent owing to the kind treatment they received at the hands of Mr McKenzie of *Poonboon*'.[30] Again at Mungin Neumayer wrote that he 'was very much pleased by some of the Blacks showing considerable intelligence while explaining to me their way of living and giving me an idea of their language . . .'—here he quoted a few words.[31]

One cannot dismiss Becker's miniature landscapes as merely topographical sketches of a scientist. It was as if he sensed his fate and, in spite of all the traumas, was determined to make some artistic contribution to life. His knowledge of meteorology gave him an understanding of the intense atmospheric effects on the Australian outback. He painted what he saw: the low horizons, the wide blue skies, the mirages, the sunlit plains. He explored the effect of the sun's rays as they penetrated the sparse vegetation and stony terrain. He worked on the sketches late into the night, for his leader forced him to drive the camels all day. Like Clancy of the Overflow, he became aware of the 'wond'rous glory of the everlasting stars'. Enlarged on the screen, slides of little watercolours, often tinged with some oil, appear to be large paintings in the grand tradition, the details meticulously painted. One finds it hard to believe they are only postcard size.

Although he sent quite lengthy reports and some letters during the journey to Dr Macadam, secretary of the Royal Society (these were not acknowledged), he wrote little about the Aborigines that was of scientific interest. But he did transcribe some specimens of Aboriginal poetry and music, a corroboree song and a creek song, both from the Lower Murray, which a young Murray black dictated to him in English.[32]

Becker's sketches remain a glorious postscript to his life, a far greater memorial than the miserable posts surrounding his shallow grave at the junction of the Bulloo River and Kooliatto Creek in south-west Queensland.

Aborigines also appear in most of Guérard's early paintings as hunters or as the family around a camp fire, demonstrating how closely their culture was connected to the land and its natural environment. Sometimes he painted in a native dog or kangaroos among the grass trees, and always birds in the late afternoon sky. These all created a feeling of peace and tranquillity.

But as the ecology changed and the station properties of the landed squattocracy expanded further into the interior, so the native people as well as the native animals receded into more distant parts. Guérard came to paint less of the old land he had once known. While the cattle and sheep replaced the kangaroos and while alien seeds produced flourishing crops and plants that swept away the indigenous plants, the European figure appeared in place of the native groups that had characterised his early romantic landscapes. Only when he went on exploratory expeditions with Alfred Howitt and Georg Neumayer was he able to recapture something of the exhilaration of the romantic tradition that had nurtured him.

Aborigines guided Howitt and Guérard through previously unexplored parts of Gippsland, in temperatures that reached $110°F$, through creekbeds infested with leeches, as far as the Moroka River valley, among the toughest and most dangerous territory in the State. None of these difficulties worried Guérard who, when Howitt suggested that there was enough inspiration before him to paint for six months, retorted excitedly, 'Dere is not seex months, dere is seex years'.[33]

In the shadow of the Australian Alps he found once more a landscape that had not changed since those primeval days when the first Australians were able to live a full life, hunting for the food that was in abundance and still living peaceably there in a state of nature. Life for them was not all harsh, as Europeans had found

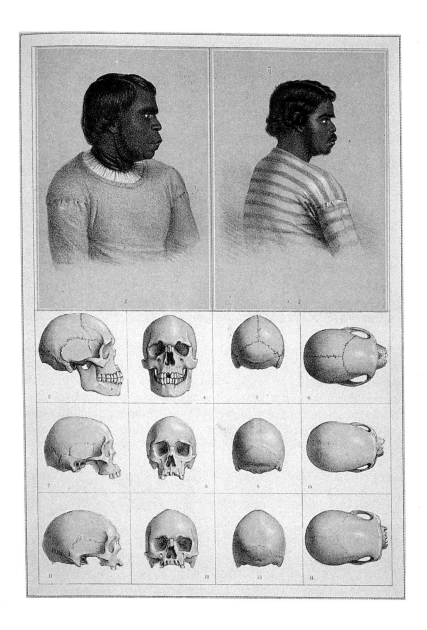

Figure 7 Billy and Jemmy (Tilki). Aboriginal skulls. Engraving and watercolour in *Report of the Committee of the Legislative Council* pp 88–9

conditions at first, for Australia was a land that provided well for
those who understood it. They were part of the landscape itself and
if Guérard found them there he made them a small but integral part
of the painting.

At every opportunity Guérard travelled in search of sublime
mountain scenery, which had inspired European artists before him
to undertake the Grand Tour. Mountain peaks in Australia or even
New Zealand, which he later visited, may not have been as high or
awe-inspiring as those in Switzerland and Italy, nor the rivers and
waterfalls as grand, but Guérard still sought the mountain gloom
and the mountain glory beloved by the Romantics. These elements
he realized in his paintings, together with every possible detail. He
defied the conventions of earlier English artists who had not experienced the same pleasures in the pathless woods of Australia nor
seen a 'wild cataract leap in glory'. Here no splendour fell on castle
walls, so Guérard replaced his former interest in picturesque ruins
and architectural devices with love and respect for the natural wonders of this continent.

Guérard was fortunate when he accompanied Neumayer who,
as government astronomer, had a well-equipped spring cart at his
disposal and took Aboriginal guides. Even so, the rugged mountain
country was a challenge to physical endurance, but Guérard was
well rewarded when they climbed the most northerly peak of Mount
Kosciusko, probably the first white persons to have achieved this
feat. He depicted them as small, insignificant figures observing the
wondrous scene before their eyes. The great outcrops of columnar-
shaped rocks inspired him to quote from Byron's *Childe Harold* in
the text accompanying the lithograph:

> Come, and compare
> Columns and idol-dwellings, Goth or Greek,
> With nature's realms of worship, earth and air,
> Nor fix on fond abodes to circumscribe thy pray'r.[34]

In scenes such as these Guérard was giving Australians an
insight into the enthralling 'architectural and sculptural aspects of
nature', as Fritz Novotny described the work of the artists of the
German *Aufklarung*, such as Guérard's former colleague, Joseph
Anton Koch. These aspects were to Guérard an extension of the
emotional and pictorial. He was well aware of the several schools of
thought in European painting, for there are echoes of work that had
influenced him and his contemporaries to be seen in his Australian

oeuvre. He was well acquainted with the literature of his time and was among the first to introduce literary notes, sometimes quoting Australian sources, to accompany his work, such as the lithographs in *Australian Landscapes.* [35]

He recognised also that science and art, as Goethe had decreed, should go hand in hand. Every detail that the artist observed was worth recording, hence the many notations relating to the time of day, colour of sea, sky or vegetation on preliminary sketches made *en plein air.* Many of these he would redraw in pencil or pen and ink, and sometimes painted in watercolour or oils in his studio. The little sketches tell one as much about the artist as the actual paintings. Over and over again he would sketch a new version of the fern tree or cabbage or grass tree, as if he imagined their tall slender trunks to be the natural substitutes for the classical columns he had often sketched in Italy, their foliage replacing the acanthus leaves that had adorned the conventional column. Goethe himself had made a plea that the column's nature is to stand free. 'Woe to the wretches', he wrote, 'who have bound their slender growth to clumsy walls.'

The figures Guérard placed in landscapes were small and mostly at a distance, but they were always distinct and not mere blobs. He never sacrificed detail for effect, which later caused some of his students at the National Gallery of Victoria to criticise him. Yet he was the first great artist trained in the European academic tradition who did recognise that in Australia there was an atmosphere that challenged those seeking to capture it on canvas. His first paintings *were* dark and dreary, and many more, hidden away in the smoke-filled billiard rooms of country houses, gathered grime and remained unappreciated for a century. But a resurgence of interest in colonial art has brought treasures out of the attics, restoring them to their original freshness, to the surprise and pleasure of many critics.

Guérard did accept the challenge which the new world offered to artists. Like Becker, his association with Neumayer gave him an insight into meteorology and probably helped in his exploration of the atmosphere. He recognised the peculiarities created by the eucalyptus tree, which everywhere exuded droplets of oil from its long leaves drooping down, unlike European trees, thereby creating a blueness in the air which native-born Australians still take for granted. Seeing it at a distance with rays of sunlight shimmering against the wide and open skies, Guérard and Becker did realise

Figure 8 Natives at Menindie 1860. Water colour. *Courtesy La Trobe Library*

that the new blue world had to be interpreted with a difference. They were the first European artists to see and understand much of that world and record it. Never again would anyone view it in the same way. It was for the next generation, Guérard's maverick students, mostly born or educated in the sunburnt country, who finally came to grips with the Australian landscape. They believed that perfect detail alone was not enough and that blobs or impressions actually painted *en plein air* could produce the spontaneous expression that Guérard had best achieved in his preliminary sketches. Yet it is doubtful whether they would have painted as well, at least in their formative years, had they not been exposed to the work of the European-trained artists: Nicholas Chevalier, William Strutt, Louis Buvelot, and in particular, Eugène von Guérard.

We as a nation are beginning to acknowledge the misdeeds of the past 200 years as they affected the first Australians. In this context it has been a salutary experience to evaluate the work and observations of the German artists who could relate to people who had occupied this land for many thousands of years. Whatever the future of those whose heritage is much longer than ours, one might also hope that the old Australians will come to learn about and appreciate the efforts of persons like Ludwig Becker and Eugène von Guérard, who tried to portray them with dignity, as human beings and not savages, and who were sensitive to the environment in which they had lived undisturbed for so long.

In Search of Carl Strehlow:
Lutheran Missionary and Australian
Anthropologist

Walter Veit

Works (on totemism) in German are numerous, but of less importance.

> —J. Hastings *Encyclopaedia of Religion & Ethics*
> vol. XII, 1921, p. 407.

Literary experts are not usually acquainted with anthropological matters . . .

> —T.G.H. Strehlow *Songs of Central Australia*
> 1971, p. xli.

My interest in Australian Aboriginal myths had led me to search for acceptable scholarly collections of myths and legends of the Australian Aborigines in English translation which could be used for comparative studies. The best example for what I have in mind is Ronald M. Berndt's philologically fully documented Djanggawul song cycle published in 1952 and at present a much sought-after title in antiquarian bookshops. Similarly, Charles P. Mountford's *Nomads of the Australian Desert* of 1976 and T.G.H. Strehlow's *Songs of Central Australia* of 1971 have vanished—like all their other works—for one reason or another into the rare book rooms of our libraries.

There existed a number of smaller collections in the past, for example Katherine Langloh-Parker's *Australian Legendary Tales*, first published in 1896 and reprinted several times, but for a long time no suitable collection was in print. The texts edited by A.W. Reed in his numerous publications are popular renderings of little scholarly value.

There are, however at least three good collections available in German, one, *Märchen aus Australien*, in the highly respected series of the Eugen Diederichs Verlag *Die Märchen der Weltliteratur*; the others as paperbacks with such enticing titles *Wie das Känguruh seinen Schwanz bekam* or *Der Tanz der Vögel*. But quite recently Ronald M. Berndt and Catherine H. Berndt have published a part of their own collection of Aboriginal tales from their main areas of research in northern West Australia, Arnhem Land and south-western South Australia under the felicitous title *The Speaking Land. Myth and Story in Aboriginal Australia*—but excluding secret myths.

It was in the German publications that I first met the name of Carl Strehlow, but it was necessary to return to Germany in order to find a complete copy of his seven-part work *Die Aranda- und Loritja-Stämme in Zentral-Australien* published by the Frankfurt Museum für Völkerkunde from 1907 to 1920. It does not take a professional anthropologist or ethnologist to realise that here was the best scholarly collection of Australian myths and legends even if they came only from a very confined area in Central Australia. But for Theodor (Ted) G.H. Strehlow's writings, nobody would know that Carl Strehlow, his father, ever existed. It was this silence about Carl Strehlow in Australian anthropology that made me look further into his work and the circumstances of his life and activities in Australia. That he was a missionary at Hermannsburg some 130 kilometres south-west of Alice Springs can be gleaned from the title page of his published books. But all further curiosity is quickly disappointed. There is no entry under his name in the old *Australian Dictionary of Biography* or any older edition of the *Australian Encyclopedia*. The volume of the new *Australian Dictionary of Biography* containing an entry for Carl Strehlow is presently in preparation. But for Johannes Stoltz' belated obituary tucked away in *Auricht's Book Almanac* of 1924 we would not even know his date or place of birth. The biographical details in publications dealing with missionary work of the Lutheran Church in South Australia or the Northern Territory

such as Everard Leske's *Hermannsburg* or Ward McNally's short
biography of Th.G.H. Strehlow *Aborigines, Artefacts and Anguish* are
completely unsatisfactory. Approaches to still living descendants
have so far not been successful. Even in the writings of his son Ted
Strehlow, dealing especially with his father's life and work, such as
the extraordinary *Journey to Horseshoe Bend* or the Introduction to
Songs of Central Australia, exact details are rare. Yet he is one of the
most important figures in Australian and German anthropology and
ethnology who—for the better part of his work at Hermannsburg—
was right in the eye of a fierce storm raised by the gods of anthropology at the time.[1]

Carl Strehlow and his work became the victims of a conflict in
European anthropology which arose long before 1900 over several
controversial issues concerning the original inhabitants of Australia,
such as their place in the evolution of humanity, their religion, their
language and their social organisation. It is my contention that it
was precisely the information contained in Strehlow's letters and
publications which brought the controversy between the representa-
tives of two different paradigms in anthropology to a head. Unwittingly, he had tripped off the avalanche of social anthropology in the
English-speaking world which engulfed and buried in all matters
Australian the older historically oriented anthropology of religion as
practised in France and Germany. For better or for worse, Carl
Strehlow continued to work in a paradigm of theory and methodology of anthropology which had been part and parcel of his training
as a missionary and contained the postulates that the researcher be
familiar with his flock and walk among the natives as a human
being among other human beings who had souls, religion and language. At the same time, Baldwin Walter Spencer and a World War
secured the dominance of the new 'scientific' paradigm of social
anthropology and empirical field studies. It is most ironic that the
very time when the new social anthropology reclassified the place of
the Australian natives on the ladder of evolution according to their
Darwinist theory from 'noble savage' to 'primitive', Carl Strehlow
recorded, translated and published the myths of the Western
Aranda and Loritja around Hermannsburg into German and described the extreme complexity of their religious belief system.

I am very much aware of the importance of the question of
colonialism in a discussion of anthropological work carried out by
scientists and missionaries alike. Publications like Klaus Bade's
Imperialismus und Kolonialmission with regard to the German

involvement, and Aarne Koskinen's *Missionary influence as a political factor in the Pacific Islands* demonstrate this very strikingly. There cannot be any doubt that European colonialist ideologies have played a considerable role in shaping anthropological theory and therefore anthropological results. Although both cannot be separated, the political parameters should be the subject of a fuller investigation than possible in this chapter.

The biography

From the published sources on Carl Strehlow's life and activities, mainly from Johannes Stolz' obituary, we know that he was born on 23 December 1871 and grew up in the farming community of Fredersdorf in the Prussian province of Brandenburg. Overcoming his father's objections to his intention to study theology, he was educated at the Lutheran Mission Seminary in Neuendettelsau, in the vicinity of Nürnberg in Southern Germany from 1 August 1888 to 31 August 1891 and designated to become a pastor for the Lutheran Church in North America.

When he was offered the chance to become a missionary among the natives of Central Australia he took it. He arrived in Adelaide in the middle of 1892 to work as second missionary of the Bethesda Mission (Killalpannina) together with the missionary J.G. Reuter among the Dieri tribe south of Lake Eyre. He demonstrated his ability for learning Aboriginal languages by translating— together with Reuter—the New Testament into the Dieri language. The translation was first published in 1897. In 1894 the South Australian Lutheran Immanuel Synod took over the Finke River Mission at Hermannsburg from the Evangelical Lutheran Synod of Australia (ELSA) which had started the Hermannsburg Mission in Central Australia in 1877, with the pioneer missionaries F.W. Schwarz, H. Kempe and L.G. Schulze from the Hermannsburg Mission Seminary in Lower Saxony, Germany. The new Mission Board chose Carl Strehlow to continue the missionary work among the Aranda and Loritja.

His work at Hermannsburg during the next twenty-eight years was interrupted first in 1895, when Carl Strehlow left for Adelaide to marry Frieda Keysser to whom he had been betrothed before departing for Australia; the second time from 3 June 1903 to 4 June 1904 when he, his wife and four children Friedrich, Martha, Karl and Rudolf went on recreation leave to Adelaide, after which two more children were born, Hermann and, in 1908, Theodor; a third time from June 1910 to 6 April 1912 when the whole family went on recreation leave to Germany from where only Theodor returned with his parents to Hermannsburg, leaving the other children to be educated in Germany. Although naturalised shortly after his arrival in South Australia and a Justice of the Peace since 1893, he had to register as an enemy alien when World War I broke out in 1914. On the recommendation of the then administrator of the Northern Territory, however, he was allowed to continue at Hermannsburg.

We do not know precisely when Carl Strehlow actually started his anthropological and ethnological work with a view to publishing his results. John Mulvaney considers 1901 as the most likely date; but considering Strehlow's translation work an earlier involvement seems likely. The question can be resolved only by studying his private papers when they become available to researchers. We are told in Ted Strehlow's *Songs of Central Australia* (p. xxxi) that: 'C. Strehlow's handwritten manuscripts have been preserved, and so have all the notes and queries addressed to him by his editor, Moritz Freiherr von Leonhardi. These reveal that in the printed volume C. Strehlow's own text has been preserved, with only very occasional minor corrections.' We shall return to the significance of the last sentence later. The first sentence, however, refers only to the letters received in Hermannsburg which I have so far not been able to see. There is no clear indication when Carl started to work on his book. There is also no indication whether Carl's letters to von Leonhardi are still extant. The Völkermuseum of the city of Frankfurt does not know the whereabouts of either and believes them to have been lost during World War II. In any case, in 1907, when von Leonhardi published several letters of Carl's in the journal *Globus* containing Aranda myths and some general remarks on field methods employed, the first two volumes of Carl Strehlow's *Die Aranda- und Loritja-Stämme in Zentral-Australien* must have been in the final stages of printing. The first volume of it appeared in Frankfurt in the same year, 1907, as the first large publication of the Städtisches Völkermuseum established just three years previously. Four further volumes appeared in rapid succession in 1910, 1911, 1913 and 1915. The last part went to press in 1920. In 1919, in the twenty-fifth year of his arrival at Hermannsburg, Carl Strehlow also completed his translation of the New Testament into the Aranda language.

Late in 1920 Strehlow sought permission to go on leave to

Germany in 1922. But sometime early in 1922 he started complaining about chest pains; too late 'dropsy' was diagnosed and help urgently requested from Adelaide. When all efforts in Adelaide to get Strehlow out of Hermannsburg failed, he left his mission with his wife and son Ted on 12 October. The journey in a buggy proved too much. He reached Horseshoe Bend, nearly halfway to Oodnadatta, where a car was expected to pick him up, and died at 5.30 on Friday, 20 October 1922. At Horseshoe Bend, he was given a simple grave which, I believe, is now in a rather bad state of repair. Ted Strehlow has described these last days of his father in his *Journey to Horseshoe Bend*, a literary work blending very effectively biography and autobiography.[2]

Carl Strehlow's widow Frieda and son Ted continued their journey to Adelaide. After Ted had completed his education, Frieda left Australia in 1931 to join her other children in Germany. She died there in 1957. This is as much as can be gleaned from published sources. The need for archival research here and overseas is obvious. The chronology of Carl Strehlow's life is only the time frame in which a forceful and dedicated missionary from Germany developed into one of the most successful if controversial anthropologists of Australia. But his work is still to be discovered by modern Australian anthropologists and phenomenologists of religion. The overbearing influence of Baldwin Spencer and his group of social anthropologists, still felt in this country today, has cast a silence over it from which his stature as a researcher has still to emerge. A few examples must suffice at this stage.

As we shall see later, Strehlow merits a mention only in the rarest of cases. He has no place in H.R. Hay's survey of Australian anthropology; A.P. Elkin, in his authoritative survey given during the all-important Research Conference in Canberra in 1961 which had brought together almost all important researchers in Aboriginal anthropology including Ted Strehlow, demonstrates the general ignorance of Strehlow's work when he writes: 'To this phase [of fortuitous, individual field projects], too, belongs Paster [*sic*] C. Strehlow, a missionary at Hermannsburg among the Western Aranda and neighbouring Loritja groups from 1892 to 1902 [*sic*], who published a series of articles [*sic*] in German recording the mythology, folk-lore and social organization of the tribes between 1910 [*sic*] and 1922. His material complements Spencer and Gillen's work on the Central and Eastern Aranda (Arunta)'.[3] In the same volume, Carl Strehlow is mentioned once more by Catherine

H. Berndt in her contribution on 'Art and Aesthetic Expression'; his work is not mentioned in the same publication by F.D. McCarthy (Ecology, Equipment, Economy and Trade), S.A. Wurm (Aboriginal Languages), A. Barnes and M.J. Meggit (Social Organization), or (worst of all) A.E. Worms (Religion), and the Index confuses him with Ted Strehlow.

In the most recent survey by D.J. Mulvaney we are told that Strehlow 'commenced his studies of Aranda religion in 1901, although the first volume was published in 1907'.[4] Further historical research should clear up the present uncertainty and recover important anthropological work for the history of science in Australia.[5]

The great silence

The silence was preceded by a worldwide 'ethnological controversy'—already so-called by A.H. Haddon in his brief reaction to Leonhardi's extracts from Strehlow's letters in *Globus* which was published in the journal *Nature*—and Carl Strehlow was in the centre of it although he may not have been aware of all its facets at the time. As we shall see later, it is not completely clear who started it all. But the two opposing groups were established very quickly. In fact, they existed before 'the outbreak of hostilities' in Europe. It is a confrontation between the mythologists and phenomenologists of religion on the one side and the empirical social anthropologists on the other. Carl Strehlow, the missionary-anthropologist, became the representative of the first group; Baldwin Spencer, the young Oxford scholar of biology whom Melbourne University Council appointed to the first professorship in biology in 1887 and who continued to become Australia's first academic social anthropologist and, in 1899, the director of the National Museum of Victoria, represented the other.

John Mulvaney and J.H. Calaby in their judicious biography of Baldwin Spencer '*So much that is new*' have carefully reconstructed the main lines of the battle that erupted in 1903 over the letters Strehlow had sent to Leonhardi who in turn had sent extracts plus commentaries to Andrew Lang at St Andrews and, as mentioned before, published them in 1907 in *Globus*. The question was whether the 'Arunta', as Spencer and his collaborator Gillen used to call the group of tribes they studied in Central Australia, had the notion of an 'Aranda (as Strehlow wrote) High God or supreme being, Altjira',[6] as described by Strehlow in his letters and later in his published works, albeit in a modified form. Strehlow's observations ran counter to descriptions given by Spencer and Gillen in their previously published works. Spencer then embarked on a campaign to discredit Strehlow;

> he countered all Strehlow's data with the unfair assertion that his unreliable informants conflated Christian doctrine and tribal tradition. Because he believed that Strehlow simply wanted to discredit Gillen and himself, [he] in turn disparaged Strehlow's work so effectively, with Frazer at least, that Frazer omitted all reference to him in his major revision of totemism. They had never met. Possibly if they had done so, Strehlow's sincerity would have convinced Spencer. His heavy-handed treatment of Strehlow was a character flaw which cannot be excused, but it may be understood in context.[7]

Mulvaney and Calaby maintain that 'Strehlow was virtually a pawn in an international debate over religious origins.[8] Strangely enough, the two protagonists not only never met—but they also seem to never have corresponded. Whether and in how much detail Strehlow and Spencer were aware of each other's writings can be decided only after an inspection of the relevant footnotes in Strehlow's manuscript of the *Aranda- und Loritja-Stämme* and of the original Strehlow letters to Leonhardi; and of the letters read in excerpts and translated by A. Lang in 1901 as well as by Spencer, according to Mulvaney on 1 December 1903.

Spencer's criticisms concerning Carl Strehlow's methods and ethnographic findings are reassessed in Ted Strehlow's *Songs* and mostly refuted without endorsing all of Carl's data. Leaving aside all aspersions on the genuineness and reliability of the informants on both sides, it comes down to a very simple though surprising fact:

> Spencer and Gillen, who have given us so many excellent pages of description of various festival rites, were forced by their ignorance of the aboriginal languages to omit the texts of the songs sung on these occasions. This was obviously very unsatisfactory. . . . Strehlow, on the other hand, was handicapped by the fact that he had never been an eye-witness of any of the sacred ceremonies. His view was that his missionary status prevented his appearance at all pagan rites. Hence his descriptions of the totemic ceremonies, for instance, had to be based purely on hearsay, and are therefore not very satisfactory.[9]

The battle line is, therefore, to be drawn not so much between the missionary and the atheist, the empirical fieldworker and some

mischievous 'opinionated social theorists [who] all claimed adher-
ence to scientific methodology, but without exception . . . seem to
have formulated sweeping and all-inclusive explanations and then
plundered ethnography to support their views,[10] like Andrew Lang
whom Mulvaney and Calaby view as the villain in the whole affair.
Rather, it should be drawn between the empirical scientist and the
philologist, or phenomenologist of religion and mythologist for
whom a Darwinist had neither understanding nor regard.

It is not surprising that at the beginning of the twentieth century
the empirical scientist should have won out. It nevertheless remains
a mystery how James Frazer was capable of eliminating Strehlow
not only from his book on totemism but even from the bibliography
of the *Golden Bough* although much of the information on myths and
legends seems to have come from Strehlow's investigations.

Australian anthropology at the turn of the century

Before we look at another example of the progressive silencing of
Carl Strehlow, we should assess the scholarly context of the whole
controversy. A selective survey of the context shows how much
Australia and the Australian Aborigines were at the centre of attention in Europe between 1880 and 1930.

The golden chain of important publications on the Australian
Aborigines constantly to be quoted in the next half century began in
1878 with R.B. Smyth's two volumes of *The Aborigines of Victoria*,
J. Dawson's *The Australian Aborigines* in 1881, and Edwin M.
Curr's *The Australian Race* in 1886–87. While these were published
in Melbourne, the following works were mostly published in
Europe. In 1887 Andrew Lang forged the next ring with his two
volumes of *Myths, Ritual and Religion* before James Frazer's first
instalment of the *Golden Bough. A Study in Magic and Religion*, (the
two volumes of 1890 were to grow to thirteen by 1936), and
K. Langloh-Parker's first collection of *Australian Legendary Tales* in
1896. Baldwin Spencer was the next with his compilation of the
*Report on the work of the Horn scientific expedition to Central Austra-
lia* in four volumes in 1896, followed in 1898 by Andrew Lang's
The Making of Religion and in 1899 by J. Mathew's study—quoted
by Carl Strehlow—*Eaglehawk and Crow: a study of the Australian
Aborigines including an inquiry into their origin and a survey of Australian languages.* In 1899 appeared also the fruit of Baldwin Spen-

cer's and F.J. Gillen's work with the Arunta: *Native Tribes of Central Australia.* The first German voice was J. Pikler with his *Der Ursprung des Totemismus* of 1900 which put the new focus of research into the title.

The next work of Andrew Lang, *Social Origins* (1903), attempted a critique of Spencer's work on the evidence of R.H. Mathew's findings, provoking an immediate reaction by all involved. Mulvaney writes: 'It seems likely that this small band of Australian ethnographers [i.e. Howitt, Fison, Roth, Gillen—with James Frazer on their side!] were drawn together in self-defence against overseas criticism.' Rightly or wrongly, R.H. Mathews was the first victim of the controversy; Strehlow was to be the next. But before that, Spencer and Gillen published *The Northern Tribes of Central Australia* in 1904. In the same year appeared A.W. Howitt's *The native tribes of south east Australia* followed in 1905 by K. Langloh-Parker's *The Euahlayi tribe: a study of Aboriginal life in Australia.*

But the hidden agenda is the battle between Spencer and Lang, and the battleground is the fascinating problem of totemism or the origin of religion. The fight heated up with another controversial book of Andrew Lang's in 1905: *The Secret of the Totem.* Lang received support from A. van Gennep who published in 1906 his *Mythes et légendes d'Australie.* It is in this somewhat excited atmosphere which can still be felt in the reviews and letters published at that time in the English anthropological journals *Folk-Lore* and *Man.* In 1906 N.W. Thomas published his two books, *The Native Races of the British Empire, Natives of Australia* and *Kinship Organisations and Group Marriage in Australia*; and Leonhardi began to edit the first two volumes of Carl Strehlow's *Die Aranda- und Loritja-Stämme* which now became the focus of and in the following volumes accompanied the controversy beyond 1929, the year of Spencer's death.

On the one side, Andrew Lang's criticism of Darwinist positivism and of the school of the Anglo-German orientalist Max Müller was taken up and developed further in continuation of German Romantic philosophy of religion by the Mechitharist father and founder of the Viennese school of anthropology, (Pater) Wilhelm Schmidt (SVD) in his books *L'Origine de l'idée de Dieu* (first published in French 1910 and then in twelve volumes in German from 1912 to 1955), *Grundlinien einer Vergleichung der Religionen und Mythologien der Austronesischen Völker* (1910) and *Die Mythologie*

der austronesischen Völker (1910). On the other side, as already
mentioned, James Frazer, on Spencer's advice, expunged any reference to Strehlow in his 1910 *Totemism and exogamy*. The title
already indicated the perspective of the study. Spencer and Gillen
on their part responded in 1912 with *Across Australia* and in 1914
with Spencer's *The native tribes of the Northern Territory of Australia*.

In the flurry of publications the first full-scale book in German
by a medically trained anthropologist, Erhard Eylmann's *Die
Eingeborenen der Kolonie Südaustralien*, which is satirically critical of
the mission establishment at Hermannsburg, appeared in 1908 in
Berlin and was hardly noticed. But it is easily overlooked that there
appeared during these years the first important works of three eminent European scholars on the same topic, all heavily based on
information gathered by Carl Strehlow: 1912 Emil Durkheim's *Les
formes élémentaires de la vie religieuse: le systéme totémique en
Australie*, translated into English in 1915; Sigmund Freud's *Totem
und Tabu* in 1912–13, translated 1919, and B. Malinowski's *The
family among the Australian Aborigines* in 1913. These, together with
other works of Durkheim, set the new tone and indicated the new
directions: the old empirical positivism and Darwinism to which
anthropology owes so much was to be replaced by a new interpretative sociology and a renewed phenomenology of religion. L.
Ehrlich followed Schmidt in his 1922 *Origin of Australian Beliefs*;
Freud was taken up by Geza Roheim in *Australian totemism: a
psycho-analytic study in anthropology* (1925) and in Malinowski's
Myth in primitive psychology (1926).

In the meantime, in Australia, Herbert Basedow asserted his
position between the front lines in his book *The Australian Aboriginal* (1925)—introducing a conciliatory spelling of the name of the
tribes in contention: Arunndta—before the parting shots were fired
by Spencer and Gillen in their massive summa *The Arunta. A study
of a stone age people* (1927) in which two Appendices (C and D) are
devoted to settle old scores on the dividing issues of 'The Churinga
Belief' and 'The Alchera Belief and Traditions'; and by Spencer's
two volumes of *Wanderings in Wild Australia* of 1928.[11]

The paradigmatic change in Australian anthropology

In a sense, anthropology and ethnology had moved on even before
the death of Baldwin Spencer, not only with regard to method but
also in their preferred areas of field studies. It seems that for the

next twenty to thirty years fieldwork was left again to the missionaries before the advent on the Australian scene of scholars like Radcliffe-Brown, Elkin, Stanner, Lommel, Petri, Hiatt and, of course, T.G.H. Strehlow. Going through the bibliographies of the Australian anthropologists it becomes quite clear that Carl Strehlow is today little more than a name. As clearly documented also in W.E. Mühlmann's *History of Anthropology*, the controversy and the protagonists have withdrawn from living memory into histories of the discipline. So much so that also in the Index to *Australian Aboriginal Mythology*, Carl Strehlow is given an entry under T.G.H. Strehlow. It is however obvious that this suppression is not only due to the monolingual education in Australia which made *Die Aranda- und Loritja-Stämme in Zentral-Australien* an arcane work. For in the meantime, Charles Chewings, station owner, amateur geologist and gentleman scholar in the MacDonald Ranges, had translated all of it into English—but these seminal works in Aboriginal studies still remain to be published in English for more than just historical interest. It is also true that the two World Wars have not helped to remember German contributions to Australian anthropology.

But beyond all elements of personal rancour and deviousness, it certainly indicates a major rift in theory and method between the British and Continental schools of ethnography, as mentioned before. The power of the paradigmatic change was such that in 1961, when A.P. Elkin gave his survey of the 'Development of Scientific Knowledge of the Aborigines', Australian anthropologists were not even conscious of the shift having occurred. Elkin distinguishes 'four distinct, though overlapping, phases: 1. a phase of incidental anthropology [1770–1870]; 2 a compiling and collating phase [1870–1900]; 3. a phase of fortuitous, individual field projects [1897–1926]; and 4. a phase of organized, systematic research [1926 ff.]'.[13] The recommendations from this conference on urgent further research in Aboriginal studies do not mention the necessity of historical studies at all. There is no hint that 'organized, systematic research' could have taken place in other systems, eg. the missionary system, by the universities or other state-funded research institutes. It was left to Catherine H. Berndt to at least suggest 'indirect' implications of anthropological studies for an Australian identity in the present.[14] For very similar reasons, I suspect, for John Mulvaney in 1988 anthropology exists only before and after ANZAAS.

However, there is also the influence of at least one other much-neglected element in scientific work: the cognitive power of social factors in academia, the formation of groups and schools. How much the group formation has worked to the detriment of Carl Strehlow can be seen in the relevant entries in the authoritative *Encyclopedia of Religion and Ethics* (*ERE*), covering almost exactly the time of our concern.

The article 'Alcheringa' by N.W. Thomas in vol. 1, p. 298 (1908) is based only on Spencer and Gillen, van Gennep and Durkheim without any reference to Carl Strehlow, or Andrew Lang for that matter. This is particularly serious because Thomas introduces the term 'Dream-Times' as translation of 'Alcheringa' into the *Encyclopedia* in spite of the philological objections to the concept raised by Carl Strehlow already in his 1905 letter to Thomas and in the first volume of *Die Aranda- und Loritja-Stämme*. In vol. 2, pp. 889–91 (1909) of the *ERE*, Andrew Lang took great delight in remedying the situation by introducing Carl Strehlow's findings and the contentious issue of the 'All-Father' in the article 'Bull-Roarer' pushing his own cart at the same time.

The next articles of any interest here are E. Sidney Hartland's 'Totemism' and N.W. Thomas' 'Transmigration' in volume 12 of 1921. Thomas makes extensive use of Strehlow's findings, quoting directly from vol. 1 in criticism of Spencer's position; while Hartland, writing on the much more important issue, did not even want to know the name Strehlow and, in the bibliography, produces the interesting statement: 'Works in German are numerous, but of less importance.' He gave expression to a new perspective which was to remain dominant for the next decades. That perspective of British empiricist social anthropologists took no cognizance of the growing interest in myth and the 'Sacred', and therefore found no use for Carl Strehlow's work, but this interest lives on in writers like W. Schmidt, C.G. Jung, Rudolf Otto, Friedrich Heiler, van der Leeuw, Mircea Eliade, Walter F. Otto, Karl Kerenyi and a host of others writing from the beginning of the century.

The missionary–anthropologist

It is obvious that there remains much to be done with regard to the mere biographical data of Carl Strehlow's life and also to the research context of his work. Even the suspicion surrounding the authenticity of his work has to be laid to rest—'Spencer's slur' as

Ted Strehlow has called it.[15] But in spite of the son's assurance that
a comparison of the manuscript, which I assume to have survived
but have not been able to peruse, confirms Leonhardi's assurance
given in his Introduction to volumes 1 and 2, that—in Ted
Strehlow's words—'in the printed volume C. Strehlow's own text
has been presented, with only very occasional minor errors'. In fact,
Leonhardi, knowing full well the territory of research to be a
minefield of scholarly contentions (hence his many letters to
Strehlow requesting verification and clarification) could have aver-
ted the whole controversy by refusing to print the word 'God' in a
work on Australian anthropology. But Spencer's claim in *The
Arunta*[16] that it was actually written by Leonhardi based on
Strehlow's notes is—albeit in a more cautious form—reiterated by
Spencer's biographers: 'It [Strehlow's vol. 1] was much expanded
and edited by Leonhardi. Because Strehlow's original draft was
roughly expressed, Spencer expected the editing to prove "rather
free".[17] Nothing of the sort can be read out of the editor's words in
the Preface to vol. 1.[18]

There is however, in my opinion, much more important research to be conducted into an area which is almost completely
neglected and not only with regard to Carl Strehlow. It is something
I wish to pursue more vigorously in the future when I shall have
access to essential archive material. I am talking of the hermeneutic
conditions of Strehlow's research, the horizon of expectation that
surrounds it. In the absence of an autobiography or a biography
interested in these aspects, these cognitive parameters of his work
can only be established through documented evidence about his
education, both in secular and ecclesiastical matters. It boils down
to the questions: how were the future missionaries prepared for
anthropological and ethnological work? What are the instructions
they received? Every history of anthropology, every history of journeys of discovery and exploration at least mentions the work of
missionaries. Obviously, some missionaries hold that the work in
anthropology was already done before the advent of the professional
anthropologist. One could refer here to the instruction issued to
L.E. Threlkeld by the London Missionary Society in 1825.[19] But
then: where are such instructions to be found? So far, bibliographi-
cal research has turned up very little useful material for the period
in question, at least with regard to missionaries of the Lutheran
Church. However, some pertinent information, albeit of a much

more recent provenance, was obtained from interested and knowledgeable churchmen. I propose to look at these instructions for and
autobiographical accounts by missionaries in some detail in order to
identify the guiding cognitive topoi of their research and thus come
to a better understanding and appreciation of their findings and
achievements.

Such topoi—which may guide directly or indirectly specific
research methods but, above all, our attitudes and approaches towards our research objects in a principle fashion—appear already,
as expected, in Spencer's criticism of Strehlow's approach. Speaking in modern hermeneutical terms: Spencer saw Strehlow's work
as being fundamentally flawed because he was a missionary, while
he himself laid claim to truth as a scientist. I shall argue that the
change in paradigm is based on a change in the content of the
dominant topoi.

Language

At the heart of the dispute between Spencer and Strehlow is the
question whether an intimate knowledge of the language of the
Australian natives under investigation was necessary or not for anthropological research. It is certainly a question with regard to the
accurate gathering of information in the field. It must have been
particularly galling to Spencer to find his observations challenged
on the grounds of philological extrapolation inaccessible to him.

The very centre of Aboriginal mythology, the fabled 'Dream-
Time' is a case in point. I have already mentioned that
N.W. Thomas in his *ERE* article 'Alcheringa' called on Spencer's
authority: 'According to Spencer-Gillen (*Nor. Tr.* p. 745) the
word alcheri means "dream" (but cf. *Folk-Lore* xvi. 430), and
Alcheringa is equivalent to "Dream-Times".' The *Northern Tribes of
Central Australia* was published in 1904. There is, however, in
Folk-Lore xvi a communication 'Religious Ideas of the Arunta'
which N.W. Thomas had read in a meeting of the
Folk-Lore Society on 17 May 1905 in the presence of Andrew Lang
and A.C. Haddon. This paper is particularly important as Thomas
publishes in it extracts from two letters (11 February and 3 August
1905) received from Carl Strehlow.

The second letter refers critically to Spencer and Gillen. '[They]
assert (*Nor.Tr.*, p. 745) that alcheri means dream, and Alcheringa,
the dream times; this is a mistake. Dream is aljirerinja, a dreamer,
altjirarena; a "dream time" is unknown to the blacks.' One wonders

why N. W. Thomas suppressed this correction in his *ERE* article. In addition, there is among the papers of Spencer, dated 20 December 1901, an 'Extract from a letter of Herr. C. Strelhow [*sic*], a missionary of the New Delittsemer [*sic*] body of Missioners, at Hermannsburg Finke River South Australia' which contains all the elements of description and etymology of 'Altjira' in the opening paragraphs of Strehlow's volume 1 without making the conclusion equally explicit. Very generously, John Mulvaney has made available to me transcripts of letters and documents from the Tylor Collection which show that this extract plus commentaries must relate to the extracts made from Strehlow letters by 'a German'—I assume by Leonhardi—and sent to Lang on 20 December 1901. On 19 October (1903?) Lang sent a copy to Tylor describing them as 'notes on Arunta religion' and commenting: 'It does not suit Spencer and Gillen and puts a very different face on matters.' And again on 28 October (1903?) he reports to Tylor: 'I sent the original German to Prof. Spencer in Melbourne. Does he know Arunta? His book (Native Tribes of Central Australia) has no philology in it, I think.'

In my opinion, both extracts—the one Mulvaney found in the Tylor Collection and the other in the Spencer Collection of the Museum of Victoria—are different translations of extracts made, I assume, by Leonhardi from letters received by Strehlow and supplied with notes. However, a good look at the 'original German' extracts—kindly supplied to me by Dr Kingsley Rowan, Spencer's grandson—which Lang sent to Spencer reveals that we are in fact not dealing with Leonhardi's original communication to Lang but with transcriptions in two different hands and by people of limited knowledge of German handwriting and grammar. When trying to translate the sometimes very garbled text, Spencer's philology was put several times and very successfully to the test. In any event, the content of the extracts coincides somewhat with the letters Strehlow had sent to Leonhardi in 1905 and 1906, who published them in extracts in *Globus* in 1907 as mentioned earlier.

Only if the original letters of Strehlow can be compared with Leonhardi's and Spencer's excerpts and translation can a proper sequence of events be established. But for the time being it is clear that in 1903 Spencer seems to have known more about Strehlow's work and the implicit criticisms of some of his own findings than he was willing to accept or acknowledge in his forthcoming book. And if we entertain, for a moment, the thought that he owed his knowledge of the philology of 'Altjira' and 'Alcheringa' to the findings of the missionaries, then Strehlow's 'Anmerkung' on page 2 of volume 1—which essentially repeats what he had maintained all along and passed on in his letters—must have come like a full blow to Spencer's efforts in his controversy with Andrew Lang and the continental anthropologists. For in this note, Strehlow argues on grounds of etymology that Spencer got it all wrong: 'When Spencer and Gillen (*Nor. Tr.* p. 745) maintain: "the word alcheri means dream," their contention is incorrect . . . The word "alcheringa," which according to Spencer and Gillen is supposed to mean "dream-time" is obviously corrupted from altjirerinja. Furthermore, the natives do not know anything about the "dream-time" as a period in time; [alcheringa] denotes this time during which the Altjiranga mitjina walked on this Earth.[20] I am not in a position to report whether Strehlow's etymology is acceptable to Aranda specialists today. But if it is correct, as is suggested by Charles P. Mountford, our present-day use of 'Dreamtime' would be wrong—and a legacy of Spencer's linguistic misinterpretation and his contempt for missionaries.

But our observations have to go one step further. I have quoted the example only in order to demonstrate the difference between the cognitive parameters of the social anthropologist and those of the linguist-missionary for whom the word is everything. The belief that it is language which unlocks the doors of understanding of the foreign is traditionally basic to the studies of theologians—the preacher knows the power of the word. For the European anthropologist trained first in linguistics, language becomes the first and foremost tool of this work.

Moritz von Leonhardi states this with perfect clarity in his introductory notes to volume 1, as he had done already in *Globus*:

> During his activities among the two tribes over many years, Mr. Strehlow has acquired a perfect command of their languages; he also has had printed some texts for use in divine services . . . The knowledge of the languages enabled him during his research to communciate with the natives in their mother tongues—an advantage which cannot be valued too highly; because the tasks are to comprehend, contemplate and preserve in writing these difficult and, in part, rather sophisticated ways of thinking of the Aboriginal peoples.[21]

The last sentence is the most important because it states explicitly the three tasks of anthropology as these European scholars saw them. The example of Strehlow is supported by the evidence from many reports and writings of other missionaries. I can only refer to the earlier Western Australian missionary Dom Rosendo Salvado OSB who published his memoirs in 1851. But a little over one hundred years later, Eugene A. Nida in his book *Customs and Cultures. Anthropology for Christian Missions* still has a chapter on 'Learning a Foreign Language' which he concludes with the following words, bringing together the essential elements: 'Languages can and must be learnt if the Word of God is to be communciated in the words of men, but this cannot be done outside of the total framework of the culture, of which the language in question is an integral part.'[22]

I wonder whether the reason given by Nida for the secular anthropologists' failure to make adequate use of the native language elucidates also the hidden basis of the difference between Spencer and Strehlow. Nida wrote:

> The numerous problems and techniques for learning a foreign language are quite beyond the scope of this discussion, but we should note briefly the fact that failure to learn foreign languages results primarily from false attitudes towards culture. A superiority complex fortified by a paternalistic air is about the worst liability for effective language learning. Our ethnocentrism makes it difficult for us to 'let ourselves go,' for we dread mistakes, not realizing that languages cannot be mastered until we have thoroughly murdered them . . . [23]

In short, the attitude of the 'modern' Darwinist scientist of the turn of the century was characterised by a scientific interest and a deep human contempt for the subject of his investigations which, ultimately, prevented him from taking the indigenous culture seriously. Spencer was 'right' in considering the missionary Strehlow as belonging to a different, pre-scientific era in anthropology; but he did not and perhaps could not reflect the hidden cognitive frame of his own approaches.

Bernard Smith has put this very succinctly in his Academy Paper *Art as information*:

> It is commonplace to regard the elevated, neo-classical style as a device appropriate for an artist of the stature of Reynolds to apply to the depiction of Europeans of rank, influence and power, but we implicitly accuse his minor contemporaries such as Cipriani and Bartolozzi of a false or 'Europeanized' perception should they apply the same device to the elevation of non-European people. It is important in this regard to realize that the ennobling of so-called Pacific savages contained a latent, but salutary, critique of Europo-centric

attitudes. It enshrined a vestige of that view of the dignity and potential godliness of all men, as Pico and the Renaissance humanists had
defined man, a view which remained eminently respectable doctrine
until Europe experienced its first real taste of popular democracy in
action in the years that followed the outbreak of the French Revolution. As a result of the great fear that followed, notions about noble
savagery and universal brotherhood became subversive, being replaced by theories more congenial to Europe's powerful, hierarchical
societies during the age of colonial expansion. Such was Darwin's
theory of evolution. It provided an empirical, secularised version of
the theological dogma of original sin; God's election was replaced by
nature's selection. That, surely was one of the more sinister aspects of
the triumph of empirical naturalism over classical naturalism. Those
who had been portrayed like gods came to be portrayed like
monkeys.[24]

It would not be too difficult to find similar views expressed by
A.P. Elkin in his early pamphlet *Missionary Policy for Primitive
Peoples* which he and others repeated in 1961 during the Canberra
conference, or in W.E.H. Stanner's 1968 Boyer Lectures *After the
Dreaming.*

Religion
It seems superfluous to mention religion among the cognitive topoi
of missionary anthropological research. We take it to be a matter of
course and anticipate the consequences, for example biased and,
therefore, scientifically unacceptable results. This is exactly Spencer's critique of Carl Strehlow. The opening sentence of volume 1 of
Die Aranta- und Loritja-Stämme in which Strehlow states:
'According to the tradition of the elders there exists a highest good
(mara) being, Altjira,' would have been inoffensive to the fraternity
of anthropologists, had he not continued three paragraphs on:
'Altjira is the good god of the Aranda who is known not only to men
but also to women.' In the same passages and later, Strehlow uses
the term 'totem gods' (*Totemgötter*). This description is in conflict
with Spencer's observation in a letter to Frazer of 19 August 1902
which, in W.E.H. Stanner's opinion, 'put his view beyond doubt'. 'I
think conclusively, that the Central Australian natives have nothing
whatever in the way of a simple, pure religion . . . ' For that reason,
Spencer felt compelled to complain to Frazer that missionaries

> have been teaching the natives that Altjira means 'God', and that all
> their sacred ceremonies, in fact even their ordinary corrobories, were
> wicked things. They have prohibited any being performed on the

Mission stations, and have endeavoured in every way to put a stop to them, and to prevent the natives from attending them, and certainly they have never seen one performed.[25]

Stanner continues:

But the occasion, if not the cause, of his irritation was the missionary Strehlow's attempt to find a High God. The scholars who wrote as if religion did not exist, and the men of religion who worked as if it could not exist, among so barbarous a people, were not in even distant collusion with authorities who had no motive of credibility to think or act beyond a vague and ill-policed policy of protection. . . . there must have been a score of causes to Aboriginal misery. But from the early nineteenth century, none had a more devastating effect than the pervasive doctrine of Aboriginal worthlessness. That depended to a decisive extent on the specific blindness to which I have referred (i.e. the pervasive ignorance about Aboriginal religion). Yet, as R.M. Berndt has rightly said: traditional Aboriginal religion was 'a living faith, something quite inseparable from the pattern of everyday life and thought'. The connection was so intimate that 'there is no sharp demarcation between secular and sacred life'. In the words of Father E.A. Worms, Aboriginal religion 'penetrates all facets of life and has little to fear from distinctions which are both abstract and disunitive and which we, with our philosophical education, often make'.[26]

Later anthropological research has found that the notion of a High God is indeed alien to the native tribes of Australia, but that does not mean that they had no religion and, in consequence, no culture. It is clear that the notion of a High God belonged to the cognitive horizon of the missionaries, brought up in the European mythology binding together the High God of their Christian faith with the High God of their Greek and Latin studies and elevating them to the top of a religious hierarchy which put earlier 'animistic' forms of religion at the very bottom. The destruction of these earlier cultures was then equated with 'necessary progress in the development of civilization'.

But their very 'bias' allowed the missionaries to give at least an early if not quite accurate description of the native religion and culture because they knew what religion was and were quite capable of recognising a religious culture when they met one. To the missionary Strehlow the Aranda religious culture was a heathen culture, but to the anthropologist Strehlow it was anything but 'primitive'. It is well known that the term 'primitive' has undergone a considerable change, ranging from 'first or earliest of its kind' in Antiquity to 'an aboriginal; a man of primitive (esp. prehistoric) times' in 1779 (*OED*). In the end, there is the juxtaposition of the primitive or savage and the civilised or progressive. As far as I can see, Strehlow did not use the term 'primitive' at all. He prefixed the relevant concepts with the equivalent 'Ur-', such as *Urvolk* or *Urvater*. In 1907 then, 'primitive' meant to Strehlow a member of the human race living in remote areas practising a culture of considerable antiquity and complexity and in need of salvation.

To Spencer the 'primitive' was a specimen of humanity surviving from early stages of the development of *homo sapiens* living in remote areas and to be preserved for further investigation like any other natural phenomenon not yet fully explored. For Strehlow it was a living present, for Spencer the surviving Stone Age. Because the 'primitives' were perceived by the scientists at the time of having remained on an early, that is lower rung on the ladder of evolution, they could not possibly have notions such as that of an 'All-Father' belonging to a much later stage.

This 'bias', as any pre-judgement (*Vor-Urteil*), is part of the normal heuristic process. It is the denial of 'bias'—on the basis of scientific method—which has caused and still causes havoc in anthropological research. To deny it is part and parcel of the semantics of the 'scientific' and the root-cause for the fact that the experts of Aboriginal studies coming together in 1961 were not prepared to face the notion of the 'sacred', or reconsider their use of 'myth' from an intercultural perspective. Strehlow himself finds it necessary to inform the reader about his own particular restrictions, obviously taking for granted that everybody concerned knows that the goal of the missionaries was the replacement of the native religious world with a different, imported faith and culture.

One case is particularly telling. In volume 2, Strehlow describes the various forms of the 'tjurungas' of the Aranda and informs us that they are kept in secret and sacred places, in stone caves—*arknanaua*—which are prohibited to the uninitiated.

> These caves are regarded as sacred places, as places of cults. That the natives connect the latter concept with that word I conclude from the fact that when during my translation work I looked for an expression for 'church,' two baptized blacks suggested to me in all seriousness the word arknanaua, after I had explained to them the concept of church in detail; but because the blacks associate too many heathen

perceptions with the word arknanaua, I declined to use the expression.[27]

These examples must suffice to demonstrate again the clash of two paradigms in anthropology: while some anthropologists were wondering whether the Aranda had a proper language or religion at all, Strehlow translated the Aranda myths into German and the Bible into Aranda. This difference in perception is a fundamental one.

Instructions for missionaries

But the search for the cognitive framework of the missionaries-turned-anthropologists has to go much further and beyond the topoi of Language and God just discussed. Although further archival research has still to be conducted in order to gain a better and more representative understanding of the attitudes and approaches guiding the research of the missionaries, in the case of Carl Strehlow some paradigmatic inferences can be made on the basis of a 'Guidelines for missionaries' (*Leitfaden für Missionare*) appended to Christian Keysser's book, *Eine Papuagemeinde*, published first in 1929. It is significant for us because it was published in the series of the *Neuendettelsauer Missionschriften* and dedicated by Keysser to the 'Deutsche Gesellschaft für Missionswissenschaft'. Neuendettelsau was the place of Strehlow's studies and preparation for his missionary work. Keysser, Strehlow's brother-in-law, refers particularly to Pastor Johann Wilhelm Löhe (21 February 1808 to 2 January 1871), the founder of Neuendettelsau in 1841 as a seminary for missionaries in Brazil and New Guinea. I assume that Löhe had also been the guiding spirit in Strehlow's early studies.

Keysser's *Leitfaden* moves almost completely within the anthropological guidelines of the French Jesuit missionaries to East Asia in the seventeenth century who received the following instructions regarding their work among the natives in 1659:

> Beware of determining in any way those peoples, to change their ceremonies, customs and manners albeit that they violate directly religion and virtue. Is there anything more preposterous than wishing to transplant France, Spain or Italy or any other European country to China? We do not want to carry our customs into this empire but our faith, which does not look at or violate the manner and customs of any nation but rather wishes to preserve them. Because human beings are inclined that they treasure and love more their own nation and all that is their own than the foreign there is no stronger reason for aversion

or hatred than the change in their national habits—particularly if they recommend themselves by their age.[28]

I shall quote some passages from Keysser without any further comment in order to demonstrate not only how closely the thinking of the missionary in the late nineteenth century resembled that of the seventeenth but also in order to draw attention to the inherent topoi of the missionary instructions which set them apart from contemporary 'scientific' instructions and 'scientific anthropology': 'When you begin your work, you have to begin it as human being among human beings, not as master among servants, not as official among numbers and not as preachers among listeners.' (Anybody familiar with German literature of the eighteenth century will recognise the enlightenment topos of *Mensch unter Menschen*.)—'Love the heathens and bring them their God.'

> The first prerequisite is the gaining of their confidence . . . —In order to gain their confidence a profound knowledge is necessary. Knowledge of the individual! Therefore visit the villages, the homes. Talk in detail with the people and devote yourself to them. Never walk casually through the villages! Do not make any empty priestly noise. Rather show interest for the people, their work and their problems!— Make every effort to gain knowledge of the entities of the people, that is their villages, their tribes!—Indispensable is a knowledge of their manners and laws, their sins and weaknesses, of the good and evil.— Always place yourself on the ground of the laws of the natives!— Important is, furthermore, the knowledge of the language, expressions, images, songs and myth.—All that is part of the soul of the people [*Volksseele*] and the cultural goods of the people [*Volksgut*]. Disregard or even contempt shows lack of love and is detrimental. Love grows with the knowledge of the people.[29]

It is my conviction that but for late Romantic notions like *Volksseele*, *Volksgut* or *Volksordnung* and other such composita, these instructions given to the Neuendettelsau missionaries, such as Strehlow, continue the spirit of the Enlightenment anthropology and the early Jesuit method of field research, the participatory observation which earned the Jesuits the strong disapproval from Rome when they tried to replace the sacred language of Europe, Latin, with Sanskrit or Chinese. These Jesuits were later sworn to a Rome-centred notion of Christianity. Strehlow became the victim of a Eurocentric science which, at the time, took pride in its 'value-free' and 'scientific' method and attitude.

It is also most interesting that if it comes to biblical guidance in social anthropology, Keysser turns to the Old Testament, invoking the transition from the Old to the New Testament as a metaphor for an advancement in political as much as in religious progress.

> Not all of the baptized [natives] and certainly not at the same time will have the experience of the grace and Christ of the New Testament, but some only at the end of their lives. But a participation in the piety of the people [*Volksfrömmigkeit*] is possible for everybody. This piety of the people will always be in accordance with the Old Testament. For the great mass of the people and its education the Old Testament and its values are indispensable. It is and remains even today the precondition and supplement of the New Testament . . . In the Old Testament we read of the 'becoming of a people' [*Volkswerdung*] under the guidance of God. That is an important insight for the mission among the primitives . . . The Ten Commandments are primarily the order of a people [*Volksordnung*]. In any case, according to the OT, religion is the business of the people [*Volkssache*] . . . There are pagan ethnic customs [*Volkssitte*] and ethnic morality [*Volkssittlichkeit*] . . . They have value that should not be underestimated and give strong support . . . Beware of destroying pagan customs! . . . Only after the tribe has experienced God, is it able to create better customs . . . In this you are the guide and helper, but the work has to be achieved by the tribe itself.[30]

Thus the missionary work is strongly guided by the traditional political interpretation of the relationship of the Old Testament and the New Testament. Israel's progress to nationhood is held up as an example and parallel to be followed by the indigenous peoples. This analogy sets the agenda for missionary activities, for the transition from the old to the new with the consent of the people concerned.

For this very reason, Keysser sees a dichotomy between the tired and bored old christianity of Europe and the vitality of new christendom among the primitives. It is the missionary's experience of the creation of the 'new man' far away from Europe which makes him turn critically against Europe. Keysser thus continues also the cultural criticism which we find in Enlightenment literature, in Denis Diderot and Georg Forster, but also in many missionaries in Australia and the Pacific before Strehlow. It is the constant battle against the moral depravity and greed of the European colonist and settler, their total contempt for the lives of the natives based on a Darwinist theory of superiority. Keysser, therefore, warns constantly against the theological and institutional errors of the home church (*Heimatkirche*) on all levels of missionary work. In view of the continuous development of the congregation (*Gemeinde*), which is to be regarded as an organic whole, towards its religious goal, Keysser remarks:

> Exactly that is the scandal of the home church [*Heimat*] [of the missionary], that the congregations have no goal, at most that 'they should conduct their lives in silent quietude and good peace as befits Christians.' But what lives, has to move, work, create and grow. . . . The goal of your work should be 'the complete adulthood in Christ' . . . [31]

The home church (*Heimatkirche*) always thinks first of external enemies but disregards the danger of the internal enemy of complacency. Keysser stresses the importance of the church assembly (*Gemeindeversammlung*) which was institutionalised by St Paul and Luther but 'which has been dropped by the home church to its own detriment'.

Therefore, pastoral care (*Seelsorge*) is particularly efficient in the 'congregation' (*Gemeinde*) while 'Unfortunately, the *Heimat* only knows private pastoral care (*Privatseelsorge*), but that is not enough'. Generally, the home church of the missionary is in deep trouble itself without knowing it. The missionary, therefore, has a task that is directed as well towards the pagans as towards the home church. At present, really living faith can only be experienced away from the home church. Thus the educational methods employed by the home church are ethnocentric and, therefore, useless in foreign countries. That is particularly true for the predominance of the intellect in Europe:

> The home method (*heimatliche Methode*) which believes that one can drum in the Christian faith using only the intellect and which, therefore, attaches great importance to the mass of facts is really non-Lutheran. Decisive is only the faith as the living relationship to God. Never ever take the situation at home (*Heimatverhältnisse*] to be an example, but on principle always return to the Bible.[32]

Conclusion

Since the critical attitude of the missionary towards his home base becomes obvious even in his religious work, we are entitled, in my opinion, to search for the cognitive basis of this attitude in the missionary impulse and motivation of the missionary, but also for the effects of it within the cognitive frame which must dominate all anthropological research, not to speak of the effect it had on the lives of the natives. We can assume that Carl Strehlow, like Keysser a student of Löhe and Neuendettelsau, was imbued with the spirit of critique of eurocentric christendom. This attitude fuelled at the same time his intense interest in and guided his cognition of the native tribes of Central Australia.

Spencer was right in his assumption that Strehlow's religious motivation was bound to influence deeply his findings, and he was right again in his suspicion that Strehlow's approaches were not in keeping with the latest methods in empirical research. But he was wrong in his belief that his own attitude and cognitive frame as well as his method were free of value judgements. It is precisely in the juxtaposition of the different cognitive frames and topoi of both protagonists that their relative merit, their perspectives, the basic tenets of their anthropology become apparent. On the basis of a Darwinist evolutionary theory, Spencer had to assume that the primitives had of necessity no higher religious notions. Therefore the findings of Strehlow were offensive to him and his group. Phenomenology of religion, on the other hand, as practised by Strehlow and others is not bound by such a restrictive ideology and method and is therefore able to understand much better the phenomena of the sacred and their meaning among the natives. No doubt, it is hampered, at this early stage, by a too narrow Lutheran understanding of religion. In the case of both, Strehlow and Spencer, we find a eurocentric perspective in the approach to the non-European world. In terms of modern hermeneutics and the methodology of intercultural studies, the dilemma is unavoidable—quite on the contrary: without such a perspective—whatever its ideology—no understanding at all would have been achieved.

At the same time, tragedy lurks in the dilemma. I do not think that it is correct to speak of a 'cult of forgetfulness or disremembering' in which the white man in Australia is caught when considering the principles and history of his relationship to the original Australians. I believe that I have shown that the catastrophic relationship between black and white people in this country is the result of a culture clash which is born out of the scientific mode of thinking which became dominant in the nineteenth century: it is not accidental but systematic and, therefore, tragic.

It is for both these reasons that a renewed study of Carl Strehlow and his contribution to Australian anthropology is of greatest importance. Such a study not only allows us to reflect the

conditions under which this country was and still is studied, but it
also allows us to recover an alternative but long-forgotten approach
which in spite of its deeply rooted problems takes humanity more
seriously. Furthermore, it also permits us to subject the ideological
base of the topoi identified earlier to a hermeneutic critique which
might uncover further pre-judgements not discussed here. It most
certainly does not close but opens up emancipatory insights into the
basis and history of the cultural conflict between Aboriginal and
immigrant Australia. It would also provide an opportunity of recov-
ering historically important intercultural relations between Australia
and the German-speaking countries. Some progress in the development of a historical consciousness could be initiated by the publication and study of a philologically faithful translation into English of
Carl Strehlow's work.

The study of Australian Aboriginal culture by German anthropologists of the Frobenius Institute

Silke Beinssen-Hesse

In 1938 the Kulturmorphologisches Institut in Frankfurt am Main, headed by the renowned ethnologist Leo Frobenius (1873–1938), sent the first Frobenius Expedition to Australia to study tribal Aborigines in the Kimberley region. The Institute had hitherto concentrated its research efforts on Africa, where Frobenius had personally led twelve major expeditions between the years 1904 and 1935. Though Frobenius himself never planned to take part in the Pacific expeditions—he died in 1938 when the first expedition was under way—there is no doubt that this new direction in research was due to his initiative and that his specifically German approach, which combined *Kulturkreis* (culture complex) and morphological methodology and which stands in a tradition reaching from Goethe to Oswald Spengler, gave the expedition its initial orientation.

The team of five anthropologists and painters sent out in 1938 managed to make it back to Germany before the outbreak of war. Their work, however, could not be written up and published before the fifties, and then not without war-related loss of material. Three members of the original team later continued their Australian

specialisation with further expeditions and a considerable number
of publications; others joined the group after the war. From joint
beginnings, two very different approaches to Australian Aboriginal
culture emerged. The one, in close communication with the Australian research community, has always placed strong emphasis on the
study of various forms of culture contact and shown a concern with
understanding the conditions necessary for the survival of the Aboriginal people and their way of life. The other, which refers back to
the *Kulturkreis* method and retains a persistently European orientation, has had considerably greater popular coverage in Germany.

The first indication that Frobenius was turning towards the Pacific
came in April 1936 when he wrote the following note to my father
Dr Ekkehard Beinssen, who had recently moved to Sydney after
years of adventuring in various parts of the world. 'I want to send
someone by plane over New Guinea—by the way, this is only
between the two of us—to find our village of Stone Age people. I
am counting on your help . . .'[1] The Stone Age people referred to
are the Kuku-Kukus whom Beinssen had encountered on an expedition into unexplored country in central New Guinea, undertaken
between August 1929 and February 1930. He had described the
ultimately tragic adventure in a book, *Kolun Neuguinea. Drei Männer
suchen Gold*, published in Berlin in 1933 with a foreword by
Frobenius in which the latter had written of his hope of one day
joining the author 'on a journey to the oceanic tropics'.
     It appeared that Frobenius was about to make good his word
after a 1932 offer to manage an African expedition had fallen
through due to lack of funds. On 9 June there is a slightly more
detailed description of the new project by a member of the Institute's staff, Dr Rhotert:

> Frobenius is hatching plans for major expeditions and is very much
> hoping that you will participate, as he is convinced that they will
> prove rewarding and offer success to you too. For we now have a very
> fine position in Germany and enjoy considerable prestige and influ-
> ence. Only the necessary cash is unfortunately still hard to come by.
>   First the following questions.
>   There was formerly a great ethnological collector and observer in
> Australia, in Hermannsburg, the missionary Strehlow. Could you find
> out whether a comparable person, with whom one could collaborate,
> exists there now? Secondly, are the economic conditions such, that a
> group of people might be found in Australia, or more specifically

Sydney, who could assist us with our work financially? Finally, would there be a group of preferably non-Jewish Frankfurters in whom a particular interest in our work could be kindled?

A letter written by Frobenius himself two days later gives a long and detailed account of the intended project.

> To clarify things, I should first tell you that the DIAFE has been terminated and that a DU [Deutschlands Umwelt] is being created, which at present is working in Spain and France as a dainty little embryonic start, but is then to launch out into the world on a grand scale.

The research conducted by this new organisation was to concentrate on New Holland as the seat of totemic civilisation and Melanesia as the seat of manism (ancestor worship). The focal points were to be East India, an island in Dutch Indonesia (probably Seram), and Sydney as the centre and point of departure of all Melanesian expeditions. A smaller base would be located in Amsterdam to provide the foreign exchange funds for the Dutch undertaking, whereas Sydney, to be directed by Beinssen, was to provide the funds for the Melanesian and Australian work. The projected time-span was twenty-five years. Initially Melanesia was to be directed alternately by Dr Rhotert and Dr Jensen from the autumn of 1937 on. Frobenius went on to suggest that Consul Asmis[2] who had himself published in the field of ethnology, should be approached. He mentioned that the Frankfurt Institute had ethnographic collections provided by Carl Strehlow. 'We are therefore a German centre of leadership and achievement in New Holland research', he pointed out and naively promised: 'we will be in a position to express our gratitude to anyone who is of assistance to us, in a manner that will receive unconditional and complete respect everywhere abroad, as the leadership of the Reich is supporting my endeavours and a considerable expansion of our area of prestige is likely to take place.'

Beinssen's answer to this proposal has not survived but I know from conversation with him that he was well aware that at that point in history a German organisation sponsored by the government of the time would be seen to be, and up to a point would in fact be, a Nazi organisation and consequently something that could not be supported. The political opportunism that chose to exclude Jews as sponsors could not be condoned, particularly by someone whose opposition to the regime had forced him to leave Germany in 1933.

On the other hand, Beinssen was willing to lend his assistance to any research undertaken by the Institute.

By December 1936 plans for Australia were beginning to take shape, though the New Hebrides still seemed to have priority. New Guinea had been given up, partly because the central highlands were at that time closed to all white men. Dr Helmut Petri,[3] who had been placed in charge of the Australian expedition, wrote:

> As regards our plans on Australian soil, the most suitable area seems to be the north-west, that is the plateau country of the Kimberley Division.
>
> As point of departure for a traversing of this almost unknown region there is a mission station at the mouth of the Prince Regent River, which can be reached by schooner from Broome. The missionary who lives there has already done ethnographic work with the Worora tribes and if the situation arose could probably help us in a number of respects. Since this area is not the research province of any one of the Australian universities, in contrast to all other Aboriginal areas, it should not be too difficult to get entry and work permits from the Australian Government. Mr Tindale, the 'ethnologist' at the South Australian Museum of Adelaide, who recently spent a few days in Frankfurt, assured us that it was quite possible that the project would receive substantial support. We would be very grateful to you if you could make inquiries at the relevant departments to what extent this plan can be realised. Perhaps you could also contact the Board of Anthropological Studies at the University of Adelaide, which can apparently give exact information on the research and technical aspects of the undertaking. Of course we would also be interested to know whether the press or any other Australian agency would be prepared to give some financial support. The likely departure time would be late 1937 or early 1938 as, according to Mr Tindale, you can only work in the north-west between the months of March and July.

Six months later Beinssen had apparently not replied to this letter. The plans for the expedition had been finalised, though as yet only Helmut Petri and Douglas Fox, an American expert on cave photography who had accompanied Frobenius on a number of African expeditions and collaborated with him on two English language publications, had been named as participants. Petri wrote that Frobenius would like to know as soon as possible to what extent they can count on the assistance and participation of Beinssen. Beinssen declined participation, presumably on the grounds that he was planning a trip to Germany in 1938, but in the following

months he procured maps and grammars, negotiated with departments and offered to pay a surety demanded by the West Australian
Government. He was also asked to arrange private accommodation
and lectures for Petri and Fox in Sydney. By October 1937 all
members of the expedition had been chosen. They were a third
anthropologist, Dr Andreas Lommel,[4] and two women painters,
Agnes Schulz and Gerta Kleist. An Australian student, Patrick
Pentony, later also joined the group for a time.

On 30 August 1937 the West Australian Commissioner of
Native Affairs had written to say that permission had been granted.
He mentioned the restrictions applying to native reserves:

> 1) refrain from unduly interfering with or molesting the native peoples
> to be found on the native reserves, 2) abstain from obtaining or
> removing any ethnological specimens from such reserves—though a
> limited collection would probably be permitted, 3) refrain from the
> taking of photographs on native reserves, though again limited per-
> missions may be granted on the condition that the Department
> receives a print of every photograph to use as it sees fit.

He added:

> I do not anticipate that there is anything in these restrictions which
> will prevent the expedition from carrying on its legitimate work. If
> treated fairly the natives are approachable and amenable to any
> reasonable requirements, but it must not be forgotten that if their
> social prejudices and family customs are interfered with to any extent
> or disregarded, trouble is likely to arise.

He warned that firearms may be carried only with a permit. He also
gave a useful list of government and mission stations and explained
what transport facilities were available, described conditions in the
area and offered to send copies of linguistic material supplied to the
Department by Professor Elkin. He closed by assuring 'that as far
as possible we will do what we can to facilitate the movements of
the party'. Unfortunately the Frobenius expedition—then financed
by the Notgemeinschaft der deutschen Wissenschaft—could convert
only two thirds of its funds to foreign exchange. In February 1938
Frobenius wrote to say that the party had left and to invite Beinssen
to the anniversary celebrating forty years since the foundations
of the Institute were laid, that is since the *Kulturkreis* and
Kulturmorphologie theories were first launched. Frobenius died
unexpectedly in August of that year.

The 1938–39 Kimberley expedition was led by Helmut Petri and studied in depth the Nngarinyin and Wunambal tribes, leaving the Worora to the resident missionary at the Kunmunya Mission, J.R.B. Love. Petri also recorded what could be ascertained of the culture of the almost extinct Nyigina. Andreas Lommel published his monograph *Die Unambal* in 1952. Petri's book on the Nngarinyin came out two years later.[5] The two tribes are neighbours with an almost identical material culture and many mythical and language elements in common. They have trade relations and celebrate important festivals such as initiations together. But, wrote Petri, 'on closer examination a great variety of differences emerge so that we must postulate different cultures with their own historical determinants'.[6] Both writers made an effort to record all aspects of the cultures they were studying and in this way to find the *Paideuma* (as Frobenius might have called it) or cultural soul of each tribe. But even at this stage their very different approaches and interests had begun to emerge and would inevitably colour their findings.

To begin with, the scholarly practice of the two men differs. Lommel had taken over a habit, for which Frobenius was often criticised, of not referring to secondary sources relevant to his field of study. This included Petri, with whom he must have had opportunity for extensive discussion, if not during his stay then on the long journey back. Similarly, he does not give us insight into the process of acquiring information. Since he had several interpreters, not all of them equally reliable, a fact that is only mentioned in a preamble, this would almost certainly have been relevant. In contrast, Petri is well informed about secondary literature and refers to it in his arguments. He also acknowledges discussion and note-swapping with Lommel. Wherever relevant, we are told who his informants were and to what extent they were in agreement. The problems facing the researcher and his relationship with the Aborigines are also described, so that we can form opinions on the probability of error. In these matters Petri is without a doubt the more mature fieldworker and scholar.

Of central concern to both these researchers was the rapidity with which native peoples, who resided in their ancestral lands with full freedom to live according to their own traditions, were approaching extinction even though they were hardly affected by white civilisation and its diseases. There seemed to be no immediately obvious explanation.[7] Again their opinions diverge. Lommel saw

their susceptibility to psychic powers as the distinguishing characteristic of the Aboriginal people and consequently accepted their
own explanation that undue preoccupation with the white man in-
terfered with the father's dreaming of spirit children. He concluded
that for the Aborigines potency depended upon that dream.[8]

Lommel seemed to accept as irreversible the fact that the Aborigines were a dying race; he admired the artistic form they gave to
their sense of doom. In what is perhaps one of the most interesting
sections of his book, he recorded two corroborees.[9] The first, by a
leprous poet hiding in the bush so as not to be deported from the
place of his dreaming, has the recurring refrain-like lines 'I am tired
and sick and I am still alive, oh, why am I still alive, if only I were
dead'. The enormous popularity this corroboree enjoyed and the
speed with which it was learnt by neighbouring tribes suggest that it
expressed the prevailing feeling. A second popular corroboree about
the culture heroes Kurungali and Banar tells of the constant threat
of catastrophe faced by Kurungali. He is stranded on a rock with the
tide rising, is separated from his people by a flood, or climbs an
exhausting mountain, conscious that his effort is purposeless.
Finally he leaves on a French ship, telling his people no longer to go
hunting and to submit to the new men that have taken over the
country. Lommel added that the departure of a culture hero can
only mean death to his tribe.

After this perceptive rendering of contemporary corroborees
Lommel goes on to contrast them with the lyric poetry of his
interpreter, a man who has adapted to the white man's way of life,
so we are told. Sitting in a cinema the poet thinks of a girl and says
'forget the cinema, kiss me'; seeing fish-nets hung out to dry he
warns 'careful, don't be caught in the trap', or watching a black
baker through a window at night he remarks 'in the light, lit up, the
baker from Kalgoda'.[10] Surprisingly, Lommel implies that this
poetry is degenerate and inferior. He does not see it as a sign of new
creative energies developing, nor does he see in these poetic comments, that show a rejection of the white cinema in favour of a black
woman, a realisation of the need for caution, and an appreciation of
the shining beauty of a black man, statements as relevant to Aboriginal concerns as those made by the corroborees. One begins to
suspect that this is because they throw doubt on his theory of the
doomed native, a theory to which he adhered so tenaciously that he
named his 1969 popular account of the Aborigines *Fortschritt ins
Nichts* ('Progress into Nothingness').[11] Degeneracy is a concept

Lommel had taken over from Frobenius and which he applied liberally but very subjectively to Aboriginal creativity.

Both Petri and Lommel were able to observe and study the rapid spread of the new Kurangara cult, a cult of black magic that originated in the central Australian desert and spread with astonishing speed. Among the Nngarinyin it was already reasonably well established; they had at the time begun to trade it to their northerly neighbours, the Wunambal. Since there is such a direct link, one would expect great similarities in the interpretation given it by the tribes, but the two anthropologists present very different accounts. Lommel sees it as a direct attempt by the natives to come to terms with white culture. He points out that the Djanba or desert spirits at the centre of the cult are white, their magic pointing sticks are infected with hitherto unknown white man's diseases such as leprosy and syphilis, and are kept at hidden locations near white stations. The Djanba themselves live in corrugated iron houses, their cult foods are tea, flour and sugar, and wherever possible the sticks are to be transported by modern means, such as trains, ships and aeroplanes. According to the Aborigines the world will come to an end once this cult meets up with the earlier Mai-Ungari cult. There is, however, another way in which this apocalypse can be induced, for the Djanba have also made female sticks. If these are ever deployed a new law will come into force. Women will gain authority while men will do women's work, women will dance corroborees and thereby acquire a power that will annihilate the men unless the women cleanse themselves with smoke before meeting them again. Men may not watch these dances. Every time they sleep with their wives they must go off and live alone in the bush for a year. This total reversal of ancient law also spells doom.[12] In the light of modern feminism, it is interesting to hear that for the Wunambal women appear to have been quite as threatening as the invading stranger.

Unfortunately Lommel tells us little else about the status of women in this tribe. He reports but does not comment on the fact that a man is known by his mother's name, even though it is his father who finds him and from whom he inherits his totems. If one looks closely, there are many things Lommel does not investigate fully. One cannot help noticing that his interpretation of the Wunambal bears a curious resemblance to the preoccupation with *Götterdämmerung* mythology that was beginning to catch the German imagination in the 1930s. The emphasis on an artistic rather than sociological interpretation of phenomena is also obvious. It was to lead to a specialisation in that area.

Petri gives a different account of the Kurangara cult. He draws attention to the fact that 'Kurangara' means poison and that its origin, the so-called Warmala, is not a geographical site, as his informants claim, but the central Australian word for blood vengeance feuds. According to the Nngarinyin, the Djanba are restless nomadic spirits who speak an unknown language. They are immortal, omniscient and omnipotent, by nature old and their own creators. Though they resemble humans, they are thin as skeletons and high as trees. Their skin is fair and they have long beards which are hitched up at knee level. Their toes are turned upwards and when they walk they leave no tracks. Their favourite food is human flesh. The waterless desert is a result of their excessive drinking habits. They always travel on moonless nights or at high noon for only their shadows are vulnerable. They never rest and they can turn themselves into any plant or animal. They work their destructive magic by means of Tjurunga sticks. The Djanba, as Petri describes them, show little direct resemblance to the white man's world, though Petri too sees the cult as open to aspects of white culture. Perhaps the fact that one of Lommel's interpreters was himself a poet attempting to come to terms with the white man's world could account for the bias.

In contrast to the traditional benign magic of the rainbow serpent, the Kurangara magic is destructive but, and this appears to be its attraction, immensely powerful. Petri is cautious about interpretation, but implies that it gives a sense of strength to people only too conscious of their weakness and vulnerability. It is, however, he suggests, dangerous to their culture because it undermines the old order, embodied by the benevolent ban-man or witch doctor. Among other things, it was beginning to replace the traditional initiation ceremonies, which were lengthy and painful, including circumcision, subincision and scarification, with a much less arduous ritual. Whereas traditional culture was based on caring for the land entrusted to each tribe by the ancestors and preserving its fertility, the new cult creates deserts and brings death. Petri sees Kurangara as a social and spiritual force and not simply as a symbolic expression of hopelessness. All the same, the rapid spread of the cult is the sign of a deeply disturbed consciousness for which the advent of the white man is ultimately responsible.[13]

Like Lommel, Petri too is preoccupied with the reasons for the apparently unnaturally rapid decline of a culture that is so rich and wholesome and so little subject to direct interference by the white man. He sees the problem in the Aborigines' orientation towards the past and their traditional resistance to change. Petri understands the creative period of the world, the mythical Dreamtime of the Aborigines, to be located in the past. It was Aboriginal man's duty to keep the world and his own spirit as close as possible to this exemplary state. Thus the rock paintings of the Wandjina are touched up each year but never replaced by new drawings. Whenever their power was activated, the ancestral spirits provided for their people, who did not need power in their own right nor the concept of a future that differed from the past. Consequently they were singularly unequipped to cope with change. Since their traditional religion left them helpless in the new situation, they turned to cults which promised some kind of power. Petri is of course aware that even the traditional culture had never been static. There had been earlier cult movements; but these had, with time, been assimilated to the older myth and had enriched it. The rainbow serpent, the Wandjinas, the heroic pairs, the more recent Mai-Ungari cult were probably all originally separate myths that had combined to create a multifaceted, flexible and ambiguous view of the world, which Petri sees as typical of specifically the Nngarinyin.[14] Lommel tends to interpret related phenomena ahistorically. He tells us, for instance, that the Wunambal believed a man to have five souls, which on his death dispersed in different directions to fulfil different functions.[15] It is possible that a closer examination may have shown that here too separate cultural layers had left their mark, creating a sense of multiple possibility rather than simple plurality. The historical perspective made it possible for Petri to credit the Aborigines with the mental flexibility necessary for survival in spite of the trauma of white intrusion.

Petri and those working under his influence and direction continued to show particular interest in the Aborigines' ability to adapt to change. Subjects investigated include traditional intertribal trade contacts, new cult movements, the mingling of residual tribal groups, and the adaptation to white work practices. Parallel with this runs the attempt to record all aspects of the traditional culture that can be observed, deduced or reconstructed, both as a preservation of the past and a way of leaving open the possibility of an eventual at least partial return to older ways. This dual focus seemed to be validated by a new cult which arose in the area in the early sixties and which Petri and his wife, the anthropologist Gisela Petri-Oldermann, describe in a joint article.[16]

It appears that Jinimin, to be identified with Jesus Christ, revealed himself to tribal Aborigines of the Wonajagu or Woneiga territory in July 1963 as a being whose skin was both black and white in keeping with his message of reconciliation. While in the beginning all land had belonged to the Aborigines the future would bring racial equality between black and white and a fair distribution of land, but only on the condition that the Aborigines remained faithful to the law of their ancestors, as defined in the Dreamtime, while at the same time acquiring enough political power to push for change. Petri and Petri-Odermann conclude:

> ... in a widespread area of Australia's north the beginnings of a new syncretistic religiosity are taking form, encouraged by missionary activities ... The material from our area suggests ... that we could be faced with a synthetization of revivalistic, millenarian, xenophobic-nativistic trends, and even an element of social revolution.[17]

The Jinimin cult suggests a willingness on the part of Aborigines to assimilate Christianity as a further cult, to come to terms with the irreversible fact of the white man's presence and yet to remain true to their own tribal law and, where necessary, return to it.

In the same article the Petris describe the assimilation process as they encountered it at La Grange mission south of Broome, where they worked regularly every three years from 1960 onwards. It appears that, with the exception of a single dedicated Catholic, the Aborigines perceived no conflict between Catholic teachings and traditional rituals, which they continued to carry out in secret. At one point the mission's resistance to initiation rites had led to serious discussion of the origins and importance of subincision among the men. The Petris write:

> Widely divergent viewpoints, concepts, and attempted interpretations were put forward ... Such discussions ... demonstrated that these Aborigines, contrary to still widely held ideas, are in no way bound to a fixed and unmodified pattern. These and similar findings discussed elsewhere, permit us to recognize that Australian Aborigines are quite prepared to question their traditional values and moral code, to discuss these and, if necessary re-interpret them.[18]

They also point to the physical mobility, in the form of constant migratory activity, among the north-western Aborigines which leads to the spread of religious cults and which must be seen in the context of the pressure of European contact. They are suspicious of the socialist and anti-colonial teachings of Don McLeod because these appear not to be properly assimilated by the Aborigines.

> Dooley Bin-Bin's eloquence ... was confined to monologues and recitals of studied programme mottoes and slogans, arranged one after another without logical sequence ... If one, however, discusses with Dooley Bin-Bin questions relevant to mythic historic traditions of his people and the cult and ritual systems which vivify them, then he displays an intellectuality, free from Western doctrinairism, flexible and open to discussion, such as is often apparent among today's Aborigines.[19]

It becomes clear here that the Petris favour a reformist rather than a revolutionary model, as might be expected of ethnologists concerned with the preservation of what is essential to the identity of a culture. They sum up:

> A total assessment of Australian Aboriginal cultures within the per-spective of the present, with its pressures towards assimilation, does not permit us at this time to [give] a general prognosis. The two polar concepts of 'stability' and 'change' stand in a relationship to each other which does not conform to certain theoretical expectations of the social sciences.[20]

A methodology which gives primacy to empirical research and makes eclectic use of theory to organise and explain the material collected, rather than allowing theory to guide observation, is char-acteristic of their scientific approach.

As a researcher in her own right, Gisela Petri-Odermann has made a significant contribution to recording the Aboriginal way of life. Her publications include work on the concept of ownership, on medicinal practices, on the sea in the life of traditional Aborigines, on wooden and stone markers, and on Aboriginal women.[21]

Andreas Lommel and his painter wife Katharina also returned to Australia in 1954–55, this time to concentrate on Aboriginal art. Their work is summed up in the publication *Die Kunst des fünften Erdteils. Australien* published in 1959 by Lommel's employer, the Staatliches Museum für Völkerkunde in Munich. His findings are recapitulated in *The Art of the Stone Age*. Here he attributes two basic styles to Australia, the geometric of the centre and south-west, and the naturalistic anthropomorphic and zoomorphic art of the north-west, north and south-east, which he assumes to have been imported. The fact that the geometric style, in the form of losenge and herring-bone patterns, is increasingly dominating naturalistic bark paintings of the north suggests to him that it is more in keeping with the Australian Aboriginal mentality. His verdict on the quality of Australian art is harsh:

> As a rule it may be said that nowadays Australia appears to be in the grip of a tendency towards schematization, which is cramping all artistic expression, so that works of art charged with living tension are very rare ... In anthropomorphic art this tension was only able to survive in the oldest examples and in the north-west, the area where contact is thought to have been made with the outside world. Anthropomorphic art continues up to the present day, but all of it, both rock art and bark paintings, seems degenerate, lacking in inspiration and vigour of artistic expression.[22]

In his 1967 contribution to the volume *Prehistoric and Primitive Art* Lommel looks at Australian art solely within the disparate and consequently somewhat distorting context of Oceanic art.[23] His method derives from the geographical *Kulturkreis* approach of Frobenius, but concentrates on significant motifs rather than on the interrelated complex. These are the X-ray style, movement in profile, the spiral, the skull motif, and the squatting figure. According to Lommel all these motifs have their origins in Europe, usually in the Magdalenian period, and then diffuse via central Asia to southern Asia and finally Australia, as the last outpost of human culture. His most recent publication *L'arte dei primitivi dell' Australia e dei Mari del Sud* (1987) is still a variation on this approach. In an article in *Diprotodon to Detribalization* (1970) Lommel suggests two chronologies, one based on time, the other on place. He again stresses the dominant influence of Europe on Australian rock art and asks:

> Have these contacts only influenced and changed Australian art, or have they also changed Australian mentality, social habits, and other aspects of the way of life? All conceivable evidence points to the contrary. The typical Australian characteristic seems to be the inability to change and assimilate ... If any element of the plant cultivators came too close to Australian Aboriginals to be neglected, it was misinterpreted and misunderstood, so as to avoid the necessity of assimilating it, as is.[24]

There is an unproven assumption here that motifs from planter cultures reached Australia in a form that would have permitted the Aborigines to deduce from them an entire unfamiliar culture. Similarly there is an unwillingness to see the assimilation of foreign cultural elements to a way of life suited to a harsh land—to the extent that it did take place—as an intelligent and creative activity. Lommel is also too little concerned with evidence regarding the mechanisms by which styles and motifs are assumed to have reached Australia. There is a total disregard of absolute chronology.

Lommel's work has elicited an angry reaction from the Australian anthropologist Lesley Maynard. Not only does she object to his "impressionistic amalgam of value judgments and *Kulturkreis* theory of the most old fashioned and simplistic kind" but she deplores the tactlessness of stressing the incompetence and unoriginality of Aboriginal art, particularly if this is done in publications intended for a wider Australian public.[25] Declaring a living people as doomed to extinction could perhaps also be seen as tactless. There are times when one suspects Lommel of a downright dislike of Australia, about which he writes:

> Anyone who has ever been in the Australian bush and seen those ugly, misshapen kangaroos fly along in great bounds will have felt that gnawing sense of horror that takes hold of him, who has caught nature in the process of becoming, or more accurately, of committing a mistake ... And the atmosphere of this continent is determined precisely by the way in which it is half baked, misconceived; and anything new that comes has to submit to this.[26]

This attitude is unfortunate, particularly as in the field of Australian Aboriginal art Lommel has had a virtual monopoly not only on the German but also the international popular market, which has given wide exposure to his prejudices and his idiosyncratic theories, that have never been defended in scholarly confrontation with other theories. It should be added here that his book on the shaman, as the prototype of man the artist, deserves to be placed in a different category.[27]

Another German specialist on Aboriginal art, Agnes Schulz, who had trained as an ethnological painter under Frobenius, was indebted to yet a different part of the complex Frobenius heritage. She was again a member of the 1954–55 Frobenius Expedition, once more led by Petri, but worked separately in Arnhemland, where she painstakingly copied rock paintings. Her attempt to establish a chronology of the art of the area is guided by her competence at her craft.[28] She takes careful note of the sequence of overlapping paintings in the caves she studies and of the brightness of colours in relation to degree of exposure and painting techniques used, to come to the following conclusions. The most recent paintings are the big group of X-ray animals, usually well preserved and uppermost on the rock faces. Reciprocal overlappings prove that they are simultaneous with the stick figures, whose equipment also indicates that they are more recent. The profusion of X-ray figures on some rocks, the faintness of the lower layers, and the consideration that they were probably only painted on special occasions suggest to her that the style must have been practised for at least 200 years. Anthropoid figures shown in movement, sometimes running, sometimes in ceremonial poses, their bodies 'elongated and curved', differ from the stick figures and are older. Groups of anthropoid figures in yet another style, their headdresses suggesting participation in a yam ceremony, are also older than the X-ray paintings. A beautifully painted kangaroo, a frieze of five waterbirds, and a pair of brolgas seem to be the oldest pictures. They are executed in a different technique where an initial outline is filled in with hatching that gives shape to the bodies. Summing up, Schulz makes the point: 'The chronology established by colour differences parallels that suggested by differences between expressive and stiffer movements: the former coincide with the faded or probably repainted figures, the latter with the more freshly coloured ones.'[29] Her findings contradict many of Lommel's assumptions, though they also suggest that the earlier art showed a higher degree of skill.

A final member of the Frobenius research group can only be mentioned in passing. Franz Joseph Micha spent a year as a guest on Gordon Downs station in the south-west Kimberleys in 1959–60 to study Aboriginal workers on the station. He admits that gratitude for hospitality and lack of access to financial records made it difficult for him to present an accurate picture of the situation. His article on Australian prehistory is oriented towards Australian research and assumes only one major wave of immigration. He also undertook a thorough study of Aboriginal trade as a mediator of culture change. His work acknowledges the influence of the Petris.[30]

Our examination of the Frobenius group of anthropologists has revealed that they separated, forming two quite different schools. Andreas Lommel has increasingly concentrated on providing well-presented books on Australian Aboriginal art to a wider public. Unfortunately they have been flawed by ideosyncratic and judgemental commentary and an almost total reliance on fieldwork done in the thirties and fifties. As director of the Völkerkundemuseum in Munich his concern has clearly been with the simple and effective organisation of material from a dead culture for an audience whose point of orientation was Europe, and to whom Aboriginal art could best be sold as an aesthetically degenerate outlandish curiosity, ultimately indebted to Europe but incapable even of maintaining the standard of the original import, moreover deriving from a culture inexorably doomed to extinction and therefore not worthy of concern in its current living manifestations. Since these publications have virtually monopolised the German market and critical book reviews have been either suppressed or published in inaccessible journals,[31] Lommel's views can be assumed to have had considerable influence in shaping German attitudes to Aboriginal Australia. In contrast, the far more competently conducted research of the Petris, that has always been characterised by a strong commitment to the welfare and advancement of surviving Aboriginal groups, has suffered from an almost total lack of resonance because it has tended to be published in the German language and in fairly inaccessible scholarly journals.[32] This is regrettable for it is not only a valuable document of changing or disappearing customs but it also opens up new perspectives on Aboriginal culture made possible by the traditionally somewhat different concerns of German anthropology.

Part 3

Literature and Identity

Hugo Zöller: A German View of Australian society

Irmline Veit-Brause

The rapid transformation of conditions in Australia is something frightening to observe for someone who grew up with the belief in Europe's unchallengeable superiority.

It is a totally new world which is developing in Australia at an unimaginable pace.[1]

Nineteenth-century German language publications on Australia[2] may be grouped into four categories: reports on the migrant experience; travelogues; naturalists' studies; and studies of a social science bent, that is, systematic analyses of Australia's emerging society, its economy and politics, as well as anthropological studies of Aboriginal culture. By and large, these early publications were based on first-hand experience, in contrast to a number of early-twentieth-century dissertations which based their analyses on evidence published elsewhere.

The genres reflect some dominant characteristics in the various authors' perspectives on and personal experiences in Australia, their coverage of topics of interest, and the intended audience. Naturally, individual publications often defy any clear and exclusive

subsumption into one or other category. Travelogues contain observations of a sociological nature; sociological or economic studies are
based on eye-witness accounts, and so on. Still, the basis of evidence, the vantage point of observations and the occasions for
writing on Australia produced characteristically different bodies of
evidence, and hence characteristically different images of Australia.

This list of genres—from reports on the migrant experience to
studies of a sociological kind—is also a rough indication of the
sequential appearance of these different genres, one after the other
adding to the variety rather than replacing each other. In short,
travelogues with their 'tall stories' and episodes of adventure are
still written today, mostly as information by and for the short-term
tourist. The migrant experience, too, still generates intense interest,
either as a topic of literary productions or in the austere prose of
social scientific studies.

The point of this chapter is to introduce Hugo Zöller as the
person who made the very first contribution to the fourth genre. His
reports on Australia in the 1880s, based on first-hand experience,
are more systematic and analytical than the usual travelogue. They
present a view of Australia, its people and politics in a proto-
sociological perspective. Hugo Zöller, the journalist and propagan-
dist of German colonialism, was interested above all in the social
and political character, the distinctiveness of this emergent polity
and the future role it might play in world affairs.

Hugo Zöller was born in 1852 into a Rhenish family of foundry
owners in the Eifel. He began to study law at the university of
Berlin. In 1872–73, he interrupted his studies for health reasons to
travel to the South of France and Spain. Observations in Algeria
made him realise for the first time, so he claimed in his autobiography, that Germany needed its own colonies. After his return to
Germany, he decided not to complete his law degree, and took up
an appointment as journalist with the *Kölnische Zeitung*, a paper
with national distribution, good contacts to the Government and
often for the propagation of semi-official Government views. In this
position he became a vocal defender of German colonialism, one of
the first in the press, as he maintained. In this cause he travelled
widely across the world, seeking to make a name for himself as an
explorer, and to find territories suitable for the foundation of
German colonies.[3]

Hugo Zöller's view of Australia in the 1880s deserves special attention for a number of reasons. There was a definite purpose to his visits, over and above the romantic motive and unfocused curiosity of the adventure-seeking globetrotter, or the scientific curiosity of the naturalist. Both of his journeys, the first in 1879–80 on a round-the-world trip, and the second in 1888–99 en route to New Guinea, were part of his assignments as journalist for the *Kölnische Zeitung*.[4] His articles on Australia in 1888 were published only in this paper.[5] In his book on his round-the world-trip the section on Australia takes up about one tenth of the first volume. His eighteen articles of 1888 varied in size from half a page to a full page of the B4 format of the *Kölnische Zeitung*.

There is no evidence which would allow us to say with certainty how Zöller prepared himself for his Australian assignments, what he read before he left, from whom he sought information, except from Georg Neumayer, then director of the *Seewarte* in Hamburg, before he set out on his journey in 1888. There are no clearly identifiable references either to Australian publications, literary or others, though he seems to have studied the statistical yearbooks quite thoroughly. For Zöller, investigative reporting for a large general audience was a primary motive, not an afterthought, as it may have been, for example, for Reinhold Graf Anrep-Elmpt who travelled through Australia at about the same time. As a journalist, Zöller was naturally most concerned with the human aspects of this new continent in contrast to the focus on the physical conditions of geography, geology, climate, flora and fauna which so preoccupied other travellers and not only naturalists. Georg Seelhorst, for example, who visited Australia in his capacity as secretary of the German *Reichskommissar* to the 1880 exhibition in Melbourne, spent a disproportionately large part of his book on the flora and fauna of the continent, despite his ostensible purpose for writing, namely his interest in the social and economic conditions.[6]

The focus of Zöller's obervations was sharpened by the specific occasions of his visits: the International Exhibitions in Sydney, in 1879, and in Melbourne, in 1880, and nine years later, the Centennial International Exhibition in Melbourne, 1888.[7] Moreover, Zöller was in a unique position to observe and assess the 'immense progress' which had been made in all the Australian colonies in the short time of a decade. Clearly, the specific occasions of international trade fairs—in which German industry participated on an unexpected scale and with considerable success—determined the vantage point and principle of selecting relevant information. Put

briefly, Zöller's perspective on Australia was geared to the question
of what this emerging society with its economic potential meant to
Germany, especially to Germany's foreign trade. Zöller certainly
also recorded very personal reactions to landscape and people; but
his main stance is that of a man on a public mission, conscious of
his responsibility as someone on an *Informationsreise*.

This consciousness shapes the tone of his account and the
selection of his topics. Looking back fifty years later, Zöller was
quite explicit about the reasons for his travel to and the length of his
stay in Australia. After all, he said in his autobiography, in 1930,
'Australia had to be seen as a point of departure for all prospective
colonial enterprises in the Pacific'. Given this task, Zöller felt no
inclination to embark on explorations of the uncharted interior of
the continent, as Georg Neumayer, whose advice he had sought on
all matters, had suggested. Nor was he tempted, or rather permitted
by his brief as a journalist of the *Kölnische Zeitung*, to delve into a
journey of personal discovery or reveal much of his private impressions. As he admitted later on, his reports for the *Kölnische Zeitung*
were marked by a 'rather too severe concentration on the facts and
figures (*Tatsachenmaterial*) and a pushing aside of personal experiences'. It was, as he explained, a consciously imposed restriction. It
conformed to his paper's editorial policy which insisted that 'in the
new circumstances [viz. of colonialism] the amiable art of narration
practised by a seasoned traveller like Gerstäcke, was no longer
apposite.'[8]

Zöller thus represents a new type of traveller to Australia,
different from the migrant, the adventurer, or the scientist. Zöller is
an explorer of the social world of this transplant of European, or,
more precisely, English civilisation at the ever-expanding periphery
of the European-dominated world. It is this aspect of Australia, as a
successful instance of British colonialism, which captures his primary attention, not the exotic, inhospitable environment, nor the
encounter with a 'pre-civilised' culture which held such disconcert-
ing challenges to the European 'superiority complex'. Intent on
educating his audience in the lessons of colonialism, Zöller was
inclined, even keen, to emphasise the likenesses between the far-
away country and the European situation, to demystify the supposed
strangeness of the continent and its people, to assimilate the new to
the familiar, by constantly comparing its outstanding features to the
already well known. He comprehended and presented Australia's
civil society, *Land und Leute*, as a variant, a slight variant at that, of

Englishness, and as a realisation of common trends emerging from the modernising impulses of European civilisation. In several instances, he recommended Australian institutions as models to be imitated. In short, his representation of conditions and life in the Australian colonies was meant to shorten the psychological distance between the new world and the old, and largely succeeded in doing so. The bridge he built for the German reader's understanding is constructed by the notions of 'Englishness' on the one hand and modernity on the other. The pervasive message, so it appears, is one of lowering the psychological barriers of German philistine provincialism against a reaching out into the wider world. His ultimate message was to demonstrate over and over again the viability of colonial ventures, and Germany's need for colonies of its own.

As noted before, Zöller reported twice on Australia. The range of themes he covers in these two reports is similar. On both trips he concentrated on the urban centres: Adelaide, Melbourne, Sydney. In 1888, en route to New Guinea, he stopped in Brisbane and went on excursions to the German settlements in the Queensland hinterland. His interest in and exposure to the Australian 'bush', the countryside, rural life, is peripheral, confined to passing comments on the 'monotonous landscape', experienced from the safety of the overland trains in 1888; the beauties of Sydney, the glistening light and the terrible dust in Melbourne. Focusing on urban life, he made no mention of the urban/rural split that became such an obsession of Australian national self-definitions.

Given this political vantage point and, as a consequence, this focus on Australia's urban life, there is little understanding or sympathy for the colonies' local identity and the intense Anglo-Australian regionalism.

> At first glance, the stranger perceives 'Australia' as such. He is struck by the many similarities between Victoria, New South Wales, South Australia etc., while the differences which are so less marked become noticeable only after a prolonged stay [in the country]. It makes little sense to [a foreign observer] that these seven state-like entities are kept separate from each other by tariff and other barriers. Australia is so fortunate to have an extremely homogeneous population, much more so than any other colonial country I know.[9]

He was struck by the fact that there were hardly any natural frontiers marking the political division between the colonies, and therefore presented the typical features of Australia, especially characteristic social features, as belonging to Australia as a whole.

Distinguishing features were relevant only with regard to political structures and policy orientations.

Zöller concentrates on three major thematic complexes:

1. Urban life, and its material, social and intellectual conditions, including long excursions into the situation of the press in Melbourne and Sydney;
2. The economic situation, with particular reference to German-Australian trade and its prospects;
3. Germans in Australia, a choice of topic not so obvious for a German observer then as it may seem today.[10]

The physical conditions of the continent which figure so prominently in other contemporary accounts are passed over almost completely; the Aborigines are mentioned only in passing, as in most other contemporary travel literature—with one notable exception, Anrep-Elmpt.[11] The history of discovery, a much repeated topic in other accounts, is merely sketched as a preliminary to observations on Australian politics in 1888, not mentioned at all in 1881. There are other notable silences in Zöller's accounts, and little is made of the standard topics of Australian folklore, though Ned Kelly is dutifully mentioned, the 'lost in the bush' motive, the awesome bushfires, the goldfield diggers—the stock-in-trade of travelogues get a mention in 1881, but are, understandably, missing in 1888. On the whole, it is not the quaintness but the utter normalcy of Australian civil life which is conveyed to the German reader.

Civilised normalcy, verging on the exemplary, characterises the image Zöller projects of urban life in Sydney, Melbourne, and Adelaide. Zöller is impressed by, even enthusiastic about, the two great urban centres, Sydney and Melbourne. In 1879–80, they both epitomise the 'Typus Grossstadt', with respect to the size of their population and of the built-up area, the number and grandeur of their public buildings, the quality and variety of architectural styles, the efficiency and comfort of their public transport systems—the coaches, horse-drawn bus lines in 1879–80, the steam-powered cable cars in 1888, the trains, the busy melée of their street life, the graciousness of their public parks and gardens. A decade later, Melbourne has made 'as much progress as Berlin since 1870', and both cities have acquired some additional cosmopolitan flair deserving the laudatory epithet '*Weltstadt*'. Both belong to the same league of truly cosmopolitan centres as San Francisco, Paris, Berlin,

London, or Brussels. In some respects the metropolis of Victoria and that of New South Wales appear as quite unique, for example with respect to Melbourne's organisation of urban spaces. In other respects, they call for very favourable comparisons, especially with regard to Melbourne's splendidly built and organised commercial buildings. In other respects, again, they surpass most European cities in the quality of urban planning. Melbourne's Botanical Garden is more beautiful than the Bois de Boulogne, or the gardens of Wiesbaden, Hamburg or Baden-Baden. Not a word of deprecation for the 'urban sprawl' of Greater Melbourne, instead full praise for the lack of centripetal pulls—as in London or Paris—and the distinct impression of completeness and perfection [*Eindruck des Fertigseins*] in spite of this expansive spread. The provision of the technological amenities of modern city life, such as Melbourne's and Sydney's well-organised public transport, and the electrification of the Melbourne Exhibition Building, are praised as truly exemplary: 'If one could only get our fellow countrymen to see these things with their own eyes, the lovely asphalted roads, the clean, superwide footpaths, the general availability of gas, piped water, baths and gardens. I am afraid they might blush with shame.' (p. 203) Due credit is given to those who created these admirable and technologically progressive achievements within a mere generation.

Zöller is aware of the rivalries between Sydney and Melbourne, and eventually makes his own bet on the likely outcome. In his own assessment of their general appeal, qualities and claims—*glänzend* (splendid) versus *behaglich* (comfortable), the 'Paris of Louis XVIII' versus the 'Paris of Napoleon III'—his preference goes to Melbourne, as the more European of the two, and on the whole more beautiful and *weltstädtischer*, (more cosmopolitan) despite Sydney's greater number of monumental buildings. It is as if he senses in Melbourne, in 1880, an air of greater vitality, and is convinced in 1888 that Sydney is lagging behind, at least for the time being, just as Vienna had been overtaken by Berlin.[12]

Reading these passages today, one may well wonder whether one should be struck more by the clear grasp of Australia's self-image as an urban culture one hundred years ago, which in the intervening years had to be retrieved from so much bush mythology of Australia's national identity making, or by the pedagogical impact this favourable depiction of Australia's urban splendour was bound to have on the German audience.[13] It should be noted, though, that the pedagogy with political intent operates subtly, with seemingly neutral descriptions of the details of perceived reality, free of such value-laden concepts—except perhaps the term of praise and admiration *Weltstadt* (the metropolis with cosmopolitan urbanity)—which a later interpretation of its impact must use for brevity's sake, such as technological progress, progressiveness, civility and modernisation.

The International Exhibitions in 1879–80 and in 1888, which were the main purpose of his visits, and the overwhelming impression of a materially thriving society as evidenced in the splendour of its cities, directs Zöller's attention to more general questions of the colonies' social and economic life, their resources, trade, their commercial relations with other countries, especially Germany. This is the second cluster of observations and comments, with economic questions figuring most prominently in his account of 1888, less so in 1879–80 when he devotes much greater attention to the social contours of the new society.[14]

There are a few comments on the economic situation which are most significant for the image of Australia Zöller was trying to project. Zöller was not an economist. That distinguishes his account from much contemporary British comment on the Australian situation.[15] Zöller's natural interest and inclination was as an observer of social life. That is most obvious in his account of his first visit, where his assignment left him with greater freedom to choose what appeared significant to him. And yet, as politics and the economy belong to any comprehensive picture of a country, he dutifully touches on both even then, with the somewhat dismissive comment that he presumes the economic development of the Australian colonies to be of rather greater interest to those at home than Australian constitutional arrangements or daily politics (p. 219). A decade later, though, he recognises a need for paying closer attention to Australian political life—no longer 'embryonic' or lacking in interest from a global perspective.[16] In 1888, this interest in the emerging political directions 'which Australia is inclined to pursue in world affairs' is closely associated in Zöller's mind with Australia's economic power, often exaggerated by some flamboyant Australians, but considerably greater than some foreign travellers were inclined to acknowledge.[17]

A realistic assessment of Australia's economic development, based on the available extensive statistics, is thus indispensable, in

Zöller's view, for assessing Australia's future in a global context, or more specifically and bluntly, for an assessment of Australia's interest for Germany. In other words, in 1888, Zöller's perspective on this issue—more so than on others—is clearly determined by his interest in German expansion overseas by means of trade and/or independent colonial settlements. To present Australia's economic situation under the heading of *Reichtümer* (literally 'wealth', as used in English at the time in the sense of resources)[18] is to use a telling phrase, one which conjures up a positively valued image of resources to be developed and exploited. The articles on the Australian economy read almost like a check list of what Australia has to offer the world. For other knowledgeable people, past and present, there is nothing very new or peculiar in his respective observations, factual as they are. Rather, it is the fact that this information is presented for the first time, in a more or less comprehensive and systematic way to the general public in Germany, which deserves attention. Although Zöller guards against moralising, his own views on what is good or bad for the economic health of a country shine through his reports in 1888. They were more openly expressed fifty years later, when he still recorded his approval in retrospect that sheep and wheat were beginning to displace the prominence of gold and silver as the country's resources.[19] In his view, it is the industriousness of a nation which determines its economic strength, not merely its natural endowments. However, in 1888, he realises that one highly valued natural resource, namely gold, needs to be mentioned in the first place, 'not because of its present, not all that great importance, but rather because of its past'.

Gold was the motor for Australia's rapid development. Gold 'has made Australia to what it is today', as it led to the immense population expansion, and was the cause of Victoria's ascendency, and threatened to turn the other colonies, especially South Australia into a depopulated waste land.[20] The gold rush (a term he does not use) was followed by the exploration of silver. The phenomenal development of Broken Hill and the instrumental involvement of some Germans get a special mention, as does the 'speculative' nature of this mining company in which immense profits were made, facilitated by the British legislation on share companies. While the rest of the natural resources, such as tin, copper, precious stones, coal (as an export article of growing importance), are listed in a factually informative way, there is, no doubt, an overtone of disapproving amazement in his story of Broken Hill. That tone grows stronger, changing almost into the indignant voice of a social critic when Zöller turns to the general features of an intense 'speculation fever', the issue of the extraordinary size of the public debt, especially of New Zealand and Queensland, and the general fast buck attitude.

As for the relative value of these different kinds of resources, Zöller is not afraid to offer his evaluation of the mineral wealth: 'It is much less than that of the pastoral industry, especially wool production.' Zöller impresses on his readers the order of magnitude of this latter production. 'The Australian colonies taken together, are the most important of all woolproducing parts of the world', ranking above the La Plata states, Russia and North America. Germany, he feels obliged to add, still produces one-eighth of the total wool production of the Australian colonies.[21] Zöller's own economic prejudices show up again when he explicitly mentions Victoria as an exception to the generalisation he has just proposed, because of the 'recent shift' in Victoria's rural industry, the rise of agriculture and the resulting decline in wool production. He notes, too, the very recent interest in raising sheep for meat as well as wool, and emphasises Queensland's growing importance in the cattle industry. These observations should be read against the background of the fitting of the first German ship, *Protos*, in 1880, with refrigeration facilities for the transport of frozen meat to Germany.[22]

Quite obviously, Zöller is mindful all the time of his specific mission as a reporter on the industrial exhibitions and the expectations—deemed exaggerated by him in 1879–80—they raised in Australia, but more particularly in Germany. He therefore feels obliged to offer his view primarily on 'conclusions and lessons' about both the productivity and the demand for European imports of the Australian market.[23] In 1879–80, he appears cautiously optimistic on both accounts (p. 213). A decade later, the picture has grown much more complex and ambiguous. With regard to productivity, the diversification of economic activity both in the rural and in the industrial sectors are presented as positive developments. He mentions wheat, fruit and wine-growing which have replaced the limited number of staples; and the figures he lists on the growth of the manufacturing industry in Victoria are impressive-sounding evidence.

The picture is balanced by pointing out what can only be understood as the shaky foundations of the apparently booming business sector: speculation fever, the early 1880s mineral boom having been replaced by another boom, the land 'boom' (his term!). He notes with an air of concern that the really productive forces, namely the peasants (*Ackerbauern*) have a socially inferior position and no political voice. In his estimation, the ultimately unproductive inflow of English capital favouring the 'squatters' (his term) merely fuels land speculation, but does not benefit the country as a whole as capital gains are withdrawn to England. But Australia's development as an internationally competitive nation is inhibited in Zöller's, as in so many other foreign critics' views at the time, by the unreasonably high level of wages. 'The impact of high wages is felt in so many aspects of social and economic life.' It shows up, too, in the fact 'that not only some manufacturing goods, but even farm produce cannot compete with those of America, or of Europe, despite [Australian] protective tariffs'.

It is this paradox or dilemma of Australian productive resources—'one can produce [all these goods] in the country, but it is cheaper to import them from elsewhere'—which must make Australia appear as an uncertain market for foreign exports. The one concrete example he mentions to illustrate this point is agricultural machinery, an item very well presented in the German Court at the Centennial International Exhibition. On the one hand, 'it is fortunate for our European [!] industry', says Zöller, that Australian products are so expensive that they cannot compete in the world market. On the other hand, Zöller reminds the reader, Australian industrial products, rough and expensive as they may be in comparison, do fulfil their purpose and satisfy the domestic demand, so that 'if need be, Australia can, no doubt, stand on its own, without having to rely on Europe'.

It is the tenor and frequency of such examples which convey a cautiously pessimistic conclusion about the economic situation of 1888, although Zöller wisely refrains from any explicit recommendations or warnings. Balanced and neutral as the picture appears to be, for someone interested in doing business with Australia, a seemingly passing comment that the boom fuelled by speculation 'will by necessity be followed by a setback' must have sounded ominous enough, especially as it proved true so soon after, with the depression of the 1890s.

Zöller was certainly not in principle against the promotion of German–Australian trade. Yet by allowing the facts and figures to speak for themselves and by avoiding any sensational language he not only lent credibility to his report, but may also have influenced attitudes of German business whose engagement in the Australian market was less enthusiastic than the government and other commercial propagandists would have liked it to be.

So far we have treated Zöller's two accounts as if they were one, the later continuing on, and adding to the observations made in the earlier one. There is however, some difference between the two. In 1888, Zöller's curiosity was much more clearly focused on facts which count in world politics. His range of topics in the articles in the *Kölnische Zeitung* extends to questions of political structure, policy issues—such as colonial federation and possible separation from Great Britain which he sees unlikely to happen in the near future; even Australia's security concerns and defence preparations score a mention.[24] All these observations present Australia as a country to be taken seriously, as an emerging power in the Pacific, as a factor in world politics to be reckoned with. In that perspective, 'social mentality' and 'way of life' issues become peripheral, quite in contrast to his intense interest in just those features of Australian society on his earlier visit.

This shift of focus is to be seen in the context of the international situation which changed drastically between 1880 and 1888. Zöller's account of Australian life in 1879–80 predates the beginning of an active German colonial policy which his reports were meant to promote in one way or another. This aim determines his approach in a subtle though noticeable way. It is as if his more original, subtle and sensitive observations, in 1879–80, those which go beyond the merely anecdotal, emerge as answers to two unstated questions, namely 'what is it that qualifies the English for the successful founding of overseas colonies?' and secondly, 'how well do Germans live among the English, that is in this case, the Anglo-Australians?'[25] What reads at first like rather spontaneous and somewhat random observations and comments acquires the coherence of something like an experimental set-up for the purpose of finding answers to these questions, and furthermore, of testing his own anglophile sentiments.

> There would be very few cities in which one can live so comfortably as in Melbourne, and few people among whom one would feel at home so quickly as among the English. This is, after all, one of the main reasons why all English colonies have proved so attractive to emigrants . . . though the alien [*der Fremde*] must be familiar with the English way of life in order to feel at home. (p. 213)

And yet: 'However, one should never forget that all the advantages, all the comforts are ultimately—like Mephisto's help—acquired at the cost of a highly valued good, namely German national identity.' (p. 214)

Zöller approaches this phenomenon of Australia in a rather complex, even tension-ridden frame of mind. He is a man of cosmopolitan experiences which allow him to see Australia in global terms. He is attracted by the English way of life and nurtures a sense of envious admiration for the British predominance in the world. He is also intensely conscious of his own German nationality. Zöller, in a nutshell, is a member of a special breed: he is a cosmopolitan, Anglophile German nationalist, which, though it may appear a contradiction in terms, was more common at this time than one would suspect. His valiant attempt to work out these contradictions colours all his observations on Australia which he takes as an exemplar of Englishness. Australia's *Vorzüge*, its advantages, are, basically, those of the English and their most positive development under the conditions of colonial life. The darker side of the 'typically Australian'—on which Seelhorst, for instance, dwelt with ill-disguised disdain—is almost totally absent from Zöller's picture.[26]

By and large, Zöller's Australian experience contains nothing that could have upset his Anglophile sentiments. But the earlier and the later account differ markedly in emphases and conclusions. The resolution he works out for his psychological tensions is simple: Germany must emulate the English and found its own overseas empire. Yet, this is not to say that the text of *Rund um die Erde* is simply an imperialist tract. None of Zöller's points are dogmatically argued. Rather they emerge from the rich and lively material laid out in a kind of *parlando* style, a style which makes it extremely hard to condense his many illustrations from various different sectors of Anglo-Australian life without appearing to repeat a series of platitudinous cliches. What then does Zöller present as characteristically Australian qualities of life?

First and foremost, it is the sheer comfort of material life for all, including for example the 'poorer classes' of Germans: 'Dreimal täglich Fleisch, sagen sie . . .': 'Meat three times a day, they say . . .' It is a point too mundane for Seelhorst to mention. Zöller recognises that there are more important psychological attractions: a sense of 'liberty', the psychological release from social pressures, due to few demands put on people's social graces, education or sheer wit. It is the easy-going, relaxed way of social communication freed from the conventions and from the respect for social hierarchies which heightens the feeling of social well-being, especially for those from the lower classes. There is almost lyrical praise for the beneficial effects on social life of Australian women's emancipation from conventional role prescriptions for a proper housewife. Australian women who 'perfectly combine the dignity of a lady with the duties of a housewife' are seen to play a much freer and extremely important role in Australian social life, especially as much of it takes place within the private home, the family. Even the barmaids get a eulogy for their graces. On the other hand, the role of the all-male clubs, the social exclusiveness of the Melbourne Club, and the frictions between social and political rank orders are mentioned as well. Still, the outstanding characteristic of Australian social life is that the pleasures of daily life and the leisure-time activities are available to and shared by all classes. In some, the lower classes participate even more prominently than the higher classes—such as the sports, the races, especially the Melbourne Cup, the thrills of betting as a consuming pastime. A long explanation is provided on the new totalisator! (pp. 214–18).

Ultimately, the Australian experience is the occasion for some poignant general reflections: first about the decisive difference between European and colonial societies: the absence of social hierarchies and the openness of social contact—a precondition 'for the faster throb of life'. Here, Zöller tells his provincial philistines at home, lie the immense advantages of egalitarianism (*Gleichheitssystem*) (p. 257). Zöller's attitude to the 'democratic spirit' of such new societies as the United States and Australia, however, wavers and changes. In 1888, he has some derogatory asides on the 'freedom phrases' (*Freiheitsphrasen*) which captured simple-minded people.[27] In his autobiographical reflections, his experiences of 1888 suddenly appear in a rather different light again: 'Auch in sozialer Hinsicht hatte sich in diesem übertrieben demokratischen Lande . . . manches verschlechtert.'[28]

The second general point is spelt out in some lengthy socio-psychological speculations. They grow into a tableau of the 'social virtues' of the English brought into sharp relief by constant comparisons with the typically German character, mentality and attitudes which he saw confirmed once he was again among Germans in Australia. These reflections contain the answer to Zöller's first unstated question. The success of the English as a colonising people, he argues, is not to be explained by a more favourable 'natural endowment' (*Naturanlage*), whether materially or economically, but by some prominent traits of their social character which were reinforced by their political and social experiences. Moreover, what must appear to the Germans as culturally inferior traits—such as 'a certain intellectual narrowness', an ingrained conformism (*nach einer Schablone*), the self-centredness, i.e. the ignorance of and insensitivity to other languages or cultures or customs, the cliquishness of their church life—all these cultural deficiencies turn out to be real political strengths, because they enforce solidarity (*Zusammenhalt*), maintenance of their own, the English way of life, and reinforce self-confidence and self-discipline, all of them essential personal attributes of a gentleman, and singularly missing among the Germans (pp. 254–56).

It would be wrong to brush these points aside as topoi of a primitive social psychology (*Völkerpsychologie*). They are worth quoting, though, because they may explain why Zöller is inclined to overlook or excuse, for example, the lesser interest in the institutions of 'high culture', especially among the men (p. 217). High culture is for him a less important condition for a good life, and for political success and power, than these 'social virtues', even though he is less forgiving about the smartness in business life a decade later.[29] His praise of egalitarianism also carries over into his later assessment of political life in Australia. The division into two parties, the squatters (Queensland) and a liberal-radical party pandering to the working class, appears as something quite natural, given the English model. The absence of well-prepared and educated political personnel, the favouritism (*Günstlingswesen*) have done no obvious damage to the conduct of political affairs. Far from being signs of ingrained corruption, as Seelhorst understood them, these conditions have, in fact, often thrown up some very competent men.[30]

Needless to say, such a positive evaluation of what appeared to other observers as the most conclusive indicators of Australia's social ills and despicable crudeness is a rather unique characteristic of Zöller's image of Australia. The opposite impression is created by Seelhorst, and even Anrep-Elmpt, to mention only immediate contemporaries. Zöller expressly notes, too, that Australia, because of the generally high standard of living, has remained immune to the doctrines of socialism: '*Socialdemocraten*' there are none, 'as yet'. But he detects in the strong working-class organisations and the 'enormous influence' of their trade unions, a 'strong flavour of socialism'.[31] In this respect, and that makes for the singular interest of his observations in the 1880s, Zöller anticipates what became a major reason for German socialists to concern themselves with Australia, shortly after: the idea of a 'workers' paradise', and of a 'country of social miracles'.[32]

Given Zöller's own national consciousness, the answer to the second of his unstated questions arises with near inescapable plausibility from the dialectical construction of German character flaws in contrast to Anglo-Australian strengths. Whatever the material conditions of the Germans in Australia—'at best comfortable, never rich or well-to-do' (p. 252)—whatever the chances for social mobility (p. 247), whatever their pioneering achievements in farming, science and culture—and he has a mass of detail to demonstrate his case—the fact remains that their social and political influence and standing is nil, at best negligible, except in South Australia.[33] The cause is seen in their lack of solidarity, the absence of personal self-confidence, their timid, though solid and sober business behaviour (peasants, not squatters!) (p. 246), the low-class origin of most German migrants (p. 214) and the fact that 'there was no leadership by politically capable people' (p. 250). The lack of a natural, taken-for-granted national self-confidence and the economic necessity to give in to the assimilating pressures of the unselfconsciously prejudiced and domineering Anglo-Australian majority come together to deprive the Germans of due recognition of their objectively immense contributions to Australia's development, though without, as he stresses, any conscious intentions on the part of the English (p. 252). For Zöller, the psychological effects on the Germans appear obvious: namely having to live, half consciously, with the feeling of having 'sacrificed' their cultural identity for material benefits (p. 248).

One may well ask who among the Germans in Australia may have expressed such feelings. Zöller's admission that he has neither the courage to leave his *Heimat* permanently nor an understanding for those who do raises some suspicion that it is his own projection which authorised such conclusions, although he himself believed that the thought of returning home guaranteed his impartiality. Putting his nationalist unease about emigration aside, his observations on the social and socio-psychological conditions of German-Australians still lead him to warn quite explicitly against emigration to Australia, rather than other countries.[34] As for more general political conclusions, they are even more inescapable:

> One may acknowledge the personal amiability of the Englishman as an individual, one may enjoy living among this businesslike, curt, but polite, honest [offen] and reliable [characterfeste] people. All that does not cancel the wish that our emigrating fellow countrymen may succeed in even more favourable conditions and maintain their nationality. (p. 252)

Admittedly, there are social and material conditions which are more favourable to cultural maintenance than others, such as concentrated settlements, and their intense church life. But that is the conclusion which the experience among the German communities in Australia and his analysis of Australia's development impresses on him, namely that Germany needs its own colonies, as colonies secure the conditions for large-scale commercial activities which, in turn, lay the foundations for a 'great power' (p. 254).

Quod erat demonstrandum: Zöller's experiences in 1880 thus reconfirm what he set out to prove.

In 1888, his observations are set in a framework dramatically changed in the intervening years. In the mid-1880s the German Empire had embarked on a policy of colonial annexations, in New Guinea (annexed in 1884), in East and West Africa. Hence, Zöller no longer needs to present empirical evidence in support of his political message. Nevertheless, his belief in Germany's cultural and colonial mission still filters his perceptions.

It is consistent with his old preoccupations with the *Erhaltung der Nationalität,* that is, maintenance of national identity, that he changes in 1888 with ease to the new terminology which signalled a fundamental change in Germany's attitudes to German migrants in foreign countries. In 1879–80 Zöller still speaks of the 'Germans in Australia'. In 1888, he adopts the by now fashionable and increasingly invidious term of '*Deutschtum*'.[35] The collective singular *Deutschtum* describes and, at the same time, postulates communities of close settlement, a feeling of social and cultural cohesion and difference, a proud consciousness of their cultural background (of their 'ethnicity' as one would say today). The term also conjures up, in a vague, ill-defined sense, some feeling of loyalty to the 'home country', a role into which the German Empire was cast by German nationalists, while for many migrants memories and feelings of belonging were linked to their 'particularist' country of origin, such as Bavaria or Prussia, Württemberg or Mecklenburg, Saxony or Oldenburg.

In contrast to the—in his view—rather depressing attitudes and demeanour of the Germans in 1880, Zöller is pleasantly surprised about, at least, a new 'spirit', if not about the objective conditions of the Germans in 1888. By far the largest part of his account is concerned with the objective conditions of the German migrants, in its demographic, economic, social, political and cultural dimensions. All the details he presents go to prove that this topic has a legitimate place in any comprehensive account of Australia's new society, because of the size of this migrant group and because of the significance of its contribution in many walks of life, not merely because this particular author happens to feel 'most at home' among his fellow countrymen.[36] To make his case, he presents figures on the size of the German population, challenging the way the criterion was used in the official censuses, namely as 'German-born', to a much broader definition of 'German', including second-generation Germans and also those who renounced their German background completely and were 'submerged' in the English-speaking milieu.[37] Depending on who is to be legitimately counted, the estimates range from 2 to 3.5% of the total population.[38] There are qualitative indicators, as well, to make his case. So Zöller pays homage to Schomburgk and Ferdinand von Müller, to the Germans who have made it into the parliaments of South Australia and Queensland, to the enormously beneficial work of the German consuls, like Muecke in Adelaide, Brahe in Melbourne, or Heussler in Brisbane, to the successful businessmen in all three cities.

His sketch of the general situation of the 'Deutsch-Australier' refers in particular to the Germans in the rural settlements in South Australia and in Queensland, as his brief required.[39] He is convinced that German migrants have greater chances of success in agriculture, modest as it may be, than in the cities where unemployment among commercial clerks was widespread. The condition of the German settlers is marked by a kind of urban/rural split, especially with regard to social cohesion and cultural maintenance.[40] But Zöller is not only interested in the past contributions Germans have made to the economic and cultural development of Australia, or in their current position. He is also concerned about the likely future of this 'ethnic community'. In this respect, the reported facts are rather ambivalent. On the one hand, there is a deeply rooted Heimatgefühl, the 'clinging to customs and language', especially among the Lutherans in the rural settlements of South Australia and in Queensland, and among the 'lower classes' (*Handwerker und Bauern*) in general.[41] This is commented upon in a tone of deep satisfaction, accompanied by a recital of the usual commonplaces about the German colonists' sobriety, hard work, reliability, solidity. Zöller also detects the 'very new' sense of self-respect, and a decline in the Anglo-Australians' disdain of all things German. In an almost triumphant tone, Zöller welcomes this new national spirit as an effect of the great advances Germany has made in domestic as well as international affairs: the establishment of the Norddeutscher Lloyd shipping line to Australian ports; the periodic visits of the German South Pacific cruisers; the activities of the consuls, and the colonial policy of the Empire, obliquely referred to simply by dating this rise of national consciousness to the period between 1880 and 1888, so as not to offend any sensitivities of the Australians. These developments 'back home', so to speak, have helped to strengthen a sense of positive identification with the 'home country'. On the other hand, the picture is bleaker when he comments on the predictable loss of a German cultural identity, the progressive Anglicisation, most definitely of the second generation, the despicable betrayal of their origins even by some first-generation Germans, on the de facto discrimination illustrated by the fact that Germans if they want to succeed in business have to conform to English norms and conventions.[42] But the conclusions Zöller derives from this complicated state of affairs are anything but ambiguous:

> That this [i.e. the foreseeable decline of *Deutschtum*] is going to happen is deplorable not only from a national German, but also from a cosmopolitan point of view. Even the most English of Englishman would not deny that—just as the other way round—the German has some virtues which are missing in the English. Just as Australia owes today many a beautiful thing to his citizens of German origin, it would be of great benefit for the final shape of the great new people which is in the process of formation if this people absorbed, to a greater extent than hitherto, all that is superior to Englishness in the German way of life and in German culture. We Germans would and could be happy if our brethren who have become Australian citizens would maintain their German ways from one generation to the next. What damage could it do to Australians if a minute percentage of its population would continue to speak German while recognising English as the official language of the land?[43]

Such comments sound like an advocacy of multiculturalism *avant la lettre*, put forward, moreover, by an outsider with motivations very different from those of the migrants themselves. There are, it appears, two very different kinds of multiculturalism: one that is propagated from within, and the other from outside the society at which it is directed. The external variant uses the same idiom as the internal one, but combines it with an argument for harnessing the loyalty of those ex-nationals residing in other countries to the political causes of the home country. The *Deutschtumspolitik*—the policy of maintaining and strengthening a 'German' identity among the Germans overseas—Zöller is anticipating is a late-nineteenth–early-twentieth-century precursor of what is known today as the 'transnational politics of ethnicity'.[44]

As for this German observer's forecasts on this new society's future, there is no doubt in his mind that Australia is destined to flourish, less perhaps than some sanguine Australians believe themselves, when they dream of an Australia with the importance in world affairs as great as that of any European power; but definitely greater than any of his eurocentric readers ever stop to imagine.[45]

More important to this avid supporter of German colonialism is, however, the emergence of a new geopolitical centre of gravity in the Pacific of which Australia will be a part:

> In any case, in the next century, the [Pacific]—with such energetic peoples at its edges as the Australians, the North Americans, the Japanese and the Chileans and with one of the most populous countries [i.e. China] close to its shores—is quite likely to gain a similar importance as the Atlantic has today, especially once the Panama canal has been completed.[46]

In whatever way one reads these comments, as those made by a detached observer or by someone with very definite preconceptions, the fact remains that one hundred years later, Zöller's observations must be deemed remarkably perceptive.

Like an overture, Zöller's reports of the 1880s introduced themes into the German perception of Australian society, politics and culture which were to be developed later on, for instance by a continuing interest in Australia's solution to large-scale technological developments, such as railway construction, engineering, or the advanced methods of statistics introduced by the New South Wales Government Statistician, T. A. Coghlan. Australia also continued to attract the attention of German political commentators concerned with industrial relations and social legislation. On the other hand, writing for a general public in Germany, Zöller announced that there was a new and not all that hidden agenda for German interests in the development of this new society. From the 1880s onwards, Australia was one of the targets of Imperial Germany's worldwide trade offensive and *Deutschtumspolitik* which were part and parcel of the Empire's bid for world power status. Zöller's perception of Australian conditions thus bears witness to an image of Australia forming in the German public mind. Australia, once an item on the private agenda only of individual travellers or naturalists, now moved into the focus of political attention, at least of that section of the German public deeply agitated about German colonial expansion.

Returning to the more general question of German perceptions of Australia, it appears that they remained diverse and the total picture fragmented. There was not before World War I, and is not even now much evidence in the literature on Australia of a strong *wirkungsgeschichtliche Bewusstsein* or a demonstrable intertextuality relating one text to the other. The consecutive experiences of Germans in Australia made publicly available hardly added up to a well-established and commonly accepted 'image of Australia'. It is as if no common stock of knowledge about this new country and its people was building up in the German public despite a continuous stream of publications. In every new publication, basic information on geography, flora and fauna, the history of discovery and so on is reiterated instead of being assumed as knowledge taken for granted. Australia appears as a land forever rediscovered—almost down to the present day. In pre-1914 literature this feature of the ever-renewed novelty of the experience is particularly striking. It is as if 'Australia' represented the prototypical *fascinosum* of the exotic, with its flora and fauna quite unlike anything else that was known, as yet populated by people of European stock close enough to oneself to be constructed as the 'Antipodeans', not just the alien other, but one's counterpart. The fascination of the exotic is that it entices a longing for personal discovery, for a sensual experience through immersion unmediated through prior knowledge. For those who feel attracted by the exotic aura of a country, a rehearsal of factual information comes after the personal experience, as a kind of antidote to the romantic surrender and loss of orientation. To set out on such a journey well prepared by foreknowledge would dampen the romantic urge, and kill the *fascinosum*.[48] In any case, the remarkable lack of a somewhat stable image of Australia is an indicator of the slow reception of the available information. Every new visitor of these foreign shores felt as if they were entering a *terra incognita*. This is what remained subjectively true, whether or not it accorded with the objective situation.

Imagining an Australian nation: The German community of South Australia during the nineteenth century

Gerhard Fischer

On 16 July 1883, a gala reception and banquet took place in the premises of the German Club in Adelaide. The occasion of the event was a celebration in honour of Carl Wilhelm Ludwig Muecke, one of the most respected citizens of the colony. It was Muecke's sixty-eighth birthday, the thirty-fourth he had celebrated in Australia—for mystics and cabbalists a constellation pregnant with symbolism: Muecke was a German-Australian, and on that day he had lived exactly one half of his life in Germany and one half in Australia. After the elaborate dinner—a fourteen-course French *menu*—and following the obligatory toast to the Queen of England, a festive ceremony was staged during which Muecke was appointed honorary member of the club. The highlight of the evening was the presentation, by a delegation of the leading German-Australian citizens of South Australia, of a formal address in praise of the guest of honour. It was a masterpiece of calligraphy created by a local artist, a richly decorated manuscript contained in a magnificent portfolio bound in black velvet with elaborate gold and silver fittings. The document had been signed by 1072 colonists, representing 93 different professions and 149 towns and villages in South Australia. I quote from the address, translating from the original German:

> We see you here [in South Australia], a new Cincinnatus, humble and unassuming, tilling Australia's virgin soil ... And we see you as a pastor, as an untiring teacher of the young, as a journalist without fear, and as a concerned and always helpful friend who devotes himself with untiring love to the service of your fellow citizens. What you have achieved here as a scholar in the field of science and as a valiant representative of the education of the people will remain forever unforgotten; the fruits of your noble endeavour can already be seen in our young who proudly call you their teacher, and they can be shown in this people's political freedom that reveals traces, everywhere and unmistakably, of your creative spirit.[1]

Who was this man who was so enthusiastically eulogised by his contemporaries? And who was 'this people' to whose 'political freedom' he was said to have so significantly contributed?

Born in 1815 in Büden near Magdeburg, Muecke was a well-known journalist, editor and educational author before coming to Australia. He had studied classics and natural sciences at the universities of Bonn and Berlin, without completing a degree, choosing to work in publishing rather than following an academic career. In an age that was intensely interested in questions of education, Muecke actively promoted the idea of *Volkserziehung* (education for all) and he propagated a new curriculum which would give due weight to scientific and technological issues. As the director of the Norddeutsche Volksschriften Verein his publishing efforts were directed towards producing non-fiction books documenting and popularising the rapid advances in science and technology during the industrial revolution, aiming at a readership of artisans, workers and peasants. He was also the editor of *Pädagogische Jahrbücher*, a children's journal which pursued the same goal for younger readers. In 1847 the University of Jena awarded him a doctorate, without examination or thesis, in recognition of his work. Thirty-one years later the University of Adelaide followed suit, conferring upon Muecke an honorary M.A. degree.

Muecke was only one of a group of highly educated Germans who had chosen to begin a new life in Australia following the experience of defeat during the ill-fated revolution of 1848 which signalled, at least for the time being, an end to their dream of a democratic nation state in Germany. Among the immigrants who accompanied Muecke to Australia on the ship *Prinzess Louise*, which reached Port Adelaide after a journey of five months on 7 August 1849, were: Richard Schomburgk, botanist and ex-gardener at the court of the Prussian king at Sanssouci; Carl Linger, musician and composer; and Thomas Buring, merchant and wine grower. Others who arrived in 1849 or shortly thereafter include: Friedrich Krichauff, member of the South Australian State Parliament in 1857 and from 1884–1890, best remembered for his Forestry Act which tackled the urgent problem of afforestation; Martin Basedow, also a state parliamentarian and Minister for Education; A.H.F. Bartels, merchant, licensee of the King of Hanover Hotel in Adelaide and mayor of that city from 1871–1873; Rudolf Henning, manufacturer, pastoralist, landlord of the Globe Hotel and state parliamentarian from 1878 to his death in 1884; Robert and Herman Homburg, father and son, both active in law and politics, serving at different times as Attorney-General, Minister of Education and Minister of Industry in South Australia. Robert Homburg was appointed Justice of the Supreme Court in 1905, the first non-British immigrant to hold such an office. There was also Carl Püttmann, conductor and violinist, who had a distinguished musical career in Adelaide. Pütman had arrived in 1855 with his father Hermann, a renowned poet, editor and art critic at the *Kölner Zeitung*. A 'central figure of revolutionary socialist literature' and an associate of Marx and of poets like Heine, Gutzkow, Droste-Hülshoff and Weerth, the older Püttmann had decided to settle in Melbourne where he resumed his journalistic career to become, like Muecke in Adelaide, a prominent and widely respected spokesman of the German-Australian community of Victoria.[2]

The 'Forty-Eighters', sophisticated urban intellectuals, found little opportunity upon their arrival in South Australia to continue the work they had done in Germany.[3] Thus, initially, they took to farming in order to earn a living and only returned gradually—while the colony was becoming more established and Adelaide more of a city—to their previous interests and occupations. Carl Linger, wholly unsuccessful as a farmer, gradually managed to establish himself as a music teacher, composer and conductor of the Adelaide *Liedertafel* Choral Society. Schomburgk, after a stint as a farmer, was appointed director of the Adelaide Botanic Gardens in 1865; he held this post until his death in 1891, continuing his scholarly work in a wide range of research areas. Muecke, after taking up land at Tanunda, was soon elected pastor, a position which also involved the duties of a teacher, and he served several congregations although he was always looked upon with some distrust by the orthodox Lutheran clergy. In 1863 he founded, together with Basedow, who had become his son-in-law, the *Tanunda Deutsche Zeitung* which was renamed the *Australische Deutsche Zeitung* in 1870. In 1875, it merged with the *Süd Australische Zeitung* to become the *Australische Zeitung* (*AZ*), based in Adelaide.[4] It was the flagship of the German-language press in Australia and continued publication until it was closed by the Australian Government during World War I.

All the newcomers shared a keen interest in the political and civic affairs of their new country, soon developing an acute consciousness of their new-found identity as German-Australians, with every one of them becoming an early promoter of the idea of an independent Australian nation. They did this through contributions in their own fields of interest and expertise. One might mention as examples only the four immigrants who had arrived together on the *Prinzess Luise* on 7 August 1849. Their contributions towards an independent Australian nationalism were in the area of business and viticulture (the Burings, father Thomas and son Leo, pioneers of the wine industry who became prominent promoters of Australian wine), in music (Linger who composed the prize-winning 'Song of Australia'), in botany (Schomburgk who increased the number of native Australian species in his Botanic Gardens during his term of office from 5000 to 14 000). Muecke, finally, excelled as journalist, author and publisher who continued his work in educational and political reform by actively working towards the development of a 'national' school system. In his book *National Schools for South Australia*, published in Adelaide in 1866, he suggested that the South Australian colonists cease directing 'the public mind to the home country' [i.e. England] and to stop copying its institutions. Instead, Muecke proposed an Australian way: 'Each country must develop its own government and all other institutions from its own particular circumstances', the more so since 'our constitutional form of government appears to me to be capable of all development, and all that can be desired to render a people happy; provided, the same know how to infuse spiritual life therein, and to which a well conducted national school system forms the principal element'.[5]

The idea of a national school system was part of a larger political vision aiming at the establishment of an independent Australian nation, just as Muecke's ideas as an educational reformer in

Germany had been part of a comprehensive movement of German liberals towards democracy and bourgeois emancipation. But how could this vision be transferred to Australia? How could a German immigrant, representing a small minority within a British colony, put forward a claim to define a concept of Australian nationalism? There was no such thing as 'Australia' in the first place, only half a dozen separate colonies, situated at the periphery of a vast island continent that was hardly explored, let alone settled, by European immigrants. In 1866, the history of 'White Australia' involved at best three or four generations of European invaders who had dispossessed and decimated the original inhabitants but who felt by no means at home in or with the new country. To the overwhelming majority of white Australians, 'home' meant the British Isles; their nation was Great Britain.

Muecke and his friends, however, saw Australia as a nation *in statu nascendi*, and they recognised that it shared a common fate with the Germany they knew. To become a nation, Australia had what Germany lacked, namely a constitutional form of government based on a democratic system which was 'capable of all development' and which ensured individual freedom in order to guarantee the democratic participation of the people in the affairs of their society. What Germany had, on the other hand, was what Australia lacked or did not yet possess, namely a consciousness of its mission to become a nation. This was precisely what the German-Australians thought they were able to offer; their experiences in the struggle towards a unified democratic nation state in Germany, unsuccessful though it had been, could be made productive in the effort to infuse a 'spiritual' element into the public life of the colonies that would contribute to an awakening of a national consciousness. In the middle of the nineteenth century Germany was not politically a nation, but it could look back on a long history as a *Kulturnation* during which the achievements of poets and philosophers had defined what the nation was and could be. The Germany of Muecke and his friends was not that of the kings and army officers. It was the Germany of Luther, Herder and Lessing, Goethe and Schiller, the Romantic poets and composers, the Brothers Grimm and the Brothers Humboldt, Bach and Haydn, Mozart and Beethoven, Kant, Fichte and Hegel, of all those who had contributed to formulating the idea of a German culture which the German people living in the many states and principalities that made up the Germany of the time could claim as their own and which they saw

as a common bond. Their work had helped create an awareness of
the existence of a people as a nation. It was this vision of a national
culture that was the 'spiritual life' Muecke had in mind when he
imagined an Australian road to a national consciousness and, eventually, nationhood. Muecke's was an idealistic vision, based on the
belief in the changeability and perfectability of humankind and of
society through education and the public discourse of emancipated
citizens in a democratic state. It was the classical expression of the
legacy of bourgeois enlightenment, transplanted into a context of
European colonisation in Australia. Another part of the concept
arose out of the specific geographical and historical situation of
Australia. Nationhood had to be achieved independently, it had to
grow of and out of its own, it was incompatible with a colonial
status. Thus, a separation from the mother country and the British
Empire was, in the long run, inevitable. The final aim was the
Australian nation organised as an independent republic.

Muecke's vision can perhaps be illustrated best by quoting
from his speech of thanks in reply to the address presented by his
fellow German-Australians on 16 July 1883. I translate from the *AZ*
which printed a verbatim account of the speech a week after the
celebration:

> It has always been his [Muecke's] endeavour to uphold the idea of
> *Germanness [Deutschthum]* here in the colony. By *Germanness . . .* he
> has never meant anything but the high intellectual treasures and
> achievements of our dear mother, in the areas of science, both liberal
> and exact, of German philosophy, of the idealist art, of the religion of
> the heart, of the poetry of German authors, of the freedom of thought
> and faith. For 34 years he has striven to uphold this spiritual wealth
> [*diese geistigen Güter*] of the German nation in the colony which had
> grown up with him.[6]

The evocation of Germany as 'dear mother' and the reference to
German cultural achievements clearly demonstrate the dimension of
the *Deutschtum* which Muecke was propagating. It was not a political programme aiming at the retention of a loyalty towards the
Father-land, i.e. the state with its institutions and policies. The
German settlers had cancelled their allegiance to the kings and
governments of their respective states when they emigrated to Australia, but they could not and would not renounce their allegiance to
the *Kultur* which had formed the very essence of their personalities.
The vision contained an eloquent avowal of the intellectual heritage
of a German culture which had contributed so splendidly to the

achievements of humankind. To Muecke, this heritage was not narrowly defined by national boundaries. It included the universal declaration of human rights of the French Revolution as much as the common heritage of European scientists, artists and philosophers. Becoming an Australian could not possibly mean giving up this inheritance. On the contrary, the universal appeal of Muecke's vision implied the task of propagating it, of preserving and fusing it into the slowly growing national 'public mind' of the European settlers in Australia.

Religion also played an important part in this concept. To Muecke, a belief in God was essential to the 'spiritual life' of a nation; his insistence on 'freedom of faith' was meant to ensure, however, that the nation's development was not hindered by intolerance and theological dogmatism. Muecke's demonstrative evocation of 'a religion of the heart' must be seen as a sideswipe against the Lutheran clergy in Australia who had, ever since the first arrival of German immigrants, dissipated their energies in internal strife and futile squabbling over spurious dogmatic arguments which had resulted in numerous schisms and a fragmented community where every congregation jealously guarded what it believed to be the true faith. The reference was a subtle but poignant criticism of the pastors, a renunciation of the theological demarcation disputes among the different Lutheran synods and an appeal for unity and tolerance.

The task of promoting a cultural and national mission, of implanting it into the public life of the colony and of integrating it into an independent Australian consciousness was also seen as an act of gratitude, expressed by the German colonists who had prospered in the new land. This notion, too, found its expression in Muecke's speech:

> All of us have found in our dear Australia a new home [*Heimat*] which we sincerely love and where we can be happy, happier—for the most part—than we perhaps could have ever been in our old home country. Let us therefore return our active thanks to this our new home country. And what could our thanks be? Let us not forget that it was our fate, when it led us with broken hearts out of the old country to this place here, which destined us to help forming a new nation coming into existence in Australia, a nation made up of citizens of all nations but notably from England.[7]

Muecke's commitment to an Australian nation consisting of immigrants 'of all nations' sounds remarkably like the present-day image of a multicultural Australia; it clearly reveals the advanced position held by the spokesmen of the South Australian German community in the second half of the nineteenth century. In practice, of course, since there were only very few immigrants at the time who had come from other countries, multiculturalism meant biculturalism for Muecke and his associates; their main effort was obviously to convince both the British and the German communities in South Australia of the desirability of an independent Australia. In order to realise the aim, a synthesis had to be achieved of the best that the two communities could offer. According to Muecke, they both had to learn from one another. Comparing the two groups, Muecke stressed the supposed positive qualities of each one: theory, feeling, idealism, romanticism on the German side, and practice, pragmatism, action, pride, national consciousness on the part of the British. To quote again the correspondent's account of Muecke's speech:

> He [Muecke] believed that by wisely combining the best qualities of the two nationalities a new nation would be formed which would be a joy to the creator in heaven. Not that we should give up our Germanness, on the contrary we should hold on steadfastly to that part of our German heritage that is truthful and pure; but we should also accept and fuse with our ideals the noble English qualities which we have learned to appreciate.[8]

Mueke closed his reply by admonishing his listeners to stand united in proclaiming their identity as German-Australians, again evoking the cultural heritage of the immigrants as a source to be used in the making of a new nation. He concluded by proposing a toast to Australia:

> Let us therefore always stand as one man when it comes to declaring our Germanness in this sense, and we shall see South Australia abundantly blessed and shall always remain worthy sons of our dear old home country. Thus I ask you to join me in giving three cheers to our beloved Australia.[9]

It was, no doubt, a moving finale to an extraordinary evening, as the *AZ* reporter wrote: 'Three mighty and enthusiastic cheers with orchestral accompaniment thundered through the banquet hall and many held out their hands to each other in a show of loyalty and faith.'[10]

How, then, could such a vision which aimed at combining 'Germanness' with 'Britishness' into 'Australianness' be realised? How could German culture become a constituent element in the development of the public life of a British colony? Were Muecke's views not quite simply in contradiction with the oath he had taken upon becoming a naturalised British subject? Did not the obligation of loyalty towards the British monarchy rule out any notion of breaking away from the Empire, and were the proud expressions of loyalty towards German culture and towards the idea of an Australian nation not mutually exclusive? Muecke and his associates certainly did not believe so. They were not republican revolutionaries agitating for an abrupt break with Australia's colonial links; rather, their nationalism was a long-term project to be achieved within the constitutional framework of a political system which itself provided for the possibility of change and was 'capable of all development' as Muecke had put it. The political activities of German-Australians who served in the Parliament and became members of government in South Australia offered ample evidence of the seriousness and the commitment with which they pursued their goal within the established constitutional framework of the colony. However, British-born immigrants were not easily convinced that the argument presented by the German-Australians was consistent, and Anglo-Australian commentators did not cease to point to an alleged conflict of loyalties as a potential source of intercommunal strife. But the notion of a dual loyalty cannot adequately describe the ideological make-up of members of the German-Australian community. There was rather a triple loyalty. A cultural loyalty, firstly, bound them to the language and culture of their homeland; it was a link most strongly felt by the more recent immigrants and one which tended to wane with quick assimilation, thus the untiring efforts of people like Muecke to keep these cultural traditions alive. There was, secondly, a political loyalty to be extended to the British Crown as the constitutional head of Australia, along with an unquestioning acceptance of the political institutions of Australia. The countless declarations of allegiance to the King or Queen of England made by spokesmen of the German-Australian community were certainly genuine; they were unequivocal signs of accepting the realities of the Australian political system in preference to the undemocratic, authoritarian and often repressive governmental regimes the German immigrants had left behind. Loyalty to the Crown as guarantor of the constitution provided also, of course, the assurance of being able to participate in the political affairs of Australia and to be able to enjoy, i.e. to use, the privileges and liberties the

democrative institutions offered, including the privilege of disagree-
ing with the policies pursued by the government of the day, either in
Australia or the United Kingdom. Thirdly, and most importantly,
there was a national loyalty felt towards Australia, the country, the
land, the people, the history and culture of which the German-
Australians had become part.

I believe it is on this last level, the national loyalty of German
immigrants defining themselves as Australians, that the clearest
differences vis-à-vis the British-Australian majority can be discerned. To German-Australians, loyalty to Australia and loyalty to
the Crown were accepted and taken for granted. However, they did
not mean the same thing, and certainly allegiance to the Queen did
not automatically imply uncritical acceptance of British imperial
policies. German-Australians clearly realised that the colonial status
of the country constituted an obstacle to political, social and economic development, that the mediocrity of much of Australia's life,
its institutions and particularly its socio-cultural make-up, was due
to a large extent to its dependency on Britain, to its continued
existence as a society which was based on importing, copying,
duplicating from only one source, thus stifling originality and independent creativity. To the Australian who would 'suck wisdom'
from London, as Donald Horne has put it,[11] the German-
Australians could hold out Berlin, Munich, Hamburg and Frankfurt
as competing sources for the input of ideas, as well as methods and
technologies of research and production, an input designed not to
replace but to complement the traditional supplier of ideas to Australia, in the hope that a choice of the best that was available might
provide a more promising platform from which an original productivity could emerge, in cultural matters as well as in all other
areas of life. The nationalist perspective of the German-Australians
thus contained a vision of cooperation between Australians both of
British and German origin with the aim of developing Australia into
a prosperous, independent country with its own cultural identity in
which the best influences that could be imported from Europe were
to be creatively integrated and allowed to progress into something
that was to be seen as uniquely Australian.

The concept of nationalism developed by Muecke and his associates in South Australia after their arrival in 1849 had a number
of things in common with the Australianism propagated by some
Anglo-Saxon Australians from around 1890. It shared a belief in
singular Australian identity, based on an experience of the land, its

climate and unique geographical, floral and faunal features, as well as a consciousness of the European part of the history of Australia. All of this was inherent, for example, in the vision of the *Bulletin* or of the Australian Natives' Association. It also shared an exclusivist, racist view: 'Australia for the White Man', as the *Bulletin's* motto proclaimed, in which there was apparently no place for people from Asia and Oceania.[12] The Aborigines did not appear in Muecke's vision either. They were left to the attention of the anthropologists and to the care of the missionaries who devoted their energies to saving the souls of their wards rather than educating them about political and social matters and about their civil rights as human beings which the German immigrants had been demanding for themselves as a matter of course.[13] It is doubtful, however, whether other Anglo-Saxon Australians, such as the editors and the readers of the *Bulletin*, were even aware of the efforts of the spokesmen of the German community in Australia, or whether, indeed, they would have been willing to listen. It seems there was no line of communication which could have bridged and linked the two debates on the question of Australian nationalism. The thrust of the *Bulletin's* nationalist campaign for independence and republicanism, at any rate, seems to have been primarily anti-British *establishment*, and it is open to debate whether such a policy would have been liberal enough to include an expression of cultural autonomy for non-British groups and their integration with full social and political equality within Australian society. The experience of World War I showed that this was not to be the case.

To Muecke's listeners in the Adelaide German Club, the message delivered in 1883 by the guest of honour would have been a familiar one. It was a story that had been advocated consistently for over thirty years; it had been publicly debated in the newspapers and in the Parliament of South Australia. But it was a complex and sophisticated vision, not easily communicated to a British community which held different traditions. The integration of the German immigrants in Australian society and the success some of them had in politics and public life had not come about without struggle; it had to be fought for, and it is an open question whether it was ever fully accepted by a majority of Anglo-Celtic South Australians. On more than one occasion the German-Australians had to find out that their ideas were not acceptable to their fellow colonists who had emigrated from the British Isles.

The issue of 'German Rights' was discussed in South Australia as early as 1855, in the context of introducing a bill to establish 'responsible government'. The German immigrants protested against plans to exclude them from standing for election to the proposed Parliament; they were supported by a number of British-born South Australians, including the current Governor, but there were also many who voiced opposition, arguing 'the Germans should be grateful that they were even allowed to come to South Australia and stop demanding equal rights with Englishmen'.[14] One 'sexagenarian Briton' wrote to the *Adelaide Observer*:

> Our teutonic friends have very good reason to be thankful for the refuge South Australia has afforded them . . . and they ought to gratefully acknowledge and quietly enjoy their freedom. I would naturalize no more Germans until they made the English language a professed object in their education . . . To have the rights of Anglo-Saxons they must cease to be Germans.[15]

There can be no doubt that the writer's sentiments represented a substantial popular feeling, one which would re-emerge time and again in the decades to come. In the 1850s, the German-Australians carried the day: they were granted the right to stand for Parliament, and in the elections of 1857 F. Krichauff became the first of many legislators in South Australia who was of German descent. The victory in 1857, however, did not mean the end of the struggle for political equality and for equal rights. Only ten years later, the *Tanunda Deutsche Zeitung* provided a pertinent comment on the state of 'community relations' that pointed to a continuing and constant element of friction. The editors 'maintained that the German community had a right to suggest alterations and improvements in the public life of South Australia without being opposed simply by the argument that it was against English feelings'.[16] In another article published a few months later, which contrasted the experiences of immigrants in the United States and Australia, the same criticism re-emerged. In Australia, the paper stated, 'in closed phalanx the Englishmen oppose the immigrants from foreign countries'.[17]

The comparison of the different conditions facing German immigrants in America and in Australia was a point that was repeatedly made by the journalists who were contributing to forming the opinion of the German-Australian community; it concerned in particular the question of naturalisation and nationality and was thus a key issue in the discussion of an emerging Australian national identity. There was a major problem due to Australia's colonial status of which the German migrants were acutely aware. Naturalisation meant becoming a British subject in and of one Australian colony; it had no validity in other parts of the country.[18] And even after Federation, naturalisation only meant becoming a British subject in Australia, and only in Australia: it did not confer the status of a citizen of the United Kingdom nor was it accepted in any of the other colonies of the British Empire. This contradiction had sharpened the views of German-born migrants with regard to the issue of Australian independence. It became a major argument in the claim for a separate Australian nationality, repeatedly invoked in a series of articles devoted to the topic of Australian independence that appeared in the *AZ* between December 1884 and February 1885. The comparative analysis between US and Australian-British citizenship clearly suggested a deficiency in the status accorded to 'Naturalised British Subjects of Australia'. As the *AZ* put it:

> The acquisition of citizenship in the U.S. affords full equality and protection. This is not so in British colonies where the German immigrant gives up his German citizenship for a thing of little significance ... If a naturalized German leaves his own colony, he is completely homeless, a pariah, a member of no nation, whereas the British colonist remains a Briton.[19]

To the editors of the *AZ* the conclusion to be drawn was clear. The unsatisfactory status of British colonial citizenship could only be resolved by Australia's breaking away from the Empire. On 28 February 1885, the paper concluded its series of articles on the issue of Australian independence with a final, eloquent call for Australian sovereignty in which the alternatives, Australia as a 'free' nation or as an inferior colony under the tutelage of Great Britain, were clearly spelled out: 'Only with independence can a truly national life develop in which immigrants from everywhere fuse into one free nation. This is impossible as long as there is a mother-country to which Australia is politically subordinated.'[20]

The question of national identity and independence was, of course, directly linked to the problem of Australia's role within the British Empire, and it is in this area of contention that examples of conflict and disagreement between British and German Australians emerge most clearly. Arguments regularly arose at times of international conflict, in particular when differences among the major European powers were at stake, immediately threatening the status

of Australia's German community. Superficially, there seemed to be
little to be worried about before 1871, considering the cordial relationship as among relatives that existed between the ruling dynasties
of Windsor and Hohenzollern. A policy of intermarriages and of
frequent state visits from court to court, eagerly reported by the
illustrated journals to an equally keen readership in both Germany
and England, as well as all the colonies of course, were widely
interpreted as evidence of an harmonious understanding between
Imperial cousins that seemed to augur well for a future of peaceful
cooperation between Great Britain and Germany. However, the
underlying conflict of interests was substantial, and the establishment of the German Reich under Prussian domination set into
motion a political development in which England and Germany
appeared as major opponents whose growing differences could be
concealed only with increasing difficulty.[21] It was particularly
Germany's aggressive naval rearmament with its clearly implied
imperialistic overtones which was seen by London as a direct
threat, a position that was naturally shared in dominions like Australia which believed it was dependent for its security on the vessels
of a Britannic Empire that could, in fact, still 'rule the waves'.

The coronation of Wilhelm I as Emperor of Germany meant
the beginning of a new phase in European history; it forced the
Adelaide "Forty-Eighters' to reflect anew on their relationship to the
old country and on their position as Australians of German descent.
The victory of Germany over France had certainly not brought the
dream of Muecke and his friends any closer to realisation; unification had not brought democracy, a German republic was still a
distant ideal. But they saw it as at least a step in the right direction
and believed that it had come about not by aggression but after a
defensive war which had been forced upon Germany, as the general
consensus among the German population had it. The Forty-Eighters
had no difficulty joining the chorus of celebrants. In South Australia
like everywhere else, Germans held Thanksgiving services and
organised patriotic receptions to herald the new Reich. In Tanunda,
a 'Day of Peace and Jubilation' was observed on 13 October 1871,
five months after the signing of the Frankfurt peace treaty. Muecke
was once again the principal speaker. On this day he had chosen to
address his fellow German-Australians not as a pedagogue, pastor
or scientist but rather as a poet. He had written a *Festgesang* for the
occasion, not exactly a lyrical masterpiece but a poem that remains
a remarkable document of German-Australian history. It has the

unexpected title "Die Wacht am Südseestrand' ('The Guard on the South Sea Beach'), immediately evoking the famous 'Wacht am Rhein'. The persona of the poem, using both the singular and plural forms of the first person, hears the cry of a mother in distress: the mother is Germany threatened by France, the children are Germans everywhere, including distant South Australia. However, since the call for help has been received and the support of all children, at home and abroad, is assured, victory is swiftly at hand, with mother and children sharing both the suffering and the moment of glory. For Germany—thus the lyrical narrative continues—the prize of victory is the Fatherland, i.e. the new Reich; for the children it is a new fatherland, Australia, yet to be built on the shores of the south sea. But whereas in Germany it was the arms that won the day, it is going to be the peaceful German 'spirit' which will be victorious in Australia, by infusing the effort of building an Australian fatherland with the humanist traditions of German culture. Stanzas 6 and 7 read as follows:

> Wie du gesiegt, so siegen wir:
> Dein Schwert daheim, dein Geist dahier.
> Heut an dem deutschen Friedensfest,
> nimm unsere Hand und halt' sie fest;
> Nimm uns'ren Schwur vom Südseestrand
> Treu hält und fest die deutsche Hand.
>
> Das deutsche Reich ist aufgebaut;
> Und wo ein deutsches Auge schaut,
> Ist Deutschland. Reicht die Hand zum Bund,
> Ihr Brüder, in der Feierstund.
>   Lasst bauen uns am Südseestrand
>   Durch deutschen Geist ein Vaterland.

> (As you have won/So we shall be victorious:/Your sword at home/ Your spirit here./On this day of our peace celebrations/Take our hand and hold it tightly./Accept our oath from the South Sea Strand/ Loyally and firmly we offer our German hand.

> The German Reich is founded/And wherever German eyes behold/Is Germany. Let us hold hands,/Brothers, in this hour of celebration./ Let us build here on the South Sea Strand/Through German spirit a Fatherland.)[22]

The 'Wacht am Südseestrand' clearly demonstrates that the events of 1871 had not changed Muecke's commitment to Australia and his nationalist vision. The poem forms a missing link that joins the argument first developed in the 1850s to the debate on Australian independence of the 1880s, revealing an extraordinary consistency. Even the rhetoric is the same: Germany as the mother, references to the 'German spirit' and the idea of the *Kulturnation* which exists independently, outside the geographical and socio-political reality of the Reich, and the inevitable appeal to build a new fatherland, Australia, which is to be animated with the ideas of German poets and philosophers.

Muecke's choice of 'Die Wacht am Rhein' as a literary vehicle to convey his message must be regarded with some apprehension, however. Schneckenburger's original song had been written already in 1840 in response to the *Rheinkrise* which had been engineered by an unsuccessful Adolphe Thiers to divert attention from the failure of his policies in the Near East.[23] It rose to prominence again in 1871 when it became something of a national song, appropriated by nationalist extremists and supporters of Bismarck's *Reichspolitik* who used it to give expression to their message of military prowess and imperialist expansionism. Muecke's use of the German model obviously meant to capture the enthusiasm of German patriots in the wake of the Reich's foundation and to recreate the same feeling on the south sea shores with the difference, of course, that it was not Germany which was being evoked as the fatherland but Australia. The question, apart from the adoption of a model with dubious ideological content and of doubtful aesthetic value, is whether the literary packaging added or detracted from the clarity of the ideas presented by the author. Muecke's vision, complex as it was, could not be served by being associated with a popular song which had become identified with German militarism. One doubts whether his South-Australian fellow colonists of British origin would have been able to appreciate the subtlety of his ideas: their vision of Germany, more likely than not, would have been more closely associated with the image that was later connected to the 'Wacht am Rhein', namely the statue of a martial *Germania*, towering above the Rhine with her arm and sword stretched out towards the West, rather than Muecke's mother-figure embodying the peaceful German spirit. Of course, the *Festgesang* was not meant to be performed to an English-Australian public. However, a line like "Wherever German eyes behold, is Germany" might have been misinterpreted by any audience. In an atmosphere of growing tension between England and Germany after the Franco-Prussian War it could have been wiser perhaps to construct a text that would not have presented such obvious chances for misunderstanding. It seems curious that Muecke might not have been aware of these implications, but perhaps he had allowed himself to be swept away by the patriotic fever as well. There were, after all, not many liberal democrats in Germany who remained unaffected by the events of January 1871.

The year 1871 constituted indeed a *caesura* that marked a heightened awareness of the deterioration of Anglo-German relations. In Australia, the 'German victories and the proclamation of the German Reich at Versailles were greeted with jubilation' and 'patriotic fervour'[24]by all the German-language newspapers; however, such displays of emotion were frowned upon by the commentators of the mainstream Australian press. For the first time, the spectre of war between England and Germany appeared. In an editorial on 13 January 1871, the *AZ* speculated, after reporting about British assistance to France: 'Anti-German feeling will undoubtedly also communicate itself to the Colony. Should war really break out, which *we doubt*, our position would be fraught with peril. *Our feelings would be with Germany but our oath and our national duty range us against it on the side of England.*'[25] The paper went on to denounce the 'local press', citing specifically the Melbourne *Argus* which had spoken of the 'stubborn Germans' in Australia, stating that it was necessary to 'counter untrue opinions' and to make 'our attitude' clear to 'them'.[26] It is as well to remember that these lines appeared in print forty-four years before was actually broke out; they go a long way towards explaining the dormant hostility and alienation between Australians of British and of German origin during the prewar decades before the experience of 1914 actually transformed the latent tension into open aggressiveness.

In the periods of international crisis that were to follow, similar arguments reappeared. The position expressed by the spokesmen of the German community remained consistent, but it was not successfully communicated to a majority to whom an understanding of 'Australian' was synonymous with 'British'. The position of the German-Australian community was that of a small but clearly defined and highly visible minority which was constantly being made to feel that it was 'different'; as a consequence, it was allowed to express its self-identity only in terms of 'us' and 'them'. Within the framework of a discourse defined by an overpowering majority, German-Australians thus felt compelled, almost ritualistically, to

state their loyalty to the British Crown whenever moments of friction arose. However, their attitude towards Australia did not
change. When Muecke or the other writers in his paper expressed
their loyalty to the Crown the basis of their commitment was loyalty
towards Australia. At the same time they did not cease questioning
the policies pursued by the British government when they believed
they were not in the interest of Australia. Another principle that was
consistently defended by the *AZ* was the conviction that the
Australian-German community had the right to speak up and to be
heard in matters that affected Australians at large. It was a right,
they argued, that was legitimised both by the democratic privilege of
political equality and by the participation of German-Australians in
the development of the colony. This point of view, stated with
confidence, had become an essential ingredient within the self-
understanding of the German-Australian community. After all they
had come to experience, since their departure from Germany, the
advantages of a democratic system of government; through becoming naturalised they had accepted the duties and responsibilities
along with the benefits of the system, and they had now no intention
of foregoing their constitutional rights, all the more since they were
sufficiently self-assured about the contribution they had made, indi-
vidually as much as a group, to the material and cultural progress of
the continent.

Thus the claims made first in 1855 were reiterated, but perhaps never so vehemently as during the 1899–1902 crisis caused
by the British Boer War in South Africa. In November 1899 the *AZ*
wrote: 'Should we be silent because, though full citizens, we are
Germans (Helots?) and for that reason should cower under, in other
words keep our mouths shut or dissimulate?'[27] A few weeks later,
the editorial writers made the same point yet again: 'We are asked
for unquestioning approval of all that the British are doing in South
Africa. If a German is of different opinion and proclaims this in
preference to hypocrisy he is without further ado called disloyal, if
not immediately stigmatised as traitor. An unworthy position is
being demanded of us.'[28] The article closed, however, on a defensive note, foreshadowing an attitude that was to become more widespread in the years to come. As if resigning themselves to the fact
that their views would not be acceptable to the British majority
anyway, the editors of the *AZ* called upon their readers not to
provoke Britons during this time of 'heightened sensitivity'[29] by
offering to discuss the war. It was a signal to suspend communi-

cation, an admission that in the jingoistic climate of imperialistic fervour experienced during the Boer War a rational and democratic exchange of opinions was no longer possible.

In 1909, an editorial of the *AZ* commented on the rapid deterioration of Anglo-German relations are a result of the escalating naval arms race. Here, in a mood of gloomy premonition of things to come, one can find again a succinct statement of the peculiar nationalist ideal of the South Australian spokesman of the German-Australian community: 'We who live as German-Australians among Englishmen and with them carry the building stones from which in the future a great independent Australian *Reich* and Nation will arise, feel most strongly the sorrow which the estrangement of the Teutonic races causes.'[30] The writer, employing the racial vocabulary prevalent at the time, bemoans the differences separating the 'Teutonic races', that is, the Germans and the English, but the insistence on the racial similarities nevertheless provides ground for the optimistic belief that the future would see Germans and English, both as Australians, cooperating in the effort of nation-building. There is, again, no mention of anybody else who might play a part in constructing the 'great independent Australian *Reich* and Nation', and there seems to be no room either for the Aborigines or for the Kanaks and Chinese. But the suggestion of a common fate linking the 'Teutonic races' also shows the fallacy, perhaps the naiveté of the writer whose sentiments, in 1909, simply were no longer in touch with the political realities. It seems almost like a last resort to construct a meaning to the existence of the German community in Australia, and it emerges as a vision that can really only be described as wishful thinking. To Anglo-Saxon Australians who had been taught to believe in the supremacy of the 'British race', in the purported civilising mission of the British Empire as guardian 'of the weak nations of the earth',[32] the notion of the British as a Teutonic race would have appeared ludicrous, if not offensive: they were 'Britons'; the 'Teutons' were the Germans who constituted the only threat to the image that Imperialist-minded Britons had of themselves all over the world. In Australia, too, 'Britishers' who felt alienated in their new environment and who overcompensated their colonial experience of isolation and inadequacy by developing an exaggerated, aggressively pro-Imperial ideology, saw their supreme task in building the British Empire rather than an Australian nation.

The Australian nationalism of the German-Australian community thus provided no common basis to establish mutual understanding and trust. Among British-Australians there was a rise in
nationalist sentiment during the pre-war decade, but it was a nationalism that 'had been integrated with a rising Imperialist fervour'.[32]
Due in part to the 'very high immigration from Britain in the years
1906–13' which 'had accelerated the "Britishness" of the population', the majority of Anglo-Saxon Australians had become 'more
British and more Imperial-minded'.[33] Their vision of their new
country was that it was part of the old, as British as Scotland or
Wales, peopled by 'Britishers' who proudly saw themselves 'as
citizens of the world's vastest and mightiest Empire'.[34] In this
vision, the presence of other groups of white immigrants in Australia, negligible quantities as they were, could at best be acknowledged in terms of a paternalistic attitude of benign tolerance; the
Britishers' view of Australia had no place for a concept which
aimed at reducing the dependence on the Empire by working towards a sovereign Australia based on the political equality and the
cultural self-assertion of all Australians. There were other reasons as
well why the communication between the two groups did not succeed. Many British settlers had brought their traditional feelings of
insular seclusion with them, and xenophobia and racism were of
course easily exported as well. In the colony where they constituted
the overwhelming majority these transplanted Britons saw no need
to open up to and begin a cross-cultural dialogue with other groups
of immigrants in Australia. German-Australians were thus often met
with icy indifference and sometimes with outright hostility even
before the War. There was also the colonial experience, a deeply
ingrained mentality of inferiority and insecurity sharpened by the
consciousness of Australia's remoteness on the periphery of the
Empire, which had the effect of Anglo-Saxon settlers closing ranks
and of trying to prove their bona fide British credentials by developing an aggressive stance of 'being more British than the British',
overcompensating for the feeling of rejection and neglect which they
experienced as a result of the relative lack of interest on the part of
the government of the United Kingdom in matters Australian.

When war between England and Germany finally did break
out, there was no place for sentiments regarding Australian independence. According to the majority of British Australians, Australia
had a role to play within the Empire, and Imperialists like William
Morris Hughes, who was to lead the Commonwealth Government

through the war years, were to make certain that it would do its share to increase the glory of the British Empire and to increase Australia's standing in it. Now that Germany had been finally and officially, as it were, declared the enemy, the fearful premonitions of German-Australians as to their future in case of war involving the 'Teutonic races' were to become reality.[35] The dream of Carl Muecke and his friends was finally revealed as the idealistic illusion that it had always been.

CHAPTER 11

The 'Vossification' of Ludwig Leichhardt

H. Priessnitz

When Henry Turnbull, who had accompanied Ludwig Leichhardt on his second journey in 1846–47, was invited to give a panegyric on the missing explorer in Launceston, he closed his speech with the following sentences:

> Ladies and gentlemen, ye hero worshippers, ye admirers of true greatness, here is a real hero, a truly great man. His shrine alone is wanting! In the long list of navigators and captains there is no name that has been more neglected than Leichhardt's. There is none more deserving of all honour, and I hope yet that something will be done to honour his memory in some suitable manner. Let it be a monument of some sort or other—a statue if you will—not of bronze, however, but of marble—pure marble—pure as the unsullied reputation of the man whose memory it would perpetuate![1]

Midnite, the protagonist in Randolph Stow's children's novel of that name, published in 1967, meets, while travelling in the outback with his friend Khat, a strange explorer and two camels:

> When at last they overtook the explorer, he did not look at all pleased to see them, and he said to Midnite: '*Ach, du lieber*, what do you do here without your Papa?' This explorer was a rather miserable

German man called Johann Ludwig Ulrich von Leichardt [sic] zu Voss, but in Australia he had called himself Mr Smith, and his two bad–tempered camels were called Sturm and Drang. While Mr Smith was talking to Midnite, Sturm and Drang made faces at Red Ned and the other horse, and spat at them, for no reason whatever.

'I am exploring,' said Midnite, feeling shy that he looked so young [. . .] 'May I ask, where you are going?'

'I too am exploring,' said Mr Smith. 'I am exploring me.'

'How can you explore you?' asked Midnite.

'I will not explain,' said Mr Smith. 'You would have to be me to understand.'

'Well', said Midnite, blushing, 'I am sorry if I seem stupid. But at least you won't mind, will you, if I ride along with you?'

'I can you not prevent,' said Mr Smith. 'The desert belongs to everyone.'

'I think you are mistaken,' said Midnite. 'The desert belongs to Queen Victoria, and I have named it after her, and made a note in my Diary.'

The explorer laughed a hollow laugh, and handed Midnite his own Diary, in which Midnite read: '*Today have I this desert the Cosmic Symbolical Desert named.*'[2]

The picture of Leichhardt is as far removed from reality in the one passage as in the other, but differently in each. Turnbull is addressing a colonial audience steeped in Victorian ideals; his portrait of the explorer is not only free from any hint of moral weakness—Daniel Bunce's account[3] was yet to be published—but, 'like a knight errant of old',[4] his Leichhardt, armed with a sword, does battle with, and vanquishes a mighty dragon in the form of a giant kangaroo. He names Leichhardt among the ranks of the navigators who, both before and after Cook, drew the map of Australia, and thus establishes him from the very beginning on a par with the continent's other discoverers.[5] In the end Turnbull's Leichhardt is a thoroughly Anglo-Saxon hero; all that remains of his Prussian origins is the passing remark that '(. . . he had a surgeon's diploma from a Prussian university) . . . '.[6] Where Turnbull '*de*-prussianises', Stow '*re*-prussianises'. His Johann Ludwig Ulrich von Leichardt zu Voss is recognisably German right down to his idiosyncratic speech patterns, and the names of his two camels, Sturm and Drang, mark him as not only German but a German of the Romantic period. The melting together of the two figures, Leichhardt and Voss, shows the enormous influence of Patrick White's novel on the Leichhardt image in twentieth-century writing. The two fragments show that the literary process of transforming the historical Leichhardt into a symbolic figure—and this is what I mean by 'Vossification'—had begun long before Patrick White's novel and has continued after it. The stylisation of the explorer as a knight of the Round Table parallels the picture of the strange ego-centric who is journeying into the interior not of a country but of his own soul. Both pictures are abstractions: comparing them, we become aware of a change in the literary interpretation of Leichhardt, and this suggests questions about the social and histor-ical motives underlying the various metamorphoses of this historical figure in the course of Australian literature.

Leichhardt's contribution to the discourse of colonial *itineraria* with the land.

In his study, *The Road to Botany Bay*,[7] Paul Carter has examined the linguistic colonisation of Australia in accounts of seafarers, explor-ers and settlers, and shown that the apparently so matter-of-fact and scientifically exact presentation conceals an ideologically condi-tioned need to come to terms, and highly subjective terms, with a country which had been opened up for possession and settlement. Far from being objective reports of what certain individuals found, these documents are, as it were, the speech acts of a collective social discourse, an imperial discourse transforming geographical reality into a purposeful and revealing text. Their subjectivity is rooted in the distinction between 'discovery' and 'exploration': 'While discov-ery rests on the assumption of a world of facts waiting to be found, collected and classified, a world in which the neutral observer is not implicated, exploration lays stress on the observer's active engage-ment with his environment: it recognizes phenomena as offspring of his intention to explore.'[8] The account the traveller gives of his journey is therefore not a cross-section through any geographical reality, but 'a "telling" of the journey: a narrative',[9] with the per-spective of a narrative. Its object is not so much the country itself as the process of exploration, the translation of a land into the gram-mar of a particular culture.[10] The narrative perspective, determined by that of the explorer, by his personal make-up, his attitude to-wards the getting of knowledge,[11] determines the structure of the grammar concerned.

Like other explorers Leichhardt was under pressure to bring back worthwhile results from his journeyings; his geographical dis-coveries were expected, at least in part, to be economically fruitful:[12]

Explorers were not despatched to traverse deserts, but to locate objects of cultural significance: rivers, mountains, meadows, plains of promise. They had a social responsibility to make the most of what they saw, to dignify even hints of the habitable with significant class names. They were expected to arrest the country, to concentrate it into reversible roads which would summarize its content; they were expected to translate its extension into objects of commerce.[13]

Leichhardt was doubtless aware of these expectations when on 5 March 1845, after a difficult journey of about seventy miles he noted: ' . . . we shall not probably find a country better adapted for pastoral pursuits [. . .] the wells of the natives . . . and the luxuriant growth of reeds in many parts of the river [i.e. the Isaacs], showed that even shallow wells would give a large supply to the squatter in cases of necessity . . . '[14] Such descriptions were intended to draw 'a line of communication by land, between the eastern coast of Australia, and the gulf of Carpentaria . . . ',[15] declaring the land open and available for settlement.

The naming of geographical objects was an attempt to individualise them as points of meaning; but the peculiar difficulties of the Australian landscape, its monotony, its alien contours rebuffed those designations which might have expressed the physical uniqueness, the unmistakable immediacy of what the observer saw. He was obliged, frequently, to have recourse to Bunyanesque projections: names like Point Upright, Cape Manyfold, Thirsty Sound, Point Danger, Cape Tribulation, Repulse Bay, Cape Flattery, Cape Catastrophe, Mount Misery, Retreat Well, Lake Disappointment, Mount Deception, Plains of Promise, Lake Salvator and Mount Hope[16] say more about the inner state of their authors than about the nature of the phenomena described: 'What was named was not something out there; rather it represented a mental orientation, an intention to travel. Naming words were forms of spatial punctuation, transforming space into an object of knowledge, something that could be explored and read.'[17]

Leichhardt's own system of nomenclature was different inasmuch as he preferred to domesticate his surroundings with the names of friends and patrons who had helped and supported his journeys. Mount Nicholson was called after Dr Charles Nicholson, who had brought the plan for an overland expedition before the legislative assembly of New South Wales; Benjamin Boyd gave his name to the Boyd; the Mackenzie was named in honour of Sir Evan Mackenzie, who helped prepare the journey, the Isaacs in

acknowledgement of the support of F. Isaacs. The Burdekin owes
its name to the generous assistance of Mrs Burdekin from Sydney;
another patron provided the name for Mount McConnel;
Leichhardt's longstanding friend, R. Lynd, was remembered in the
name of the River Lynd. The Nicholson is so called because Dr
William Nicholson from Bristol had enabled the young Leichhardt
to study natural science and to migrate to Australia; the Robinson
because J.P. Robinson had equipped his expedition.[18] Such strategies of naming function according to Carter as 'the agent of a
linguistic fifth column, infiltrating and dividing the space stealthily
... [like] an outpost supplying a ramifying network of grammatical
and syntactical connections'.[19] The initial act of naming gave rise to
images, comparisons, metaphors, associations with which the discoverers colonised their geographical world linguistically, taking
possession of it, transforming it into something it was not yet but
could and was indeed intended to become: 'Possession of the
country depended on demonstrating the efficacy of the English language there. It depended, to some extent, on civilising the landscape,
bringing it into orderly being. More fundamentally still, the landscape had to be taught to speak.'[20] English governors, politicians
and patrons structured a geographical reality. When the explorers
traversed the furnace of the deserts it was the fiery furnace of the
European Christian tradition that coloured it; when nature provided
glimpses of paradisical beauty, it was the Eden of puritan Prot-
estantism that spoke, to those pilgrims through the Vale of Tears,
the reward of a just-minded Providence.

Leichhardt also translated Australia into English, but into the
English of a German Romantic. His letters show the spirit both of
the age and of his particular roots: in Paris he quotes enthusiastically from Byron's *Childe Harold*;[21] the landscape of Florence, the
Swiss Alps, Lake Geneva fill his soul to overflowing;[22] *en passant*
he accuses the Prussians of political immaturity;[23] and, once landed
in Australia, he writes ecstatically about the elegance and force of
Schiller's language.[24] Even in the absence of any other indications
of direct influence than those provided by Colin Roderick in chapter
2, it is scarcely probable that a student of philology and natural
science in the Berlin and Göttingen of the 1830s would not be
affected by the ideas which at that time were in the air, especially if
his teachers happened to be Franz Bopp, Johann Friedrich Herbart,
Jakob Grimm and Georg August Ewald.[25]

Two areas in particular of Leichhardt's linguistic colonisation

of the country bear the unmistakable stamp of German Romanticism: his pictorial descriptions of nature and his religious interpretations of nature's workings and its force.

On 22 February 1848 he writes to his brother-in-law:

> I leave it to others to pass judgement on my book. It's a simple
> account of our journey, and just as simple a description of the country
> and the things we saw. The traveller who just tells the truth earns the
> thanks of scholars at home. He cannot enlarge Nature, so he can't
> describe the insignificant mountain ranges of Australia as if they were
> the giant mountain chains of America. I've never striven for effect,
> and it was hardly worth my while to attempt the description of a
> kangaroo or emu hunt in the glowing terms of a poetical huntsman.[26]

Leichhardt was no 'poetical huntsman', but his descriptions of
nature are anything but the simple reflection of 'the things we saw'.
He looked on nature, whether in Australia or in Europe, as, in the
strict sense of that word, picturesque. The term 'picturesque' occurs
with some frequency in his letters.[27] This pictorial principle was a
poetic ordering force imposed on the chaotic impressions of nature
in order to cultivate and so to europeanise them. In a letter to Carl
Schmalfuss of 21 October 1847 Leichhardt expresses his admiration for the interpretative power of Schiller's language, to which he
now explicitly allies the force of music, which can transform the
chaos of nature into order and progression:

> After my three years in the wilderness I've been re-reading Schiller's
> poems. What mastery of language, and how he stands out for his
> nobility of feeling! I've never been so deeply moved by music as I once
> was during my passage from England to Sydney. It was on a stormy
> night, and the waves were pounding and foaming under the very keel
> of the vessel as she strained onward. I had been listening intently to
> the confused uproar for a long time when I suddenly got up and
> stepped into Mr Marsh's cabin. He was one of my fellow passengers,
> and a gifted harpist. And there he was, improvising on the harp. The
> measured sounds, after the rushing and roaring disorder of the wind
> and the waves out there in the dark, moved me with such strength and
> reassurance as to bring tears to my eyes. I had the same feelings when
> I read Schiller again. With that instinctive, clairvoyant understanding
> he was able to interpret situations in which his own life could never
> have placed him . . .[28]

Such passages recur in Leichhardt's *Journal*;[29] the entry for 18
January 1845, in particular, refutes the alleged objectivity of his
descriptive technique:

We had travelled so much in a monotonous forest land, with only now
and then a glimpse of distant ranges through the occasional clearings
in the dismal scrub, that any change was cheering. Here an entirely
open country—covered with grass, and apparently unbounded to the
westward; now ascending, first, in fine ranges, and forming a succession of almost isolated, gigantic, conical, and dome-topped mountains, which seemed to rest with a flat unbroken base on the plain
below—was spread before our delighted eyes. The sudden alteration
of the scene, therefore, inspired us with feelings that I cannot attempt
to describe . . . [30]

On 27 January 1845 he notes 'a most remarkable and interesting view of a great number of peaks and domes . . . ',[31] which
reminds him of the extinct volcanoes of the Auvergne. The starlit
sky of Australia fills him with memories of homesickness:

The starry heaven is one of the great features of nature, which enter
unconsciously into the composition of our souls. The absence of the
stars gives us painful longings, the nature of which we frequently do
not understand, but which we call home sickness—and their sudden
reappearance touches us like magic, and fills us with delight.[32]

That homesickness is not a 'painful longing' for Europe—
Leichhardt had in any case grown beyond this—but a metaphor of
the quest for moments of convergence between cultural grammar
and historical experience. At the same time it was an admission that
translation into the language of European Romanticism did not
always succeed.

Where it does succeed, it has the quality of a 'visual cultivation
of an aesthetic history with a civilized future'.[33] To paint the scenery
of the Australian wilderness in the tones of German Romanticism is
simply 'to attribute to them [the scenes] the observer's own heightened sense of possession, his sensation of suddenly being at home
in the world'.[34]

Unlike many explorers Leichhardt was filled with a passionate
desire to penetrate the secrets of the nature he encountered. He
writes to his brother-in-law on 20 October 1847: 'My passion for
the study of my environment here, and my ambition to solve the
riddles of this continent, are boundless and beyond control.'[35] To
his sister he had already, on 15 May 1844, written in the following
terms:

Yet what am I to tell you of the life I lead here? You say that you love
the beauty and smell of the flowers; that you rejoice to see the trees
coming into leaf and casting shade; that when you gaze across the

woods and the fields, or look up from the ground to the starry sky,
you are deeply moved, because you are receiving so many intimations
of a hidden but infinite Being. If Nature stirs you to such pleasure, just
think how much she must stir me, in my chosen task of penetrating
her secrets and discovering the laws that govern the everlasting might
and splendour of her workings! Would it not be sin in me to give you
any other answer but that of our Redeemer to his anxious Mother
when she found him in the temple? 'Wist ye not that I must be about
my Father's business?'[36]

With his conception of nature as God's temple and of his own
duty there, a duty which he developed in the image of nature as a
sacred and mysterious book waiting for its reader, he shows himself
to be in the tradition of Novalis[37] and Jakob Boehme, both of whom
attributed to nature the status of a divinely ordained scripture. If
nature reveals the Godhead, it is because the Godhead dwells
within it: in the empty desert, for instance, which Leichhardt
endows with a divine presence and thus subjects to a religious
ordinance, taking possession of the land not only commercially, by
nomenclature and aesthetically, but also metaphysically, as Henry
Turnbull half mockingly confirms:

> Like the ancient Chaldean, this Leichhardt wandering through the . . .
> desert . . . felt and saw that *God* was in all things—to him there was
> no loneliness—*he* could never be alone—*God* was with him
> everywhere—*God* in the thronged city—*God* in the untrodden
> solitude—*God* in the calm and in the tempest—in the quietness of
> green smiling valleys, and in the awfulness of the wild raging sea—
> *God* here, *God* there, *God* everywhere.[38]

Turnbull underlines the fact that the divine Providence on which
Leichhardt, like other explorers of the time, frequently called,[39] was
not, for him, a 'convenient device to gloss events that cause-and-
effect explanations seemed unable to plumb',[40] but the hand of God
revealing itself in the laws of nature, and nothing less than this
eternal Presence was the goal of his quest.

The continuation of the discourse with the land in Leichhardt poems of the nineteenth century

The collective discourse of a society with its land was pursued not
only in the *itineraria* of the explorers but in the work of the historians, artists and writers who followed them. There is no other literature in the Anglo-European tradition in which the theme of the
journey and of the physical and spiritual settlement of the country

plays so large a part as in that of Australia. Indeed, Australian literature may in large measure be characterised as the imaginative dialogue of a traveller with a country which, although settled, has not really been occupied and possessed.

In this dialogue three factors are especially important: the space to be reclaimed, the path or plan of settlement and the actors in the theatre of conquest. The *itineraria* civilised Australia by declaring its spaces to be the Garden of Eden, a pastoral Arcadia wide open to settlement. They equipped the stage with scenery and sketched in the plan of action. All that was needed was heroes for the drama. The authors of the *explorer poems* peopled the stage with suitable protagonists.

These nineteenth century poems, dedicated to the great figures of the early Australian experience, employ similar strategies to those of the expedition journals; with this difference, that the journals, for all their common elements, still retain a certain individuality of accent. If the language of colonisation is one, the voice which speaks it is distinct. That distinction is no longer evident in poems about the explorers; it is hard to tell a poem about Leichhardt from one about Mitchell or Sturt or any of the other figures. In the pantheon of Australian heroes the building was of more importance than the individual statues; at the very most a few biographical details might help one determine who the subject was. So long as he had passed the test of nature and the elements, conquered in a superhuman struggle which opened up the way to commerce and colonisation, he was qualified for entry into that assembly; it mattered little if his journeys had been by sea or land. Gerald H. Supple's William Dampier who, like Dr Erasmus Darwin, foresees the rivers, towns, streets and towering palaces which an industrious race of English tongue will build and populate,[41] stands in this pantheon alongside John B. O'Hara's Matthew Flinders, in whose poetic dreams the banners of England unfurl majestically upon the winds of conquest.[42] Mrs Lewin's Abel Tasman[43] takes his place in the ancestral gallery irrespective of the fact that he was a Dutchman and not in the service of the British admiralty at all.

The achievements of the great explorers of the interior of the continent were naturally treated as a continuation of the deeds of their predecessors at sea. The protagonists in this poetic drama of colonisation were superhuman figures beyond error and reproach, the embodiment of Victorian ideals, mythical in dimension, removed from reality. Quite obviously they were of British origin.

Colonial Victorians thought of the world in much the same terms as their fellows in the homeland; heroism at least was measured in the same terms. The Victorian hero possessed 'Toughness of muscle and toughness of heart', an ideal 'combination of force and firmness'.[44] Life was regarded as a battle, and man as a being born to do battle.[45] Napoleon, Nelson and Wellington were the great models.[46] Henry Turnbull, then, was touching on a familiar sentiment when he compared Leichhardt's death to that of the French soldier-hero Latour d'Auverque, who had fallen on one of Napoleon's numerous battlefields and was honoured later as the apotheosis of military courage:

> But for poor Leichhardt dying—not upon the battlefield, but upon a far nobler field—dying far away from friends and home and country, in the lone wilderness—starved—it may be murdered, 'a thing o'er which the raven flaps its funereal wing', perhaps the last of his band—dying, too, without an effort made to ascertain his fate, neglected, forgotten, unwept, unhonoured and unsung. Poor Leichhardt who is there when the muster role of the illustrious dead is called, who is there save some humble unheeded individual like myself to respond: *Mort sur le champ de bataille.*[47]

Goethe's *Götz von Berlichingen*, Schiller's *Die Räuber* ('The Robbers'), Shelley's *Prometheus* and above all Byron's heroes inspired Carlyle in his admiration for the man of superior strength and titanic will,[48] and confirmed the Victorians in their conviction that human beings belonged to two categories: normal mortals and the chosen few, those towering personalities of puritan religious mythology[49] whom the young colony, too, was eager to number among its citizens.

'The Victorians,' Edmund Gosse has asserted, ' . . . carried admiration to the highest pitch. They marshalled it, they defined it, they turned it from a virtue into a religion, and called it Hero Worship.'[50] In the enthusiasm and idealism of this cult there was no place for human weakness:[51]

> Much about the explorers' lives was not the stuff out of which, in the popular mind, heroes were made. Charles Sturt was a fusspot and a bit of an old woman; Edward Giles and McDouall Stuart suffered from the same infirmity that almost cut short the life of Michael Cassio in Shakespeare's *Othello*; Robert O'Hara Burke had a reputation for losing his way in the bush, and often had attacks of the 'sillies'; Ludwig Leichhardt had extravagant metaphysical longings, a conviction that he would find fulfilment in death's embrace, and a

temptation to indulge himself in the sugar bowl and other luxuries of
the stores. John Forrest was a clockwork man; Edward Eyre had a
touch of the poet; Hume and Hovell walked from Gunning in southern
New South Wales to Port Phillip and back . . . loathing and distrust-
ing each other.[52]

It need hardly be said that not all of them were convinced
democrats. But this did not prevent the colonial Victorians from
raising them to the rank of heroes. Charles H. Eden is quite explicit
about it. In his 'calendar of Australian heroes', based on the work of
the English Comtist Frederic Harrison,[53] he reviews the entire history of Australian exploration, whether by land or sea, with a view
to familiarising his English readers with the great deeds 'that have
been done by his countrymen in that part of the globe that is now
commonly regarded as the "Fifth Continent"'.[54] From Captain
Cook to Ludwig Leichhardt the qualities that mark this generation
are the same:

> Such is the map even at the present day; and in studying it the terrible
> hardships to which the early pioneers were subjected, and the number
> of brave men who lost life or health in the unknown interior before it
> reached its present condition is too often lost sight of, although a
> subject of greater interest can hardly be presented to those who rev-
> erence perseverance, courage—nay heroism, for all these qualities are
> to be found burning bright and clear in the breasts of our Australian
> explorers.[55]

Apart from the shortcomings which Daniel Bunce has extensively portrayed in his *Travels with Dr Leichhardt*,[56] the explorer
suffered, of course, from not being of British stock; but this did not
keep him, any more than it had kept Tasman, from the final acco-
lade. Before Charles H. Eden accepts him, however, into the ranks
of those who had given their lives in the pursuit of knowledge, he
degermanises him by pointing to his British upbringing: 'Ludwig
Leichhardt, by birth a German, but brought up principally amongst
the English . . . '[57]—a compensation that more than outweighed the
defect. For G. Firth Scott,[58] Leichhardt's Prussian origins do not
even deserve a mention. Henry Kendall's poem 'Leichhardt' is the
only place where they do; but Kendall is interested in the affinity of
the German to the Australian Romantics, not in the nationality of
his blood. He emphasises, not Leichhardt's British upbringing, but
his education by Nature among the German hills:

> Born by hills of hard grey weather, far beyond the northern seas,

German mountains were his 'sponsors', and his mates were German trees . . . [59]

In the mother country the cult of heroes was a sort of surrogate religion; in the colony it had a further function, that of supplying the missing evidence of a longstanding human culture, that past, rich in great deeds and men, on which British society prided itself. As Louis Esson wrote in 1907:

> The human past. Australia has been born too late in the world's history ever to become a beautiful country. All beauty, says Carducei, dwells in the Past. Australia has no past. I mean no great epochs like Periclean Athens, Florence under the Medici, like England in Shakespeare's time. It has no romantic glamour, legends nor folk tales, castles, abbeys, nor battlefields—no Louvre nor Vatican; with all its beauty of Nature, it is an empty country.[60]

For the colonial Victorians, history was an experience available only in shadow and substitute, through nature:

> Here Nature is to me the only link
>   With other days, and in this oldest land,
>   She bids us go like pilgrims to some peak,
> And dream of when it touched the curved sky's brink;
>   Or 'neath some forest patriarch to stand
>   And let its aged presence richly speak.[61]

To fill this empty country the Victorian Australians built graves and monuments, erecting upon its surface the sign language of a civilised and meaningful past. Just as the *itineraria* had translated the virgin deserts from timelessness into history by imposing on them the cultural grammar of names, comparisons, associations, hopes and visions, so the literati of the Victorian colony cultivated their inheritance with the poetic predicates of a burgeoning Anglo-Australian code, both moral and aesthetic. The explorers, as path-finders of European civilisation,[62] became the 'founding fathers', a generation of whom neither Homer nor Ossian need have been ashamed.[63] Henry Kendall's 'The Fate of the Explorers' is a literary pilgrimage to the graves of Burke and Wills, at whose sight the speaker of the lines utters the solemn admonition:

> Let them rest, for oh! remember, that in long hereafter time
> Sons of Science oft shall wander o'er that solitary clime!
> Cities bright shall rise about it, Age and Beauty there shall stray,
> And the fathers of the people, pointing to the graves, shall say:
> 'Here they fell, the glorious martyrs! . . . '[64]

The names of the explorers now played the same role in the cultivation of the land as had the names of their patrons and masters for them. Indeed they too now became geographical as well as literary landmarks: the highway from Sydney to Melbourne was called after Hume, that from Port Augusta to Darwin after Stuart and that from Gundagai to Adelaide after Sturt. Electoral districts were called after Leichhardt and Kennedy (Qld), Forrest (WA), Cook and Mitchell (NSW), Wills (Vic.) and Sturt (SA); suburbs of Canberra and Sydney bear the names Hume and Leichhardt.[65]

In these nineteenth-century Leichhardt poems one notices three distinct processes of cultural colonisation, each of them typical of the nineteenth century: the use of the epitaph as a means of Christianisation, the raising of monuments to the fallen hero as acts of military conquest, and the setting of his achievements within the perspective of a future national history.

Leichhardt's first epitaph was a premature obituary in the *Sydney Morning Herald* of 3 July 1845[66]—an entry he read with some humour.[67] Its author, Leichhardt's friend of long standing, R. Lynd, portrays a pilgrimage to the death-place of his supposedly murdered comrade in order to give his whitened bones a fitting burial. Like Turnbull, he brings out Leichhardt's religious traits: the great force which in his life he served so faithfully sanctifies the earth on which he rests. The act of poetic burial transforms the wilderness, despite the absence of ecclesiastical insignia, into a holy and Christian place. For here lies one who is great in the sight of God as well as man, a hero to whose grave one owes unquestioning pilgrimage.

Henry Kendall's 'Leichhardt' is without doubt the most memorable of the otherwise rather undemanding tributes paid by the nineteenth century to the great explorer. Written thirty-two years after his mysterious disappearance, it focuses on Leichhardt's empathy with nature, the heritage of the German Romantic. In his homeland he had learnt not only to wonder at the sublime beauty of nature but to feel an almost Franciscan oneness with it:

Grandeur of the old-world forests passed into his radiant soul,
With the song of stormy crescents, where the mighty waters roll.
Thus he came to be a brother of the river and the wood —
Thus the leaf, the bird, the blossom, grew a gracious sisterhood . . .[68]

Nature had enabled him to understand her language; for her he had left both home and country in order to come the nearer to her and God in Australia. As if he had read Leichhardt's own letters, Kendall writes:

> Here he found a larger beauty—here the lovely lights were new
> On the slopes of many flowers, down the gold-green dells of dew.
> In the great august cathedral of his holy lady, he
> Daily worshipped at her altars, nightly bent the reverent knee—
> Heard the hymns of night and morning, learned the psalm of solitudes;
> Knew that God was very near him—felt his presence in the woods![69]

Kendall too makes for the 'heroic traveller'[70] a resting place: planting in the Australian desert an English churchyard, hearing in the wild tumult of the waves and forests an ordered song:

> Down a dell of dewy myrtle, where the light is soft and green,
> And a month like English April sits, an immemorial queen,
> Let us think that he is resting—think that by a radiant grave
> Ever come the songs of forest, and the voices of the wave![71]

The second process is the honouring of the military conqueror. On hearing of the success of his expeditions, Leichhardt's contemporaries honoured him as a conqueror. He had qualified as a 'successful candidate for Fame',[72] triumphing over nature, subduing the refractory terrain as in a military action. The panegyric published in the *Port Phillip Herald* demonstrates the fusion of hero cult and military ethos. The poem's author suggests, as a welcome for Leichhardt:

> A '*monster meeting*' let us have, where all may crowd around,
> And 'hero-worship' find its vent in one commingled sound . . . [73]

Leichhardt's voyage of discovery is likened to a peaceful campaign, a conquest which has cost no lives and harmed no man, for God has protected the expeditionary corps with his mighty hand. A failure of the mission would have brought to the nation no loss in terms of suffering or indeed financial investment; conversely, its success may be greeted with truly universal jubilation:

> His mission was not to *destroy*, nor comes he back to tell
> Of fields, in which, though nobly won, our best and bravest fell;
> Far higher conquests his than these—and well he knew his God
> Would watch him all along the way his trusting footsteps trod;
> He knew too that if, after all, his labour should be lost,
> A nation would not have to bear the suffering and the cost;

That if triumphant, 'twas success might greet each listening ear,
Nor cause a single broken heart, nor one up-braiding tear.[74]

Another poem of the time goes even further, celebrating Leichhardt's victory as a sign of man's self-appointed destiny in the uncivilised wilderness of nature:

> Thou hast wrought thy work of victory, by deed of blood unstain'd,
> For man's appointed purposes a glorious world obtain'd;
> Thy step upon the wilderness, the harbinger of peace,
> Hath bid that wild and savage night of solitude to cease.[75]

The third group of Leichhardt poems draws its inspiration from the belief—or disbelief—that the explorers' achievements are the beginning of an historical development that will lead inexorably to an Australian utopia. In 'Lines Written in Commemoration of Dr L. Leichardt [sic] . . . and his safe return to Sydney' the anonymous C.D. yearns for an Australia free from the evils of the old world, a country modelled on the principles of Dr Erasmus Darwin and William Charles Wentworth, governed by 'Freedom, and Science, and Virtue . . . '[76] As in Pope's *Windsor Forest*, the peoples of the world will turn in wonderment to this realm, the offspring of the Australian dream, for which the deeds of the founding fathers are now little more than a necessary condition. Leichhardt's name is not mentioned in the text of the poem; the person of the explorer is no longer meaningful, but only his contribution to the dreamed of goal, a new and better Britain under southern skies, and one with a mission to the world:

> Thy fleets to all regions thy pow'r shall display,
> The nations admire, and the oceans obey;
> Each shore to thy glory it's [sic] tribute unfold,
> And the East and the West yield their spices and gold.
> As the day-spring unbounded, thy splendour shall flow,
> And Earth's little kingdoms before thee shall bow,
> While the ensigns of *Freedom*, in triumph unfurled,
> Hush *Tyranny's* sway, and give peace to the world!
>
> Thus, as down a lone garden, 'mid th' acacia's soft shade,
> From the din of the City I pensively strayed,
> The gloom from the face of fair Heaven retired,
> The winds ceased to murmur, the thunders expired—
> Perfumes, as of Eden, flowed sweetly along,
> And a voice, as of angels, *prophetic'lly* sung—
> Australia! Australia! to glory arise,
> Thou queen of the South, and thou child of the skies![77]

Against the backdrop of this cosmic teleology few were prepared to consider the negative aspects of the conquest of the land.
A.B. Paterson's 'The Lost Leichhardt'[78] has a double meaning in its
title. Written fifty years after Leichhardt vanished, it is concerned
less with his personal fate than with that of the ethos which determined his exploration. The 'Rash men, that know not what they
seek . . . '[79] and the 'Commercial Travellers'[80] who follow in his
tracks have indeed 'civilised' Australia, but the voices which crowd
upon the traveller's ear as he journeys into the interior are no longer
those of angels in the Garden of Eden:

> And loud from every squatter's door
>   Each pioneering swell
> Will hear the wild pianos roar
>   The strains of 'Daisy Bell'.[81]

The vision of utopia gives way to a bleak and cynical history.
Leichhardt's spirit has been lost; the pub built on his grave demonstrates how little his non-material motives for opening up Australia
now count in the minds of his successors:

> And then, to crown this tale of guilt,
>   They'll find some scurvy knave,
> Regardless of their quest, has built
>   A pub on Leichhardt's grave![82]

The discourse about the discourse with the land in explorer poems of the twentieth century

Bernard O'Dowd's poem 'Australia' (1901) takes up the common
theme of C.D. and of A.B. Paterson when he asks the youthful
nation: 'Are you . . . /A new demesne for Mammon to infest? /Or
lurks millenial Eden 'neath your face?'[83] His questions are directed
to the nation as such; their reply presupposes a collective act of
critical self-examination about the course the nation's journey was
now to take. Randolph Stow's Johann Ludwig Ulrich von
Leichhardt zu Voss, who in Australia had become plain Mr Smith,
signalling in turn that behind every Mr Smith there is a potential
Leichhardt or a Voss, is also—and still—on a journey of self-
exploration. O'Dowd's question, at a time when the politicians, with
the act of federation, had brought the discourse with the land to a
temporary halt, inasmuch as they had staked out the boundaries of
the territory they claimed, shows to what extent Australia at that
time was aware of itself as A Land Half Won[84] and nothing more.

The young nation which in 1901 presented its face proudly to
the world was a nation of travellers who had left their old home but
had not always taken root in the new. The dilemma which the
politicians had passed on to the historians, artists and writers was
the mental turmoil of a loyalty split between two hemispheres. In
Outbreak of Love Martin Boyd reduces this dilemma to the formula
'Only our bodies were born in Australia. Our minds were born in
Europe. Our bodies are always trying to return to our minds'.[85] Or,
as John K. Ewers puts it:

> ... For a generation of years
> migrant ships have brought new faces
> to become old Australians in a decade or more.
> We who have welcomed them, every one
> of us, were migrants or came of migrant stock.
> Our forbears had no thought but to remain
> forever English, but the hard bony hand
> of this country changed them.[86]

This is the central spiritual conflict, whose effects reach down to the
present day. A.D. Hope describes the insecurity to which it has
given rise:

> The roots are European, but the tree
> Grows to a different pattern and design;
> Where the fruit get its flavour I'm not sure,
> From native soil or overseas manure.
>
> And this uncertainty is in our bones.
> Others may think us smug or insular;
> The voice perhaps is brash, its undertones
> Declare in us a doubt of what we are.[87]

A poem printed in a Melbourne student magazine in 1986 is even
more explicit; it is called 'This lost place, my home':

> i went looking for my country and i
> couldn't find it anywhere [...] i'm looking out
> and what do i see? white aliens in a
> desert country. they cling to the fringe. they
> live in city. this is the heart of the white man
> country. so let's sing a song of alienation. of
> competition and first division [...] let's make a world like
> a flag unfurled
> that tells us who we are and where we're
> heading. unless we find out quick enough
> we'll be as dead as our national anthem. i
> still call this lost place my home.[88]

The explorer poems of the twentieth century are, then, quite different from those of earlier times. The linguistic colonisation which in the nineteenth century was seen as a necessary precursor of material and economic colonisation is now itself the subject of discourse, and this discourse takes the form of a critical examination of men and motives; beneath this, however, it is a quest for sense and purpose in the journey which constitutes Australian society. The poetry which shapes it is reflective and questioning, its tone no longer imperial; the explorers and seafarers are only very occasionally heroes and trail-blazers of the great political or material future.[89] More often they voice the collective uncertainties whose answers might alleviate the crisis of identity, as Douglas Stewart expresses it in the foreword to his anthology of *Voyager Poems*:

> . . . there seems to come a time in the history of nations when whatever it is that moves the production of poetry . . . demands that the poets should sing the nation itself into shape. How did it come to be? What kind of men made it? What are its ideas and ideals?
>
> It is a search . . . for gods, demigods and heroes, the men or divinities who have founded the nation and whose deeds and characters, whether for good or for ill, as inspiration or as warning, are still felt to be working through it. We are what we are, so the unconscious thought runs, because our ancestors made us so; we are where we are, even because our ancestors brought us here: and if the poets can tell us what our tribal ancestors were like, and why and how they brought us here, we shall have a better chance of understanding ourselves.[90]

Stewart brings into his volume poems on such different figures as James Cook, Abel Tasman, Frank Worsley, Christopher Columbus and Ludwig Leichhardt, showing once again how difficult it is to single out personal achievement in the search for identity; how, in the perspective of the twentieth century, one hero again looks much like another. Now, however, the great figures of the past have lost not only their individuality but their heroic status too. They have become mortal men, creatures whose tragic failure is frequently looked on as more important than their triumph. For the arena of quest and conquest has passed from the outer world to the inner; the actors in the imperial drama are more often than not passive sufferers.

This development is particularly clear in the case of Leichhardt, whose personal qualities predisposed him for the role of victim and failure which, in the changed climate of the twentieth century, was now to be his literary fate. In John Howard's panorama of Australian navigators and explorers, written probably between the two world wars, '[the] ardent Leichhardt' is still 'One of our energetic seers, / Of the Teutonic race',[91] a founding father whose image is as yet untarnished. James Devaney, too, in his poem 'The Lost Explorers (Leichhardt 1848)',[92] written in 1931, sees Leichhardt as a man condemned to failure by the sheer hostility of nature, but for all that not unsympathetic. The first real change in the picture of the explorer comes in M. Barnard Eldershaw's story, published in 1938, 'The Man Who Knew the Truth About Leichhardt . . . '.[93] Here he is an intemperate autocrat, consumed with envy for Mitchell, who punishes his sick companions with exotic medicines, grabs violently everything he wants or needs and makes others bear the blame for his shortcomings. It is as if Leichhardt must pay the penalty for the global aspirations, the power politics of the German *Reich*:

> He knew he wasn't a bushman and never would be, so he trusted to luck. He talked a lot about his star—like Napoleon. He had all sorts of poses. Sometimes he liked to think of himself as a simple, unworldly scientist, sometimes he was Don Quixote, the leader of lost causes, or he was a great leader, a Bismarck, or a martyred exile. He never could make up his mind.[94]

The war brought upon the world by Nazi Germany accelerated the fall of the former hero, or at least his translation into a man of problems and grief. In the nineteenth century Daniel Bunce's critical study of Leichhardt (1859) had been unable to make headway against Henry Turnbull's eulogising portrait; but, after Alec H. Chisholm's book *Strange New World*[95] of 1941, the process was reversed in the twentieth century, despite the fact that only three years earlier Catherine D. Cotton could still maintain, in her biography of the explorer, that Leichhardt was a worthy national hero.[96] Chisholm's book appeared at a moment when poetic cries to join battle for 'A world delivered from the Nazi yoke',[97] 'Until the Nazi hordes are hurled / Into the abyss of their own devising'[98] were not unusual. Chisholm took it upon himself to prove 'that Leichhardt was dishonest, malicious, selfish, slovenly, fanatical, autocratic, sponging, muddling and irresponsible';[99] he was indeed a 'constitutional psychopath'.[100]

One of the first literary depictions of Leichhardt to follow Chisholm was Francis Webb's *Leichhardt in Theatre* (1952).[101]

Webb does not allow himself to succumb to Chisholm's polemics, but his hero is a frail, vulnerable and guilt-ridden human being who has lost confidence in himself and in his mission, with its superhuman demands:

> Shall a man go crazy for the kiss
> Of thirst upon his throat? Shall he explore
> Time after time this death's-head continent,
> Probe the eye-sockets, skinless cavities,
> Till the brain sweats from his skull, his hands contract,
> And bone probes bone at length; bone lifted to cheek
> Knows the flesh dwindling, blasted by such a love?[102]

Webb's interest is in the theatre of the imagination and in the Leichhardt who plays in it: in the minds of his admirers. Paradoxically his poem confirms a principle of literary interpretation valid for both centuries: 'that Leichhardt had been metaphorically put unto stage by each generation in order to satisfy the requirements of the times.'[103] Where the nineteenth century paid homage to the hero and *Übermensch*, Webb draws a picture of the tragic loser whose path leads from arrogance to humility, a Christ-figure who becomes fully human only when the powers of nature, the personified Furies, wreak their anger on him:

> The Furies circle:
> Desert with bleached eyes, mountain with the hawk's mouth,
> Sea with her witching falseness; cordon him.
> He is taken, stripped, and bound.[104]

With Eyre, Burke and Wills, Kennedy and all those sea captains whose ships lay stranded on Australia's coasts, Leichhardt belongs to a race of introverted seekers who in Australia discovered only their own nothingness and the vacancy of their dreams.[105]

In Diane Fahey's 'To Francis Webb'[106] the reader is presented with three great losers, Sturt, Eyre and Leichhardt. With respect to Leichhardt the poem is a pointed reversal of nineteenth-century Romantic attitudes:

> dreading, hungering for, the final loneliness
> Leichhardt tracked its wastes with animal cunning
> threatening the void with *Übermensch* rage;
> at the end, Australia, the great mind of loneliness
> itself, bared and embraced his bones . . . [107]

The fate of such men, far from sweeping away all doubt, leaves 'a question, with only a question mark / at its end'.[108]

In conceiving Voss, Patrick White too drew on Chisholm's study,[109] but it is his own figure, in the novel of that name, that gave the decisive impulse to modern poetic interpretations of the explorer. The 'Vossification' of Leichhardt in the wake of White's novel is simply a further proof that the literary Leichhardt is and was at every stage of his career a personification of the desires, or the problems, of Australian society. In John Blight's 'Leichhardt as Voss' the speaker has capitulated in the face of nature's insurmountable power: in this wasteland a conqueror even of the titanic dimensions of a Tamburlaine would come to nothing. Where the nineteenth century had seen Leichhardt and his fellows as subjecting nature to their control, Blight draws a picture of an untameable adversary that swallows up all evidence of man and of his colonising endeavours, forcing him back into the cities whence he came. Leichhardt/Voss writes to Laura:

> There space gapes wide for daylight to
> remind me a world spins round me. I see
> no Pyramids in this Country;
> only the infatigable beyond
> blinding through void past the timid
> stars . . . [110]

Noel Macainsh's 'Doctor Leichhardt on Board'[111] presents a nature lover fascinated by the immeasurable grandeur of the Australian outback; his poem 'Voss, Also Called Leichhardt' (published thirteen years later) on the other hand emphasises the unending hostility of the Nullarbor, which compels the explorer to give up his task just as it does the travellers in a comfortable Ansett bus:

> If he had known the word . . .
> The burning houses of the masters in Germany
> would have been dearer to him than
> the flaming horizons of
> the Great Simpson Desert. Perhaps
> he had still seen it—Nullarbor
> as the sickle glinted in the throat,
> swung by an ecstatic Aborigine.[112]

In Keith Harrison's 'Leichhardt in the Desert' Leichhardt waits with vacant features for someone to tell him the goal of his journey. The poem ends as a prayer to the explorers to intercede for those still travelling:

> You mad saints who claim to know this place
> Make prayers for those on a dry journey:

Pray that our arrogance does not fail
In this hard light, in this astringent beauty.[113]

The nineteenth century raised signposts in whose shadow they could possess, and settle on, the land. But these fences, graves and monuments have fallen into decay: the land has shown itself stronger than the men who thought to conquer it, and the poets of the twentieth century have been left to seek new guidelines. The dialogue situation is now reversed: where in former times the colonisers' words rang out across a largely passive continent, it is now the land itself that has taken on the active role, bringing forcibly to men's awareness their weakness and its strength. Its message to its troubled inhabitants is that the real exploration is only just beginning, that the dialogue must be started afresh, and that in this act of speech the travellers into the interior must be driven by motives other than possession. That at least is what the dead—but still living—Leichhardt communicates to the reader of Larry Buttrose's 'The Leichhardt Heater Journey':

You
Have arrived at the start. Now you must find
The tracks of the explorer, follow them
Until you find the last message he wrote,
Scratched in the dust on a Collins Street tram
That tells you to listen to the radio for the next
Word from Leichhardt, from the centre of Australia;
To listen for your mother's voice, black mother's voice,
Somewhere in a show on television, somewhere in the middle
Australia; somewhere in the Simpson.[114]

CHAPTER 12

Leichhardt's Diaries

Robert Sellick

It has been said that we live in an age in which biography has become the dominant literary form. Certainly the signs of this immense interest are clearly in evidence in Australia at the moment: almost every academic seems to be writing one. A colleague at another university has recently published a biography to great critical acclaim: it is a study of Louisa Lawson, the mother of one of Australia's best known fiction writers, Henry Lawson. The publication details don't really matter; what is significant is the fact that this biography engages in a startlingly fresh way with the problems that face *all* biographers.

Where there is an abundance of evidence — family papers, masses of letters, fulsome diaries, surviving witnesses, voluble and knowledgeable interviewees etc., etc. — the biographer's wayward and intruding ego is held in check by the sheer weight, the directing and supervising influence of constantly attendant evidence. Where such material is largely absent — lacking very often at quite crucial points of the story — and where there is instead much rumour, hearsay, legend, family lore, the narrating biographer is under constant pressure to fill or tidy the gaps: by subtly inventing; by endlessly (and after a while tediously) withdrawing from unequivocal statement into a fog of, 'It seems . . .', 'We might speculate . . .', 'Perhaps . . .'; 'It is impossible to say if . . .'; or, above all, by quietly, unpretentiously but with ever-increasing firmness and alacrity insinuating himself onto his own stage — sliding from biography to phantom autobiography and from both into a disguised form of fiction.[1]

At first sight this extended comment would seem to have little relevance to anyone about to begin (or even someone well into) the task of writing a biography of the explorer Ludwig Leichhardt. No researcher can claim that there is a paucity of material: the Mitchell and Dixon Libraries in Sydney hold an immense store: diaries, letters, notebooks, field books; lecture notes, catalogues, chronological notes, reports. There seems no way that the biographer can escape 'the directing and supervising influence of constantly attendant evidence'. But is that really the case? Leichhardt's biographer seems rather to have the worst of both worlds: surrounding that plethora of evidence is a veritable forest of 'lore, rumour, legend': the 'base of evidence has become weighted with accretions of commentary by champions and critics'.[2] Before the biographer can begin he must first clear this away. No easy task when the commentary has had almost a century and a half to accumulate and when the accretions have attained the status of received truth. I am thinking here in particular of quite fanciful details of Leichhardt's early life, first 'recorded' (if that is the word) by Ernst Zuchold in 1856[3] and adopted and transmitted by people such as Catherine Cotton some eighty years later.[4]

And even if the immense body of evidence is accepted without question, the biographer still must face the implications of his own intrusions into the text he is writing; *I* must perforce come to terms with those 'vestiges of the narrating self' that must — however I attempt to guard against them — 'invade the notionally objective record'.[5] I have to become reconciled with my multiple selves at the same time that I am attempting to come to terms with the multiple selves of the subject of my biography — of Ludwig Leichhardt himself — multiple selves that must, inevitably, colour and shape and control the record from which I begin.

It's no easy task for me to recall exactly when it was that I became aware of the existence of the Leichhardt diaries. Clearly it was some time after 1969, when I first began my research on Australian explorers. It was probably when I began to search the manuscript

holdings of the Mitchell Library for material relating to Sturt or
Mitchell or Oxley. Or it may have been my first reading of
Aurousseau's monumental edition of Leichhardt's letters that
appeared in 1968.[6] Whenever it was, it doesn't really matter, for it
wasn't the diaries themselves but what they seemed to promise that
captivated me: a final, unchallengeable key to the explorer who was
so fascinatingly complex, so honoured at one time, so reviled at
another. And allied to this was the conviction, now so transparently
naive, that they were an undiscovered country where I, however
briefly and tentatively, would be able to make major discoveries —
chart rivers of motive, scale peaks of purpose, in the hope that such
rivers and peaks would prove different from those physical ones
that had made the task of exploration in Australia so difficult: rivers
that 'vanished in inland sands'; and peaks that demanded names
like Mt Hopeless, Mt Desperation and Mt Despair. At first the
diaries held out the promise of hope. They offered an apparently
continuous record from that first Berlin entry of 27 September 1832
to the final closure of the record immediately before Leichhardt's
departure on his final expedition in April 1847. This was a naive
conviction. Its assumptions were manifold: that the same youthful
'self' who began the entries at the start of a university career remained unchanged throughout all the experiences of England and
Europe, untouched by the impact of expectations both fulfilled and
denied there and in Australia; that not only the narrating self but
also the 'reading' self would be constant.
One was equally sanguine about the provenance of the diaries. Here
they were, housed in one of the world's great repositories of
Australiana; surely, I innocently thought, their provenance was
beyond doubt! But as it turned out, the actual path was far from
straight, and certainly not smooth. After many hours in obscure
corners of places such as the Australian Museum it was made plain
to me that the diaries had rested, however briefly, in very many
hands. 'Certain property of the late Dr. Leichardt [sic]', so the
record states, was deposited with the Australian Museum in 1853.
It had been placed there by James Murphy, the father of
Leichhardt's friend John who had travelled with him on that first
major expedition to Port Essington. The material was subsequently
lost and only rediscovered by the museum's director, Gerhard
Krefft, a decade or so later. Krefft's own story is a complex one,
including as it does tales of disputes with the Trustees and an
attempt to expel him physically from the Museum after his dismis-

sal. These items (or some of them because there is no complete catalogue of what was actually transferred although it included volumes from Leichhardt's personal scientific library which were later incorporated into the general collection of the State Library of New South Wales) were offered to the Free Public Library, Sydney, in 1902, at which time they were described as 'certain old Books, merely literary Curiosities'. A later consignment followed in 1917 and the transfer was recorded in a letter from the curator of the Museum to the principal librarian, Public Library of New South Wales.

5 February 1917

The Principal Librarian & Secretary
Public Library of N.S. Wales,
SYDNEY

Dear Sir,
  Some years ago, about 1900, I think, a number of Leichhardt documents, books & c., were transferred by order of my Trustees to the Public Library.
  Quite recently a few more were discovered stowed away in an old trunk, evidently overlooked on the former occasion. These I have much pleasure in handing over to you under the same authority leaving you, at your discretion, to place them either in the Public Library proper or the Mitchell, which ever you think fit.

I am,
Yours truly,
R. Etheridge
CURATOR[7]

The diaries acquired by the Mitchell Library included major items such as the *Tagebuch* for 27 September 1832–17 May 1840 and the Fieldbook used on the exploration journey from Moreton Bay to Port Essington, 1844–45. Other volumes came with the David Scott Mitchell collection when the library was founded, or were acquired from W.B. Clarke, the grandson of the Rev. W.B. Clarke in 1948. W.B. Clarke, a geologist, was a friend of Leichhardt's; indeed, he edited Leichhardt's journal of his third expedition and published it in *Waugh's Australian Almanac* in 1860. Many items, however, despite repeated searches and enquiries both within the Mitchell Library and elsewhere, remain tagged with the frustrating description 'Provenance unknown'.
  Such questions of provenance are clearly of interest to collectors and bibliographers, but they assume major significance for

someone immersed in the task of transliterating and editing
Leichhardt's diaries — and this for two reasons. The work that Dr
Marlis Thiersch and I did on the diaries revealed a major break in
the sequence. Mitchell Library Manuscript C152/3 records
Leichhardt's travels in France, Italy and Switzerland but breaks off
on 14 September 1841. Leichhardt resumes his entries on 1 April
1842, some six weeks after his arrival in Australia. Given the fact
that he had been such an assiduous diarist, it is difficult to believe
that Leichhardt failed to keep a journal on the voyage out or in those
first weeks in Australia, when new and strange impressions would
have flooded in on him and demanded his response. In fact, the
practice of keeping a diary on the outward voyage to Australia was
so commonplace that for Leichhardt not to have kept one would
have been extraordinary.

But there is another, more crucial reason why this question of
provenance is of such vital concern. In the early days of the project,
as we were working our way laboriously through the first volume—
and grappling (not always harmoniously) with an unfamiliar
script—we became aware of puzzling breaks, lacunae, in the text.
And these occurred, it now seems, through the not always reliable
glass of memory, at stages of enormous interest: in particular when
Leichhardt is writing about his fraught relationship with his father
or his friendship with William Nicholson on which so many commentators have focused. These interruptions to the text took a variety of forms. Sometimes they declared themselves through missing
pages, a line of thought suddenly interrupted, broken off without
warning or preparation. Sometimes one was faced with the evidence
of neat, almost surgically precise excisions in the text. One illustration only will have to serve my purposes here.

Towards the end of August 1833 Leichhardt visited his family
in Trebatsch, and spent three weeks with them. At the end of his
stay he commented in his diary on the mixture of the pleasant and
unpleasant that he had experienced there. He was particularly concerned with the gap between his view of the world and his father's:
earlier harmony had now become discord. What emerges in the
diary is an impassioned assertion of Leichhardt's individuality in
the face of his father's dominance and what to the son appears to be
the older man's refusal to profit from experience.

Trebatsch 12th September [1838]
　　For the last three weeks I have been again in the circle of my family.

There has been little enjoyment but much unpleasantness in this time. In Berlin I still saw everything through the eyes of my father. Now I am looking at it through my own ones and now I detect everywhere mistakes, big massive mistakes, which to face demands ones whole tenacity and steadfastness. But the issues involved have become too laughable to me, too trivial, and I have written so much about it that I don't want to molest my diary with one more word about it. People are a funny breed; to put it briefly, everybody has his opinion, his taste, his individuality. And everybody has the vanity to regard his own individualism as the very best — be it *privately* or *publicly*. And with people who reach what they have gained in life through their own strength' and effort, this self-satisfaction becomes so great that one tries in vain to make them see one's own view . . . And because of this bias I can't get even the most straight-forward things across to him [his father]. Well, enough of that, as my sister Mathilde always says in her simple letters when she deals with something unpleasant. For a long time I suffered from an enormous inner-torture: the disagreement between the views of myself and my father, where there has previously always been such a nice accord; this disharmony was painful to my feelings and I tortured myself with the thought that I was not fulfilling my duty as a child. Yet I will never change my mind to do a favour to somebody who errs, be it my father or the king, but I will carefully, as nature demands, attempt to lead them to the truth. It would be a pity should I not succeed but I will not grieve about it, because grief does not achieve anything but will rob my life of the basis of my quiet satisfaction.[8]

The entry breaks off at this point and resumes on the following page of the *Tagebuch* with an account of a journey Leichhardt and his brothers took from Trebatsch in the direction of the River Oder on 5 September but again terminates, suddenly and in mid-sentence. We had by this time become accustomed to such sudden breaks: there were many occasions on which we suspected that pages were missing or the ordering of the sections of the *Tagebuch* was problematic. The puzzles raised by *this* apparent break were not solved until much later, when Marlis Thiersch and I were dealing with the papers collected together in C163. Here we encountered a number of pages which appeared to have no relation to others gathered there and we eventually realised that they really belonged with C151. The account of the journey to the Oder continued from where it had been interrupted and then Leichhardt records the following incident:

> After I had been wandering around for a long time, suddenly Dorchen [his father's second wife] comes [sic] running up to me, pale, trembling, she falls into my arms and asks with a voice drowned in tears:

what shall I do, Anne [the housemaid] is lying under father's bed. My legs were shaking to the bone, I didn't say anything and went into the house where father was sitting having a talk with Neumann. He was so embarrassingly friendly as he always is when is up to something. He asked me, Neumann talked to me, but I could hardly answer. Finally Neumann left, father accompanying him; in the meantime Dorchen entered and urged me to go with her to father's room. I went, looked and caught sight of the girl lying stretched out under the bed. And as if a shyness overcame me I quickly returned to the other room. Dorchen left the light standing at the bed and followed me. Now father had entered again and intended to go to his room. Dorchen asked him — not impudently, not triumphantly, but with a trembling voice: "But father, what is Anne doing underneath your bed?" "Does she really lie under the bed?", he answered seemingly calm. — She obviously has to tell me something". — "Yes, the way you always talk to each other," said Dorchen. I left passing father without saying a word, dragged Dorchen with me, shut father's door and asked Dorchen not to say a word. She didn't. I went just as speechless to my room, barred the door and suddenly stood there alone with incredible pain. I fell on my knees and wanted to pray . . . Yet in between crying I was not able to. Mad with pain I tried to pull myself together again, stretched my hand to the sky and screamed my God, my God and something else — I don't know.[9]

It was not the dislocation of this section itself that was intriguing but the reason for the displacement. Was it due to accident? Who had been responsible? Who had found the convoluted relationship between Leichhardt's father Christian, his second wife Dorchen and the servant so distressing that it needed to be expunged from the record? The fact that Leichhardt had added a quotation as a marginal comment—a quotation from Goethe's *Torquato Tasso*—in Göttingen in 1834 provides some measure (over and above that evident in the original entry) of the enormity of the shock that Leichhardt had experienced, but it doesn't really resolve the difficulty. Had the section been removed before or after the Göttingen comment? Clearly the answer to these questions could only be settled when the provenance of the diaries was known.

Wenn Ganz was Unerwartetes begegnet,
Wenn unser Blick was Ungeheures sieht,
Steht unser Geist auf eine Weile still,
Wir haben nichts, womit wir das vergleichen.

Torq. Tasso. Goethe
Gottingen [*sic*] den 7th July [*sic*] 1834.[10]

The quotation is from *Torquato Tasso* Act Five, Scene V and establishes clearly the impact on Leichhardt of the experience at Trebatsch. It can hardly be accidental that, even after a lapse of almost a year, Leichhardt is drawn to this particular play by Goethe, a play which is so preoccupied with the notion of the divided self and the tensions that can exist between private passion and the demands of public morality and which are central to his reaction to his father's behaviour.

When this displacement and the later marginal gloss are added to a great number of similar 'editorial' interventions something quite novel begins to emerge. Clearly the diaries can no longer be seen as a simple day-by-day record; they emerge instead as the record of a continuous dialogue between one Leichhardt — the recorder, the journalist the diarist writing as near to the event as possible — and another, later, Leichhardt who judges and evaluates from a different perspective, a perspective significantly altered both in time and space. Two Leichhardts and two selves. The entire programme of revision and excision, of displacement and subsequent gloss begins to point towards the construction of a particular self: a construction not so very dissimilar from those associated with autobiography. And in the same way that current critical evaluation of autobiography concentrates on the notion of a fragmented self, so the reader of the diaries is forced to confront a *variety* of Leichhardts in the pages of the *Tagebücher*, each one in no sense less authentic than the others.

It is this overriding concern with the self and its emancipation — the emancipation of the *ich*, the individual self — that establishes Leichhardt as a Romantic, although the Romantic would have hardly acknowledged the variety of 'selves' I am referring to here. The notion of the fragmentation of the self is a much more recent concept. It is only through the recognition of the complex of ideas that shaped Leichhardt's age—the 'Romantic' basis on which he depended and from which he began—that Leichhardt's insistence on the 'inner' life falls into place. After all, for the Romantic, the true meaning of life lies in the finding and fulfilment of this inner self (a double exploration throughout his life)!

Paradoxically, though, the diaries from the outset assert that *one* Leichhardt in particular will be foregrounded: the expression 'the inner man', although trite, is as useful here as any other. It is this attention to the 'inner man' and the 'inner life' that is emphasised in the initial entry on 27 September 1832:

It is the spiritual life (which has to take the human into consideration) [which has] to purify him and lead him to his fulfilment.[11]

Farther on in the same entry the point is repeated: "Das Seelensein ist es also, was der Beobachtung vorliegen muss." Indeed, the trend of the *Tagebücher* is best seen as a turning away from the objective, the external, towards the subjective, the internal: "it is the being of the soul, that has to be presented for observation . . . . two lines further: "yet what are all these exterior things doing in the history of the internal creative spirit." [8 July 1833][12]

Nowhere is this concentration on the inner life shown more clearly than in Leichhardt's perceptions of and feelings towards women. And it is worth emphasising the frequency with which young women appear and disappear in the pages of the diary — a frequency sufficient to temper if not finally to negate the ubiquitous references by many commentators to his supposed homosexuality. The entry for 9 October 1832 almost leaps from the page in its exuberance: "Ich habe gesehen, ich habe gesehen — ich habe das herrliche Madchen gesehen!—Was sind Ideale—was sind sie?" This ecstatic response followed a visit to Cossenblatt, where Leichhardt for the first time saw Charlotte (?), the daughter of the Hern Oberförster Bock. Although she is mentioned often after this first Sunday meeting, there is no actual record of any conversation or of any exchange of feelings between them. The relationship is acted out only within the pages of the diary, it seems. Leichhardt the young and passionate lover is assembled feeling by feeling, thought by thought, upon the stage of the inner world. Certainly it's a convincing construct but one that clearly has no validity in any external, objective sense. The pattern is repeated with other young women who come within Leichhardt's orbit, William Nicholson's sister Lucy, for example. How is the biographer to find his way through such an intricate weaving of 'fact' and 'fiction'? What are the implications for the record as a whole, after a lapse of a century and a half?

It is my contention that a similar process can be discerned with other relationships that are significant for Leichhardt, notably that between the explorer and his father and that existing between Ludwig and his friend William Nicholson. Here, too, the drama is internalised and it becomes increasingly difficult to decide where the boundary between fact and fiction is to be located. Indeed, it is tempting to apply to the diaries a description that is usually held to isolate the particular qualities of the autobiography which is seen as belonging to a genre 'situated at a midway point between fact and fiction, between prose and poetry, between imagination and experience'.[13] In making this claim I am not suggesting that the diaries be read as fiction but I am wanting to claim that the suggestion is a particularly enticing one when one recalls that this is the life, after all, of an explorer, a man dedicated to the task of scientific and geographical revelation, of 'bringing into fuller knowledge' 'something previously unknown'. It is the tension which is created between this primary impulse of the explorer and the diaries' emphasis on a rejection of the external world which makes the *Tagebücher* themselves so fascinating and Leichhardt himself such an absorbing creation. And I use the term 'creation' in complete realisation of what this word implies. From the time of the first entry in the diary in 1832 until Leichhardt's eventual disappearance in 1848, he was engaged in the creation of a variety of 'selves'. Of abiding interest, of course, is the creation of Leichhardt the explorer; the pieces of that 'self' were only assembled slowly and laboriously over time: the explorer as scientist, the explorer as linguist, the explorer as medical student. But equally interesting is the construction of Leichhardt as dutiful son to a difficult father, of Leichhardt as lover, Leichhardt as friend. There were models, of course, but they resided in the realm of the ideal and were accessible only through the life of the ideal, the inner life, the *Seelenleben*.

How to measure the success of this creation? Ultimately there is no measure in the external world to which one can refer and it's worth remembering that others have been about the business of constructing other, perhaps more manageable and certainly more useful, Leichhardts, as Elsie Webster has so superbly and definitively demonstrated in her study *Whirlwinds in the Plain*[14]. Since that publication joined the long list of other studies — and the line reaches back almost to the year in which Leichhardt disappeared — the number of 'Leichhardts' has proliferated. The diaries can offer no absolute certainty and so the most useful strategy is perhaps the one I am at present following: publish the diaries and let the multiple voices speak for themselves.

Intercultural Encounters: Aborigines and White Explorers in Fiction and Non-Fiction

Volker Raddatz

This chapter has a twofold objective. First, it is intended to be a study of Australian literary and cultural history; second, it has a methodological aim: the confrontation of two different text categories, fiction and non-fiction—Patrick White's *Voss* and Ludwig Leichhardt's *Journal of an overland expedition* published in 1847.

It is not my intention to subject the novel to the criteria of an historical document, to verify or falsify it against the background of the expedition journal. Such an attempt (as reflected in H. Orel's article 'Is Patrick White's "Voss" the real Leichhardt of Australia'?) would indeed violate fiction by ignoring its specific laws of artistically created 'reality' (in particular its handling of time, place, characters, and action) and would reduce it to a mere piece of historical evidence. On a less factual and down-to-earth level, however, it seems quite legitimate and worthwhile to confront these two kinds of texts with each other as a means of establishing joint findings on people's relationships, patterns of behaviour, attitudes, scale of values and, ultimately, their cultural affinities or differences. In view of such assumptions, it is of little significance that Patrick White, in all probability, did not base his novel on Leichhardt's first expedition (which will be my frame of reference), but on his third, foundered one.[1]

If you look at both texts with a comparison in mind, selection criteria need to be established. Obviously, only those themes can be considered which occur in both the novel and the journal. This excludes a number of potentially interesting subjects which are only manifest in one text and absent in the other, such as the many visionary passages in the novel (Le Mesurier, Voss, Laura Trevelyan, Belle Bonner) or its intended social criticism (Mr Bonner's philosophy of life),[2] and, regarding the journal, the wide range of scientific observations on plants, wildlife, geological and geographical features of the Australian North-East.

Bearing in mind these self-imposed restrictions, I have tried to distil the following themes from each text in terms of their frequency as well as their significance to the narrative and to the expedition itself:

1 The Aborigines
2 The nature of suffering
3 The environment
4 The leader

All these categories overlap, of course, and form a complex unity. So the relationship between man and his natural environment implies suffering and deprivation. This, in turn, frequently originates from the conflict between Aborigines and the white members of the expedition, but also from certain inadequacies in Leichhardt's leadership. Even the Aborigines do not represent a category of their own, as—in both texts—Brown and Charley or Jackie and Dugald have to divide their loyalty (if not identity) between the expedition and their tribal commitments.

Of all the categories found to be eligible, it is the intercultural encounter between Aborigines and whites which proves to be most relevant to the message of the novel and to the outcome of the expedition — quite apart from taking up much of the space in both texts.[3]

For a start, it could be said that the Leichhardt text reveals a range of potentially communicative patterns in progressive stages, beginning with Leichhardt's random observations of Aboriginal tracks, fireplaces, and campsites, proceeding to purely accidental encounters with the natives who mostly panic and try to escape, moving on to the stage of mutual recognition involving curiosity and fear, and concluding with genuinely communicative actions, such as physical contact, the exchange of presents, and even the odd 'parley'. It should be understood, however, that practically all these forms of communication are non-verbal, thus curiously corresponding to Voss's own remark: 'In general . . . it is necessary to communicate without knowledge of the language', which is somehow ironically complemented by a later statement in the novel: 'Language did not bother the black: that is to say, generally he would not listen' (*Voss* pp. 181, 294) It remains to be seen whether the leader is eventually able to meet his own requirements, to dispense with language and still communicate adequately. It is at this point that the vast number of intercultural misunderstandings prove significant to the whole study, as they represent communication in its negative, frustrated state.

If you apply the above stages to the novel, you will find that Patrick White does not seem much interested in the descriptive elements, in the merely factual, almost encyclopaedic account of Aboriginal lifestyle. Rather, he incorporates the Aborigines into the fabric of his novel which—as in practically all his work—contains visionary and metaphysical dimensions embracing all human existence. So, it is the more advanced and involved stage of intercultural encounters which he treats with utmost sensitivity: the physical and spiritual confrontations revealing the almost unintelligible and thus unbridgeable gap between the people concerned who evoke, on the one hand, the dreamtime myth and, on the other hand, the rather merciless rationality as part of the white man's upbringing. Embarrassment, comic relief, conflict, and tragedy are the immediate and long-term results of this cultural incompatibility. What, in Leichhardt's rather self-centred perception, appears to be a curious deviation from civilised 'normality', is to White the human ordeal in its fatal consequence. So Voss and his plight are much more a means to an end (i.e. man's suffering as a prerequisite to his ultimate self-awareness), whereas Leichhardt's expedition seems largely an end in itself.

The initial, mostly descriptive stages of intercultural encounters (which the novel lacks altogether) will be recorded from the journal in brief. There is a gradual progression from the superficiality of external glimpses to the minuteness of intimate observations. The objects of Leichhardt's curiosity are mainly those which represent the Aboriginal lifestyle (with the natives themselves still 'carefully out of sight'):[4] food, clothes, household items, hunting gear, accommodation, and various traces of ritual activities:

> The fire-places of the natives were here arranged in a straight line, and sheltered from the cold wind by dry branches: they were circular, the circumference was slightly raised, and the centre depressed and filled with pebbles, which the natives heat to cook their victuals. (*Journal* p. 382)
>
> The well-known tracks of Blackfellows are everywhere visible; such as trees recently stripped of their bark, the swellings of the apple-tree cut off to make vessels for carrying water, honey cut out, and fresh steps cut in the trees to climb for opossums. (*Journal* p. 9)

Subsequently, Leichhardt begins to take a closer look at the Aboriginal campsites, the *gunyahs*, which seem to be in abundance throughout the journey. The external construction features are described as 'two-storied' with 'four large forked sticks rammed into the ground' and an 'arched roof' (*Journal* p. 290). Once curiosity is awakened, Leichhardt ventures further into the interior of these dwellings. This gives rise to speculations about the staple food, eating habits, sleeping accommodation, tools and, ultimately, social structure of the Aborigines. It is especially the 'culinary department' which, probably because of the expedition's chronic food shortage, wins Leichhardt's attention:

> We then rode up to the camp, and found their dinner ready, consisting of two eggs of the brush turkey, roasted opossums, several roots or tubers of an oblong form, about an inch in length, and half an inch broad, of a sweet taste, and of an agreeable flavour, even when uncooked; there were also balls of pipe-clay to ornament their persons for corroborris. Good opossum cloaks, strewed about; there were also some spears . . . all were forgotten in the suddenness of their retreat. I could not resist the temptation of tasting one of the eggs, which was excellent. (*Journal* p. 89f.)

Let us now move on to the second stage of the encounters involving brief and superficial recognition of each other and showing signs of timidity, fear, or even downright horror on the part of the Aborigines. Here, the novel tends to yield instances of vaguely suggestive language, such as:

> Other figures were beginning to appear, their shadows first, followed by a suggestion of skin wedded to the trunk of a tree. Then, at the bend in the river's bed, the dusty bodies of men undoubtedly emerged. (*Voss* p. 204)
>
> During the morning a party of blacks appeared, first as shreds of

shy bark glimpsed between the trunks of the trees, but always drifting,
until, finally, they halted in human form upon the outskirts of the
camp. (*Voss* p. 218)

During the days that followed, mobs of blacks appeared to
accompany the expedition. Although the natives never showed themselves in strength, several dark skins at a time would flicker through
pale grass, or come to life amongst dead trees. (*Voss* p. 357)

Unlike the evasive quality of these poetical passages,
Leichhardt records his contacts with the natives most accurately
and with an intended realism, although it remains clear that his
intercultural accounts are invariably biased and distorted because of
his rather limited outlook, his inexperience as a bushman and,
above all, his inability to detach himself from his own cultural
background and attempt a genuine evaluation of his findings. To
start with, there are some fairly patronising statements on the physique of the Aborigines. Their faces are described as 'pleasing coun-
tenances', their figures as 'muscular and powerful', but with 'rather
slender bones'; generally, they are found to be 'well made, good
looking men', occasionally 'even handsome', such as 'a fine native
[who] stepped out of the forest with the ease and grace of an Apollo'
(*Journal* pp. 28, 110, 413, 502).

In painful contrast to these notions of harmony and perfection
(which evoke the topos of *noble savage*), the random encounters
between the two cultures show all the symptoms of ugly discord
ranging from secret suspicion to outright hostility:

As we approached the place of our encampment of the 12th February,
some Blackfellows were bathing in the water-hole, but fled as soon as
we made our appearance. (*Journal* p. 147)

We suddenly came upon two women cooking mussels, who ran off,
leaving their dinners to their unwelcome visitors. (*Journal* p. 188)

[A native] took to his heels, and fled in the greatest consternation.
(*Journal* p. 222)

... we saw a party of them, but they were too frightened to allow us
to approach. (*Journal* p. 241)

The following example comprises both the visual and the acoustical
aspect of the culture shock:

Mr Gilbert and Charley, when on a reconnoitring ride, met another
party of natives; among them two gins were so horror-struck at the
unwonted sight that they immediately fled into the scrub; the men
commenced talking to them, but occasionally interrupted their

speeches by spitting and uttering a noise like pooh! pooh! apparently expressive of their disgust. (*Journal* p. 189)

Gradually, fear and horror begin to be replaced by curiosity, so that signs of a two-way communication become more numerous, even though they may be short-lived:

> As we proceeded, we came suddenly upon two black women hurrying out of the water, but who, on reaching a distance in which they thought themselves safe, remained gazing at us as we slowly and peaceably passed by. (*Journal* p. 107)
> ... they had discovered our tracks, and followed them until they came in sight of the camp; but retired as soon as they saw us. (*Journal* p. 326)
> When we were preparing to start in the morning, some natives came to look at us; but they kept within the scrub, and at a respectable distance. (*Journal* p. 333)
> The natives cooeed from the other side of the river, probably to ascertain whether we were friendly or hostile; but did not shew themselves any farther. (*Journal* p. 488)

So much for brief encounters. Mutual recognition begins to develop into larger forms of confrontation showing a wide range of sensory perceptions, an increasing number of misunderstandings, and a limited awareness on Leichhardt's part of Aboriginal sentiments. In spite of his growing efforts to act in a considerate and benevolent way, most of his policies and decisions are still short-sighted and inadequate:

> Whilst riding along the bank of the river, we saw an old woman before us, walking slowly and thoughtfully through the forest, supporting her slender and apparently exhausted frame with one of those long sticks which the women use for digging roots; a child was running before her. Fearing she would be much alarmed if we came too suddenly upon her ... I cooeed gently; after repeating the call two or three times, she turned her head; in sudden fright she lifted her arms, and began to beat the air, as if to take wing,—then seizing the child, and shrieking most pitifully, she rapidly crossed the creek, and escaped to the opposite ridges. What could she think; but that we were some of those imaginary beings, with legends of which the wise men of her people frighten the children into obedience, and whose strange forms and stranger doings are the favourite topics of conversation amongst the natives at night when seated round their fires? (*Journal* p. 190f.)

For the first time, Leichhardt's personal account reveals an instance of intercultural appreciation and concern. All his subsequent precaution, however, is of little avail, as the woman displays the usual patterns of behaviour: she cries hysterically, throws up her arms, and runs away in panic. Even Leichhardt's attempt to identify himself with the woman's emotional turmoil does not reach the quality of ethnological insight, but rather embarrassingly remains within the framework of German fairy tales with their underlying element of intimidation.

A similar attitude can be observed when a native, mistaking his own campfire for that of the expedition, feels cornered by the whites and takes refuge to a tree which he nimbly climbs and then remains motionless between some dry branches 'like a strange phantom or a statue'. After some useless efforts to make him descend (ranging from patient appeasement to open threat including the use of a gun), Leichhardt begins to realise the inadequacy of his reactions and decides to withdraw, so that the Aboriginal may come down unnoticed, 'doubtless delighted at having escaped from the hands of the pale-faced anthropophagi' (*Journal* p. 322f.).

Although Leichhardt must be given credit for trying, both physically and mentally, to bridge the gap of intercultural ignorance, he unwittingly aggravates the problem by falling back, once again, on the theme of *Angst*. His reference to 'anthropophagi', that is, cannibals, originates from his own, distorted notion of the 'primitive' which he now projects into the Aboriginal's mind in a curious reversal of stereotypes.

With the exchange of presents we are about to enter the hitherto most advanced stage of intercultural encounters showing attempts at genuine communication sporadically interrupted by outbursts of hostilities. There is a fine example of the threshold-situation, of the tentative approach and ensuing failure to establish something more than just casual recognition. For the time being, such individual efforts are frustrated by the collective forces of cultural incongruities:

> As we were travelling along, a native suddenly emerged from the banks of the creek, and, crossing our line of march ... seemed inclined to hide himself until we had passed. I cooeed to him; at which he looked up, but seemed to be at a loss what to do or say. I then dismounted, and made signs to shew my friendly disposition: then he began to call out, but, seeing that I motioned away my companions with the horses and bullocks, as I moved towards him, and that I held out presents to him, he became more assured of his safety, and allowed me to come near and put some brass buttons into his hand. ... As, however, we were equally unintelligible to each

other, and he did not appear to be very communicative, I mounted my cream-coloured horse, and left him staring at me in silence until I was out of sight. (*Journal* p. 466f.)

This passage contains several references to the delicacy of Leichhardt's endeavour which remains an abortive attempt to bring about some kind of conscious and mutual recognition. The dilemma is expressed by phrases like: 'inclined to hide himself', 'to be at a loss', 'unintelligible to each other', 'did not appear to be very communicative', 'staring at me'. Similar instances can be found throughout the journal, e.g. 'suspicion', 'precaution', 'confusion', 'aversion', 'shyness', 'watchfulness', 'avoidance' (*Journal* pp. 63, 109, 162, 179, 188, 358, 403).[5]

Before going further into the exchange of presents, we must briefly refer to Leichhardt's habit of taking certain items of Aboriginal property—mostly household accessories—from their hurriedly abandoned campsites and leaving items of his choice as compensation, objects which he finds dispensable for the expedition. This policy has aroused considerable controversy about his character:

He also had a habit of stealing food and nets from their camps when the Aborigines fled in surprise at his arrival. (In the early stages he left trinkets in exchange for the items he took, but the Aborigines probably didn't understand or appreciate this gesture. Later, he seemed not to have bothered about making a 'fair exchange'.)[6]

What is interesting here is not so much the moral or legal aspect, but the cultural one, the adequacy or inadequacy of the objects exchanged. On one occasion, Leichhardt takes two kangaroo nets and leaves behind 'a fine brass-hilted sword, the hilt of which was well polished, four fishing hooks, and a silk handkerchief; with which, I felt convinced, they would be as well pleased as I was with the cordage of their nets'. Next, he picks up two calabashes, 'leaving in their place a bright penny, for payment'. Another time, he notices three koolimans (vessels of stringybark) full of honey water, 'from one of which I took a hearty draught, and left a brass button for payment'. Later again, he discovers more koolimans, this time full of bee bread, 'of which I partook, leaving for payment some spare nose rings of our bullocks' (*Journal* pp. 45, 162, 269, 279).

Whereas, so far, rather one-sided transactions have been recorded (which, as some scholars would maintain, occasionally amounted to theft), the focus will now be on the actual exchange of presents with both parties remaining on site. A few examples will suffice to show the haphazard and often ludicrous way in which some form of mutual reassurance was sought to be established:

> The natives had, in my absence, visited my companions, and behaved very quietly, making them presents of Emu feathers, boomerangs, and waddies. Mr Phillips gave them a medal of the coronation of Her Majesty Queen Victoria, which they seemed to prize very highly. (*Journal* p. 166)

Apart from their obvious irrelevance, 'presents' of such arbitrary choice could even have an adverse, intimidating effect on the recipient:

> ... I went down to them, and gave them a horn of one of our slaughtered bullocks. Roper had saved the mane of his horse and threw it over to them, but it seemed to frighten them very much ... They threw some yam-roots over to us, the plant of which we were not able to ascertain. (*Journal* p. 248f.)

Other random articles included leather belts, tin canisters, iron nose rings, broken pieces of iron, horse nails, even a geological hammer on the part of the expedition—and goose feathers, fruit, red ochre, ornaments on the part of the Aborigines, not to forget their valuable advice on the existence of drinking water and on the itinerary in general.

Here is a rare example of an intercultural encounter which, although taking place at close quarters, does not show the usual strain of suspicion, fear, and misunderstanding on either side:

> ... I dismounted and advanced slowly to have a parley, and was met by an old man with three or four young fellows behind him. As soon as he saw that I intended to make him a present, he prepared one in return; and when I gave him some rings and buckles, he presented me with some of the ornaments he wore on his person. As our confidence in each other was thus established some of my companions and several others of the natives came up, and we exchanged presents in a very amicable manner. (*Journal* p. 413)

In spite of some hostilities (one resulting in the death of John Gilbert), a progression of communicative patterns can be observed leading to short-term cooperation and even to hilarious scenes of fraternisation. Ignorance, which has often been the source of alienation, turns into unrestrained curiosity entailing a good deal of fun and laughter:[7]

> We encamped at this pool, and the natives flocked round us from every direction. ... They observed, with curious eye, everything we

did, and made long explanations to each other of the various objects presented to their gaze. Our eating, drinking, dress, skin, combing, boiling, our blankets, straps, horses, everything in short, was new to them, and was earnestly discussed, particularly by one of the old men, who amused us with his drollery and good humour in trying to persuade each of us to give him something. (*Journal* p. 494f.)

In contrast to the lucky outcome of Leichhardt's expedition, Voss' venture appears to be doomed right from the start through to its disastrous end. This is not just because Patrick White, historically, refers' to the third, vanished expedition, but also because, artistically, he presents the Aborigines as an alien and mysterious threat to the explorer, who is ultimately sacrificed by them. Both cultures, in their numerous confrontations, not only remain totally incomprehensible to each other, but also lack the awareness of their incompatibility to an even higher degree than any passage from Leichhardt's journal could possibly suggest. Unlike the real Leichhardt's many clumsy but not quite useless efforts to establish at least some kind of makeshift rapport with the natives on daily issues such as food, clothing, or weapons, Voss finds himself engrossed in a drawn-out struggle against the supernatural. Devoid of any common sense, and also conspicuously lacking in humour (which invariably turns into sarcasm), his encounters with the Aborigines tend to assume an evasive quality. This becomes obvious at the first meeting between Voss and his two native assistants, Jackie and Dugald. In a rather naive attempt to promote each other's recognition and secure the natives' loyalty, the leader adopts his patronising stance and hands over a present of the most unintelligible kind which, to the Aborigines, appears as mystical as some object of native ritual would have appeared to the white man:

> So he got down from his shaky step, and advanced on the old black with his rather stiff, habitual gait and said: 'This is for Dugald.' It was a brass button that he happened to have in his pocket ... The old man was very still, holding the token with the tips of his fingers, as if dimly aware in himself of an answer to the white man's mysticism. He could have been a thinking stick ... The youth, on the other hand, had been brought to animal life. Lights shone in his skin, and his throat was rippling with language. He was giggling and gulping. He could have eaten the brass button. (*Voss* p. 182f.)

Instead of gaining the desired affection, Voss's message is either misunderstood (Jackie) or becomes lost in the vastness and vagueness of the Aboriginal's mind (Dugald). Naturally, the leader resents the 'ingratitude' and feels rebuffed by the natives. On similar lines, such painful embarrassment is experienced by Voss in one of the crucial scenes of intercultural misunderstanding when both the spiritual and the material presents (handshake/bag of flour) fail to be appreciated:

> 'Here is my hand in friendship.' At first the blackfellow was reluctant, but then took the hand as if it had been some inanimate object of barter, and was turning it over, examining its grain, the patterns of veins, and, on its palm, the lines of fate. It was obvious that he could not estimate its value. Each of the white men was transfixed by the strangeness of this ceremony. It would seem that all human relationships hung in the balance, subject to fresh evaluation by Voss and the black. Then the native dropped the hand. There was too much here for him to accept. Although something of this nature had been expected by his companions, Voss appeared somewhat saddened by the reception his gesture had received. 'They are at that stage when they can only appreciate material things', he said in some surprise. It was he who was in the wrong, to expect of his people—for as such he persisted in considering them—more than they were capable of giving, and, acknowledging his mistake, he promptly instructed the boy to fetch a bag of flour.
> . . . The blacks were chattering, and plunging their hands into the flour, and giving floury smiles. Then they swooped upon the bag, and departed through the valley, laughing . . . One old woman was seizing handfuls of the flour and pouring it upon her head. She stood there, for a moment, in veils of flour, an ancient bride, and screamed because it tickled . . . Such an abuse could have been felt most keenly by Voss, the benefactor. (*Voss* p. 219f.)

Whereas, so far, Voss has only felt the disturbing consequences of his self-centred disposition, his very nature eventually precipitates his tragic death. Again, it is the enigma of a formal handshake with its many implications that is used to illustrate the fatal gap between the two cultures. Towards the end of the novel, when Jackie is about to abandon the expedition in order to join an Aboriginal tribe, Voss makes a last effort to reconcile the two parties:

> 'I am a friend of the blackfellow. Do you understand? This is the sign of friendship.' The white man took the boy's hot, black, right hand in both his, and was pressing. A wave of sad, warm magic, and yearning for things past, broke over the blackfellow, but because the withered hands of the white man were physically feeble, even if warm and spiritually potent, the boy wrenched his hand away . . . Then Jackie, whose position was obviously intolerable, raised his eyes, and said: 'No good, Mr Voss.' (*Voss* p. 389)[8]

To give a final impression of the complexity of intercultural (mis-) understanding, some typical value judgements on the natives will be recorded, as they frequently occur in both texts. Leaving aside sarcastic jokes and downright obscenities,[9] comparatively sober statements on the subject of reliability have been selected, evidently a question of great importance to the members of an expedition. When looking at these statements, it is sometimes difficult to draw the line between unconscious prejudice (as a result of ignorance) and the conscious refusal to acknowledge the characteristics of Aboriginal culture (e.g. the different notion of time, or the absence of individual responsibility in the tribal structure). So, when introducing Voss to his black companions, the station owner adds a word of warning:

'I cannot recommend these blacks as infallible guides and reliable companions,' Mr Boyle was saying. 'Like all aboriginals they will blow with the wind, or turn into lizards when they are bored with their existing shapes. But these two fellers do know the tribes and the country for a considerable distance to the west. Or so they tell a man. Standards of truth, of course, vary.' (*Voss* p. 181)

This general verdict is manifest throughout the novel. Particularly when objects are missing (livestock, equipment), it is the natives who become the immediate suspects. In the case of a lost compass, Judd, the ex-convict (!), concludes: 'These blacks would thieve any mortal thing, I would not be surprised,' (*Voss* p. 194). On another occasion, when Jackie has left the camp to search for missing cattle, Ralph Angus slightingly accuses him of having forsaken the expedition and is quick to add: 'These blacks are all alike . . . In no circumstances are they to be relied upon' (*Voss* p. 303).

Again, the Leichhardt text is minute, alive with interesting details, and yet symptomatic of the inability to judge a different culture by standards other than one's own.[10] Consequently, Leichhardt's approval is limited to the Aborigines' physical qualities, such as their 'wonderful power of sight', the 'wonderful quickness and accuracy' of their memory, or their 'wonderful agility' (*Journal* pp. 5, 118, 269). Harsh criticism, however, is directed against their lack of respect and reliability. Twice, Leichhardt describes his anger and disappointment at being kept waiting by his two black assistants who, instead of helping him reconnoitre, have gone to procure honey and opossums for themselves (*Journal* pp. 71, 144f.). As to their supposed lack of respect, probably the best example is the fierce argument between Leichhardt and Charley involving physical violence on the part of the Aborigine.[11]

In spite of this and other painful experiences, Leichhardt, rather condescendingly, professes to be well acquainted with the Aboriginal character:

> ... my frequent intercourse with the natives of Australia had taught me to distinguish easily between the smooth tongue of deceit, with which they try to ensnare their victim, and the open expression of kind and friendly feelings, or those of confidence and respect. I remember several instances of the most cold-blooded smooth-tongued treachery, and of the most extraordinary gullibility of the natives; but I am sure that a careful observer is more than a match for these simple children of nature and that he can easily read the bad intention in their unsteady, greedy, glistening eyes. (*Journal* p. 506f.)

Summing up, it has become clear that—irrespective of the many differences between fiction and non-fiction—both texts illustrate the magnitude of problems as regards intercultural encounters. Leichhardt's journal is full of valuable observations which are, however, limited to encyclopaedic details. As far as communication patterns with the natives are concerned, he follows a course of trial-and-error, unable to perceive and assess the indigenous culture on its own merits. Patrick White's novel, on the other hand, attempts to grasp the Aborigines in a more spiritual way, thus probably doing them greater justice, but also driving home the message of incompatibility. In both texts, it is the frame of mind, rather than the technical equipment, which proves inadequate to the task. The ventures by Leichhardt and Voss may have succeeded in geographical or psychological terms, but in terms of cultural awareness they must be considered—perhaps inevitably—a failure.

241

NOTES

Introduction

1. Note Johannes H. Voigt, ed. (1983) *New Beginnings. The Germans in New South Wales and Queensland*, Stuttgart: Institute for Foreign Cultural Relations, select bibliography pp. 282–286.
2. This list does not claim to be comprehensive: Bardenhagen, M.E. (1988) *Lilydale. A German Legacy* Launceston; Bodi, L. and Jeffries, S. (1985) *The German Connection. Sesquicentenary Essays on German-Victorian Crosscurrents 1835–1985* Melbourne: Department of German, Monash University; Corkhill, A. 'The German Influence in Queensland', *Generation*, 5/1, 1982, 3–9, 'The Image of Queensland in the Writings of German-born Authors Stefan von Kotze and Rudolf de Haas' *LinQ*, 14/1, 1986, 12–22, 'Friedrich Gerstäcker in Australia: An Appraisal of his Fictional Writings' in *Outrider*, 3/2, 1986, 164–72, 'German Settlement in Queensland 1838–1939' in *The Australian People* ed. J. Jupp (Sydney: Angus and Robertson, 1988) 486–87, *Antipodean Encounters, Australia and the German Literary Imagination 1754–1918* (Bern: Lang 1990), xix, p. 273; Fewster, K. (1984) ' "Shut up!" die Zensurpolitik und die Haltung der Bevölkerung gegenüber feindlichen Ausländern in Australien 1914–1918' in Hüppauf, B. ed. *Ansichten vom Krieg, Vergleichende Studien zum Ersten Weltkrieg in Literatur und Gesellschaft* Königstein: Athenäum; Goth, H.J. and Thümling B.B. *100 JAHRE CONCORDIA CLUB LTD. DEUTSCHER VEREIN* Sydney: Concordia Club; Harmstorf. I. and Cigler, M. (1985) *The Germans in Australia* Melbourne: AE Press; Harmstorf, I. and Schwerdtfeger, P. (1988) *THE GERMAN EXPERIENCE OF AUSTRALIA 1833–1938* Australian Association of von Humboldt Fellows; Fischer G. (1989) *Enemy Aliens. INTERNMENT AND THE HOMEFRONT EXPERIENCE IN AUSTRALIA 1914–1920* University of Queensland Press; Jürgensen, M. and Corkhill, A. eds. (1988) *The Germans Presence in Queensland* University of Queensland: Department of German; Kwiet, K. (1985) ' "Be patient and reasonable!" The internment of German-Jewish refugees in Australia' *The Australian Journal of Politics and History* vol. 31 No 1 pp. 61–77; Lack, J., Ohles F. and Tampke, J. eds. (1990) *The Workers' Paradise? Robert Schachner's Letters From Australia 1906–1907* Melbourne University History Monograph Series No. 12; Moses, J.A. 'Imperial Germany Priorities in New Guinea 1885–1914' in S. Latufeku (ed.) *Papua New Guinea: A Century of Colonial Impact, 1884–1984* Port Moresby: University of Papua New Guinea Press, 1889, pp. 163–177, 'Isidor Siegfried Lissner 1832–1902 in Max Brändle (ed.) *The Queensland Experience: The Life and Work of Fourteen Remarkable Migrants* Brisbane: Phoenix Publications, 1991, pp. 27–48, *Prussian-German Militarism 1914–1918 in Australian Perspective: The Thought of George Arnold Wood,* Berne: Peter Lang Publishers, 1991 pp. 220; Meyer, C. (1982) 'The Germans in Victoria' (1848–1900)' *JRAHS* 68, 1, pp. 18–36; Overlack, P. (1984) 'German settlers in the Moreton Bay Region, 1838–1914' *The Journal of the Royal Historical Society of Queensland* 12, 1 pp. 103–118; Perkins, J., and Tampke, J. (1985) 'The Convicts Who Never Arrived' *The Push from the Bush* 19, (1986) 'German Liberal Intellectuals and Australian Socialism before the First World War' *JRAHS* vol. 71, 4, pp. 255–67, (1986) 'Two pastors and their flock', *Royal Historical Society of Queensland Journal* vol. XII, No. 5 pp. 379–87; Proeve, H.F.W. (1983) *A Dwelling-Place at Bethany* Adelaide, Lutheran Publishing House; Roderick, C. (1986) 'New Light on Leichhardt' *JRAHS* vol. 72, 3, pp. 166–190; (1988) *MISKA HAUSER'S*

Letters from Australia 1854–1858 Maryborough: Red Rooster Press; (1988) *Leichhardt, The Dauntless Explorer* Sydney: Angus and Robertson; Seidler, H. (1985) *Internment. The Diaries of Harry Seidler* Sydney: Allen and Unwin; Sluga, Glenda (1988) *Bonegilla, 'A Place Of No Hope'* Melbourne University History Monograph Series; Smith, Jim (1990) *The Blue Mountains Mystery Track Lindemann Pass* Winmalee: Three Sisters Production; Tipping, M. *(1984) An Australian Song, Ludwig Becker's Protest* Melbourne: Greenhouse; Veit-Brause, I. (1986) 'German-Australian Relations at the Time of the Centennial International Exhibition, Melbourne, 1888' *AJPH* 32, 2, pp. 201–216; Voigt J. (1988) *Australia-Germany, Two Hundred Years of Contacts, Relations and Connections* Bonn: Inter Nationes; Webster, E.M. (1984) *Whirlwind in the Plain* Melbourne University Press; Winter, Barbara (1986) *Stalag Australia, German Prisoners of War in Australia* Sydney: Angus and Robertson.

3. Tampke, J. and Doxford, C. (1990) *Australia Willkommen, a History of the Germans in Australia* New South Wales University Press.

Chapter 3. Georg von Neumayer and the Flagstaff Observatory

This paper could not have been written without the friendly cooperation and assistance of Herr Hans-Jochen Kretzer, curator of the Neumayer-Archiv at the Pfalz Museum für Naturkunde, Bad Dürkheim, to whom I offer grateful thanks.

1. Not Kirchenbolanden, as several Australian sources, including the *Australian Dictionary of Biography*, would have it.
2. 'Mein Prüfungsjahr', published as an appendix, pp. 51–75, to Kretzer *Windrose und Südpol*. Several other accounts of Neumayer's life and work have been published in addition to Kretzer's, the most relevant being Günther 'Georg von Neumayer'; Wislicenus 'Georg v. Neumayers Wirken'; Ross 'Our Observatory'; Heidke 'Neumayer als Deutscher und Gelehrter'; Paulus 'Neumayer als Förderer der Schiffahrt;' and obituaries in *Naturwissenschaftlichen Rundschau* 24, 1909 (by W. Köppen), *Mitteilungen der Geographischen Gesellschaft in Hamburg* 24, 1909, pp.287–97 (by L. Friederichsen), and *Vierteljahresschrift des Astronomischen Gesellschaft* 45, 1910, pp. 10–42 (by C. Stechert). These accounts do not agree among themselves on all details, so in constructing the present one, recourse has been had to original sources wherever possible.
3. Neumayer to Chief Secretary, Victoria, 15 June 1857, Public Record Office, Victoria, Series 1189, Box 744, B57/4287; Neumayer 'Ein deutscher Seemann'
4. Humboldt to Neumayer, June 1854, La Trobe Library, published in Fletcher 'Humboldt-Briefe in Australien'; Neumayer to Godeffroy, 26 August 1856, published in Wiederkehr 'Die Hamburgische Seefahrt'; Neumayer to Chief Secretary, Victoria, 15 June 1857 (note 3). Cf. Maury's *Wind and Current Charts* (1848–) and his *The Physical Geography of the Sea* New York, 1855. In contrast to Liebig, Humboldt proved unwilling to become an advocate for Neumayer's project; see Wiederkehr and Schröder 'Georg von Neumayers geophysikalisches Projekt'
5. Neumayer 'Bericht über die Erfolge . . .'
6. Smyth to W.B. Clarke, 6 August and 29 October 1857 and 9 September 1858, Clarke papers, Mitchell Library. On Smyth, see Hoare 'The Half-Mad Bureaucrat'.
7. *Der Kosmopolit* (Melbourne) 1 September 1857, p. 323, Public Record Office, Victoria, Series 1189, Box 744, A57/6210 and B57/4338; Neumayer 'Bericht über die Erfolge . . .'
8. Neumayer *Results of the Magnetical, Nautical and Meteorological Observations . . .* p.iv
9. *Transactions and Proceedings of the Royal Society of Victoria* 6, 1861–64, p.xlix
10. Neumayer *Results of the and Meteorological Observations . . .* ; *Discussion of the*

Meteorological and Magnetical Observations . . . ; *Results of the Magnetic Survey* . . .
11. Cannon *Science in Culture* ch. 3
12. Maury *Wind and Current Charts*; Spoehr *White Falcon*; Neumayer *Results of the Meteorological Observations* . . . pp.314–30, 339–43
13. Neumayer 'On Dove's Law . . .'
14. Gibbs *Origins of Australian Meteorology* p.21
15. Neumayer *Results of the Meteorological Observations* p.143
16. Cawood 'Magnetic Crusade'
17. Sabine 'On Periodical Laws . . .'; Savours and McConnell 'History of Rossbank Observatory'. It is frequently stated that Neumayer worked for a time at the Rossbank Observatory during his first visit to Australia. Since he was himself under the misapprehension, however, that the Observatory closed in 1849 (*Auf zum Südpol* p.5), it is clear that he did not.
18. Neumayer *Auf zum Südpol* p.4; Neumayer to Chief Secretary, Victoria, 15 June 1857; Neumayer 'Description and System of Working . . .' p.100
19. Dooley 'Centenary of Melbourne-Toolangi Magnetic Observatory'
20. Neumayer to Chief Secretary, Victoria, 15 June 1857
21. Neumayer *Results of the Magnetic Survey* . . . , passim
22. Home 'First Physicist of Australia'
23. The setting up of geodetic surveys in the different colonies, based in each case on the local observatory, was another important factor here.

Chapter 4. Amalie Dietrich

1. There are many editions of Charitas Bischoff's *Amalie Dietrich. Ein Leben*. It first appeared in Berlin in 1909. References here are to the 1980 edition cited in the bibliography. Although the book has been shown elsewhere to be notably unreliable in factual and scientific information on Amalie Dietrich in Australia, Bischoff does provide insight into Amalie's life in Germany and into her thoughts, emotions and behaviour.
2. ibid. pp.69–70
3. ibid. p.53
4. ibid. pp.106–9
5. ibid. pp.114–15
6. ibid. p.119
7. ibid. pp.121–22
8. ibid. p.128
9. ibid. p.123
10. ibid. p.133
11. ibid. pp.138–48
12. ibid. p.182. Bischoff suggests (pp.184–86) that Amalie also visited Wilhelm to bid farewell, but this episode is unlikely.
13. For dates see Sumner 'Amalie Dietrich. A German Naturalist in Queensland'
14. A trip to Cape York was proposed but did not take place.
15. Bischoff *Amalie Dietrich* pp.57–58
16. ibid. pp.32–33
17. ibid. p.65
18. This had been the sense used by Linnaeus (1707–1778), the great founder of natural history, who had believed that his systematic classification and scheme of binomial nomenclature would enable him to encompass, and comprehend, the whole of nature.
19. Bischoff writes as if this were for Amalie a late marriage, but recent research shows that many of her contemporaries also married at that age (G. Steinecke, pers. comm.). Charitas herself also married at 25.

20. Yet Charitas was apparently named after Wilhelm's beloved aunt who cared for him after his mother's early death.
21. Bischoff *Bilder aus meinem Leben*. It is possible that Bischoff herself felt some pangs of conscience and hoped to redress some of the wrong impressions conveyed by the earlier book. It is more likely that she had been reproached by former friends of her mother. In fact even while she strives for melodramatic effect in recounting her youth, Bischoff allows enough detail to appear so that a dispassionate reader sees that she had a childhood of great interest, variety and considerable freedom with her different, clever and loving parents.
22. Bischoff *Bilder* p.94. See note 40 re Reum.
23. Müller remained a close friend of Amalie and an admirer of her work throughout her life. We return to the connection later.
24. Naturkundemuseum, Freiberg; Staatsbibliothek preussischer Kulturbesitz, Berlin (this letter wrongly attributed to Amalie Dietrich)
25. Gertraud Enderlien, quoted by G. Wirth, *Nachwort* to 1980 edition of *Amalie Dietrich* p.306
26. *Catalogue of the Hunt Botanical Collection* vol. 2, part 2, 1961, p.99; Blunt *Art of Botanical Illustration* pp.127–29
27. Bischoff *Amalie Dietrich* pp.15–16
28. Barber *Heyday of Natural History* ch. 9
29. North *Recollections of a Happy Life*; *A Vision of Eden*
30. Rowan *A Flower Hunter*; Hazzard *Australia's brilliant daughter*
31. For example, Moyal 'Collectors and Illustrators'
32. For a list of Ida Pfeiffer's books see the bibliography.
33. Lebzelter *Die österreichische Weltreisende Ida Pfeiffer*
34. Humboldt *Kosmos*. The second reference is from Dr G. Wirth, Berlin, pers. comm.
35. Pfeiffer *Eine Frauenfahrt*, quoted in Lebzelter p.46
36. Bischoff *Bilder* p.109
37. Bischoff *Amalie Dietrich* p.150
38. Meyer *Erinnerungen an Dr. H.A. Meyer*
39. Bischoff *Amalie Dietrich* p.171
40. Sumner 'Amalie Dietrich and Queensland Botany'. Bischoff records that Professor Rheum also visited her parents. Presumably she means Johann Adam Reum (1780–1839), whose date of death makes this impossible.
41. *Isis* 1880 (Jahrgang 1879), pp.98–104. Reichenbach's son, Heinrich Gustav Reichenbach (1793–1879) also knew Amalie much later in Hamburg. He identified a number of her Australian plants for the Museum Godeffroy catalogue *Neuholländische Pflanzen* (1866).
42. Sumner, Amalie Dietrich in Australia, p.250; *Museum Godeffroy Catalog V* 1874, pp.xxv–xxvi
43. Bischoff *Amalie Dietrich* p.203
44. ibid. p.28. This may be a literary invention by Bischoff, not a true recollection.
45. ibid. p.191
46. ibid. p.203
47. Koch *Die Arachniden Australiens*
48. Sumner 'Amalie Dietrich and the Taipan' pp.262–68

Chapter 5. Robert von Lendenfeld: biologist, alpinist and scholar

1. I thank Professor Randolf Menzel, Robert von Lendenfeld's great-grandson, for introducing me to von Lendenfeld's book. He also generously supplied me with the unpublished biographical details of his great-grandfather.
2. von Lendenfeld *Australische Reise*

3. von Lendenfeld *Forschungreisen in den Australischen Alpen*
4. von Lendenfeld *Results of the examination . . .*
5. Ziegler *Snowy Saga*
6. von Lendenfeld *Forschungreisen in den Australischen Alpen*
7. Ziegler *Snowy Saga*
8. Klaus and Teichmann 'Townsend, not Kosciusko'

Chapter 6. Ludwig Becker and Eugène von Guérard: German artists and the Aboriginal habitat

1. Nicolas Baudin to Governor Philip Gidley King, 23 December 1802, in *Historical Records of New South Wales* V, Sydney, 1897, p.830. Baudin referred to the land 'inhabited by men who have not always deserved the title of savages or cannibals . . . while they were but the children of nature and just as little civilised as are actually your Scottish Highlanders or our peasants of Brittany . . .'
2. Peron *Voyage of Discovery* p.312
3. ibid. p.313
4. Guérard signed his name in several ways, but mostly in the French manner. His father had come from a French Huguenot family which had originally fled to Dusseldorf, and he himself had migrated to Australia with a party of Frenchmen. However, he always regarded himself as German rather than French or Australian.
5. Abstracts of these were published in *British Association Reports* part 2, July–August 1850, pp.72–74
6. Denison *Varieties of Vice-Regal Life* p.170
7. These are in the La Trobe Library.
8. See Tipping 'Portrait of William Buckley' pp.87–91.
9. 'Meteorological Observations at Bendigo' in *Trans. of Phil. Soc. of Vic. 1* (Melb., 1855, p.90)
10. 'Notabilities of Bendigo' in *Newsletter of Australasia* 15, September 1857, p.1
11. Eugène von Guérard's diary, 16 March 1854, Mitchell Library MS. The diary was first published and edited by Tipping in *An Artist on the Goldfields*.
12. Several of these sketches and paintings have been published in Tipping, *An Artist on the Goldfields*.
13. Becker *Men of Victoria* (opposite Plate 2)
14. See Tipping 'Becker's portraits of Billy and Jemmy'.
15. *Catalogue of the Melbourne Exhibition 1854 in connection with the Paris Exhibition 1855* Melbourne, 1854, Item 294; Melbourne *Herald* 9 December 1856
16. *Report of the Select Committee of the Legislative Council on the Aborigines* Melbourne, 1859, p.88
17. *Report of the Select Committee of the House of Commons into the condition of Aboriginal peoples throughout the British colonies*, tabled 6 June 1837. This report was most critical of conditions in Australia, especially of circumstances surrounding the conduct of Major Thomas Mitchell's men during their expedition to Australia Felix.
18. It is interesting to note that William Strutt's origins and education were not entirely British. His paternal ancestors (named Strutz) were German-Swiss and his artistic training was at the Ecole des Beaux Arts, Paris.
19. See Bonwick *Wild White Man* p.30
20. *Report of the Select Committee of the Legislative Council* pp.88–89
21. ibid. p.82
22. ibid. See also Becker's statement at a meeting on 8 September 1858 of the Philosophical Institute of Victoria in its *Transactions* 3, 21: 'Our own aborigines in Australia are of a much higher class than is usually and wrongly stated in works treating of the same subject.'
23. These are in several collections but have been brought together in Carroll and

Tregenza *Eugène von Guérard's South Australia*. See also Whitelaw *Australian Landscape Drawings*, a catalogue of the National Gallery of Victoria.

24. A facsimile of his work, together with an extensive biography and notes, appears in Tipping *Eugène von Guérard's Australian Landscapes*.

25. *Transactions of the Philosophical Society of New South Wales* Sydney, 1866. Becker sketched the corroboree, drawn on wood by Nicholas Chevalier, which appeared in the *News Letter of Australasia* 12, June 1857 and in other publications.

26. Blandowski had presented his 'Preliminary Report on Recent Discoveries in Natural History on the Lower Murray' at a meeting of the Philosophical Institute of Victoria on 2 September 1857. The Institute refused to publish the derogatory remarks on his colleagues. He left Australia in March 1859. See Krefft papers, Mitchell Library. See also Pescott *Collections of a century*.

27. *Melbourne Punch* 7 August 1856, p.4. See also Tipping *An Australian Song*.

28. 300 drawings, identified as the work of Blandowski, are in the zoological department of the Museum for Natural Science at Humboldt University. They comprise watercolour paintings and pencil drawings, mostly of reptiles, amphibians, molluscs, starfish and insects, all made on the Lake Boga expedition. Some were labelled 'Yarree! Yarree!'. Most were in a scruffy condition, but Becker's animals and birds have been preserved. The Palaeontology Museum in Berlin also holds a folder with drawings and geological objects.

29. All these sketches as well as his scientific reports of the expedition are in the Royal Society collection, La Trobe Library, and have been published in Tipping *Ludwig Becker*.

30. Neumayer *Results of the Magnetic Survey* . . . pp.10–11

31. ibid. p.12

32. See Tipping, *Ludwig Becker* p.190

33. Letter from Alfred Howitt to his sister Anna Maria Howitt, 24 December 1860. Howitt Papers, La Trobe Library

34. *Australian Landscapes* plate IV

35. See note 24.

Chapter 7. In Search of Carl Strehlow: Lutheran Missionary and Australian Anthropologist

I wish to thank Professor John Mulwaney and Dr Kingsley Rowan for their generous supply of manuscript material and critical advice concerning Baldwin Spencer; the Rev. Dr W. Metzner for access to missionary instructions; Professor Diane Bell and Professor Hans-Peter Koepping for guidance in matters anthropological; Dr T. Darragh and Ms Gay Sculthorpe, of the National Museum of Victoria, for kind assistance with the Spencer Collection.

1. The bibliography of Carl Strehlow's publications is still sketchy. The titles given in the bibliography are as much as could be verified. His anthropological publications started with the 1907 article in *Globus*, introduced in the preceding issue by Leonhardi's article. I would like to thank Prof. Barry Blake, Dr Peter Austin and Ms Jenny Green for the translation of the Dieri and Aranda book titles. See Madigan's *Central Australia* and Mulvaney and Calaby's *'So much that is new'* for further material on Strehlow's biography.

2. See Scherer 'Death on "The Line" ', a reconstruction of the events leading up to Strehlow's death in 1922. It should probably be read in defence of the role played by Pastor Johann Julius Stolz and the administration of the Lutheran Church of Australia with regard to the failed rescue mission of which Ted Strehlow is very critical in *Journey to Horseshoe Bend*. There is a critical reply to Scherer by Pastor

John Sabel, 'Damned with Faint Praise' in *Forum* 69 (1974), which I did not see. See also the assessment of the controversy by Ward McNally in *Aborigines, Artefacts and Anguish* pp.156–57.
3. Elkin, A.P."Development of Scientific Knowledge of the Aborigines," in Shiels, H. ed. 1963. *Australian Aboriginal Studies*. A Symposium of Papers Presented to the 1961 Research Conference. Published for the Australian Institute of Aboriginal Studies. Melbourne: OUP; p.13
4. Mulvaney, D.J. "Australasian Anthropology and ANZAAS: 'Strictly Scientific and Critical'," in McLeod, R. ed. 1988 *The Commonwealth of Science, ANZAAS and the Scientific Enterprise in Australasia 1888–1988*. Melbourne: OUP; p.5
5. Mulvaney, D.J. "Australian Aborigines 1606–1929: Opinion and Fieldwork," in *Historical Studies. Australia and New Zealand*. vol. 8 Nrs. 29–32 (Nov. 1957—May 1959) University of Melbourne, 1959; Part 1 pp. 131–151; Part 2 pp. 297–314; see also Hays, H.R. 1958 *From Ape to Angel. Informal History of Social Anthropology*.Westport, Conn.: Greenwood Press
6. Mulvaney, D.J. and Calaby, J.H. 1985 *'So much that is new.' Baldwin Spencer 1860 – 1929. A Biography*. Melbourne: MUP; p. 392
7. Mulvaney and Calaby, *'So much that is new*. p.393
8. Mulvaney and Calaby, *'So much that is new*. p.393
9. T.G.H. Strehlow *Songs of Central Australia* pp.xv–xvi
10. Mulvaney *'So much that is new'* p.329
11. For further material on the Aborigines, see several reviews in the journal *Folklore*, between 1905 and 1927.
12. Elkin in Shiels, H. ed. 1963 *Australian Aboriginal Studies*. p.257
13. Catherine H. Berndt 'Art and Aesthetic Expression' in Sheils, H. ed *Australian Aboriginal Studies* Melbourne, OUP pp 256–288
14. T.G.H. Strehlow *Songs of Central Australia* p.xxi
15. vol. 2, p.589
16. Mulvaney and Calaby, *'So much that is new.'* p.394
17. Strehlow, C. 1907, *Die Aranda- und Loritja-Stämme in Zentral-Australien*. vol. 1, pp.I–II
18. Gunson *Australian Reminiscences of L.E. Threlkeld* pp.178–80
19. See also Mountford *Nomads of the Australian Desert* p.53, note 12: 'We have not used the word "Dream-time" in this book. It is a term adopted by Spencer and Gillen (1927, p.592) to refer to the creation period. This particularly apt word is now being used by ethnologists under the impression that it is of Aboriginal origin. In fact, many of them are using it as a cliché to express a wide range of meanings, some being totally ridiculous.'
20. Strehlow, *Die Aranda- und Loritja-Stämme*. vol. 1 p.I
21. Nida *Customs and Cultures* p.223
22. ibid. p.222
23. Smith *Art as information* pp.11–12
24. Stanner, W.H.E. 1979, *'White man got no dreaming.' Essays 1938–1973*. Canberra: ANU Press; p.113
25. ibid.
26. Carl Strehlow *Die Aranda- und Loritja-Stämme* [presumably this is what is referred to] p.78
27. Aufhauser, Joh. Bapt. 1932, *Umweltbeeinflussung der christlichen Mission*. München: Hueber; p.18
28. Keysser, Chr. 1.1929, 2.1950 *Eine Papuagemeinde*. Kassel: Bärenreiter-Verlag. Neuendettelsauer Missionschriften Nr. 65; p.317
29. ibid. p.332
30. ibid. p.325
31. ibid. p. 328, 334
32. ibid. p.334, 328

Chapter 8. The study of Australian Aboriginal culture by German anthropologists of the Frobenius Institute

1. The letters referred to in this chapter are in my possession and quoted in my translation.

2. Consul Dr Rudolf Asmis was the author of articles and a book on tribal law and land ownership in Togo. He had also written a report for the Nazi government of Germany on Australian Aboriginal policy. See Kwiet and Reinhard 'A "Nazi" Assessment of Australian Racial Policy'.

3. Helmut Petri (1907–1986) had studied mainly under Professor Wilhelm Schmidt in Vienna. His subjects were philosophy, history, ethnology, prehistory, physical anthropology and economics. He joined the staff of Leo Frobenius as assistant at the Institute of Cultural Morphology at the University of Frankfurt and curator at the Völkerkundemuseum in 1935, and after war service returned there in 1946. In 1958 he received the chair and directorship at the Institut für Völkerkunde of Cologne. After expeditions to north-west Australia in 1938–39 and 1954–55 he and his wife Dr Gisela Petri-Odermann made further field trips between 1960 and 1984. He has published extensively on the ethnology of Aboriginal tribes of north-west Australia. See R.M. Berndt 'Helmut Petri'.

4. Andreas Lommel (b.1912) originally studied Sinology and Japanology under Bachofer in Munich, then ethnology and Japanology under Frobenius and Kitayama in Frankfurt. His dissertation was on 'Snake and Dragon in Indo-China'. Frobenius, who had employed him at the Völkerkundemuseum, encouraged him to concentrate on the cultures of the South Seas, sending him on the 1939 Kimberley expedition. He returned to the area in 1954–55 with his painter wife Katharina to study Aboriginal rock paintings. Lommel became an assistant at the Museum für Völkerkunde in Munich in 1948 and was its director from 1957 to 1977. See *Süddeutsche Zeitung* 162, 18–19 July 1987, p.15.

5. Lommel *Die Unambal*; Petri *Sterbende Welt*

6. Petri *Sterbende Welt* p.14

7. ibid. pp.8ff.

8. Lommel 'Notes on Sexual Behaviour and Initiation'

9. Lommel *Die Unambal* pp.60–75

10. ibid. pp.75ff.

11. Lommel *Fortschritt ins Nichts*

12. Lommel *Die Unambal* p.83

13. Petri *Sterbende Welt* p.256; Petri 'Kurangara' pp.43ff.

14. Petri *Sterbende Welt* pp.263ff.

15. Lommel *Die Unambal* p.39

16. Petri and Petri-Odermann pp.258ff.

17. ibid. p.273

18. ibid. pp.252ff.

19. ibid. p.257

20. ibid. p.273. See also Petri 'Gibt es eine "Historische Ethnologie" '.

21. See the list of her publications in the bibliography.

22. Lommel 'Rock Art of Australia' p.229

23. Lommel 'The Art of Oceania'

24. Lommel 'Changes in Australian Art' p.233

25. Maynard 'Archeology of Australian Art'

26. Lommel *Fortschritt ins Nichts* p.22 (my transl.)

27. Lommel *Shamanism*

28. Schulz *Felsbilder in Nord-Australien* p.100

29. ibid. p.102

30. Micha 'Trade and Change in Australian Aboriginal Cultures'. See his other works listed in the bibliography.

31. Petri reviewed *Fortschritt ins Nichts* in *Tribus* 19, 1970, Museum für Völkerkunde, Stuttgart. In April 1988 Gisela Petri responded to a bicentenary article of the same title published in the *Frankfurter Allgemeine Zeitung* 67, 19 March 1988. Instead of publishing it, the paper passed it on to Lommel, who wrote a polite but unconvincing private reply.
32. See the selection of articles by Petri listed in the bibliography.

Chapter 9. Hugo Zöller: a German view of Australian society

Research for this chapter, which is part of a larger study on German–Australian relations before World War I, was supported by Deakin University research grants which I gratefully acknowledge. I would also like to thank Leslie Bodi, A.G.L. Shaw and Stephen Connelly for comments on an earlier draft. Page numbers in brackets refer to the first volume of Hugo Zöller's *Rund um die Erde*.

1. Zöller in *Kölnische Zeitung (KZ)* 7 November 1888
2. I am leaving out of account here German translations of English publications and mere compilations—mostly geographical information.
3. For details cf. his autobiography *Als Jurnalist und Forscher*.
4. After his return from his round-the-world trip Zöller submitted a memorandum to the government in which he reviewed the possibilities for German colonial acquisitions in the Pacific and in South and East Asia. Cf. Krieger *Hugo Zöller* p.7
5. Zöller *Rund um die Erde*. In the first article for *KZ* in 1888 (9 September), he mentions that his two-year trip in 1879–80 was undertaken 'to advocate Germany's overseas interests, to study the colonial systems of the English, Dutch and French, and to explore the possibilities for German colonial acquisitions'. Cf. also Zöller *Deutsch-Neuguinea*.
6. Anrep-Elmpt *Australien*. Cf. Overlack 'Queensland in the Journals of Reinhold Graft Anrep-Elmpt'; Tampke 'Amateurs analyse Australia'; von Lendenfeld 'Australia Felix'; Seelhorst *Australien*.
7. Cf. Veit-Brause 'German–Australian relations'.
8. Zöller *Jurnalist* pp.45, 7, 254
9. 'Australische Politik II' *KZ* 28 December 1888
10. Seelhorst *Australien*, for example, has neither a chapter nor even a section on the Germans in Australia. They appear only in passing references to the agents at the exhibitions and in a general warning at the end against migration to Australia.
11. Cf. Anrep-Elmpt's comments on the destructive effects of European civilisation on the so-called savages and his hopes for the moral betterment of mankind through the 'power of philosophy', *Australien* vol. 3, p.237. Zöller does mention his pleasure about the gracefulness of the Aborigines in his autobiography, *Jurnalist* pp.47ff. Seelhorst, on the other hand, comments fatalistically, after visiting a mission station: 'These people [i.e. the Aborigines] live a miserable life [there], but it is still preferable to being shot dead as happens everywhere else' (p.149).
12. Cf. *Rund um die Erde* pp.199–219; *KZ* 16 September and 9 November 1888
13. On the fascination with urbanism in the 1880s cf. Davison *The Rise and Fall of Marvellous Melbourne*.
14. *KZ* 9 November 1888: 'Australien ist gleich allen neuen und von Engländern colonisirten Gebieten ein Geschäftsland, nichts weiter als ein Geschäftsland.' In 1888, eight out of a total of eighteen articles are set aside for the economic thematic, five specifically dealing with the Centennial International Exhibition and Germany's and Austria's part in it; two articles discuss 'Australiens Reichtümer' and one examines the current state and the prospects of German–Australian trade.
15. Cf. Goodwin *Image of Australia*.
16. *KZ* 27 December 1888

17. *KZ* 27 November 1888
18. E.G. Coghlan *Wealth and Progress of N.S.W.*; I owe this reference to Marnie Haig-Muir.
19. *Jurnalist* p.235
20. *KZ* 7 October 1888
21. Cf. *KZ* 7 and 8 November 1888; 'Australische Politik II. and III.' 28 December 1888; also 'Australische Reichtümer I. and II.' *KZ* 7 and 14 October 1888. These comments are significant in the context of a raging debate in Germany about wool imports which some East Prussian Junkers were determined to stop as destructive of the local wool industry.
22. Cf. Seelhorst *Australien* p.350
23. For the following see *KZ* 14 October 1888.
24. *KZ* 28 December 1888
25. 'Anglo-Australier' is his term, as well as 'Deutsch-Australier; cf. *LZ* 30 September 1888.
26. Cf. Seelhorst *Australien* pp.117-19 on alcohol and tobacco misuse, on corruption, on the criminal past of the Australian people, etc. Seelhorst attempts to protect himself against charges of prejudice by making the relevant points as quotations from Mortimer Franklyn *A Glance at Australia in 1880* (1881). But Seelhorst's selective quoting reinforces the fact of his own prejudice.
27. *KZ* 10 November 1888
28. 'With respect to the social conditions, too, much had got worse in this extravagantly democratic country' *Jurnalist* p.235
29. Cf. *KZ* 28 December 1888
30. *KZ* 27 December 1888; Seelhorst *Australien* pp. 122ff
31. *KZ* 28 December 1888
32. Cf. Metin *Le Socialism sans doctrines*; Manes *Ins Land der sozialen Wunder*; extracts in Tampke *Wunderbar Country* pp.42-55. German Socialists' literature on Australia is discussed in Tampke 'Pacesetter or Quiet Backwater?'
33. *KZ* 4 October and 8 November 1888
34. *KZ* 8 November 1888
35. Four articles are devoted to the topic: 'Die Deutschen in Südaustralien' *KZ* 30 September 1888; 'Das Deutschtum in Australien' *KZ* 10 November 1888; 'Deutsche Colonisten im Queensländer Gebirge I. and 26.II' *KZ* 15 and 16 November 1888.
36. Cf. *Jurnalist* p.235
37. *KZ* 10 November 1888
38. *KZ* 30 September 1888. Zöller's play with figures and criteria is only one instance of a continuing preoccupation with gauging the size of the German community 'correctly'. Cf. Veit-Brause 'Australia as an "object" '.
39. Cf. *Jurnalist* p.236.
40. *KZ* 30 September 1888; 10 and 16 November 1888
41. *KZ* 30 September 1888; 10 November 1888. The same observation was repeatedly made by the commanders of the German South Pacific cruisers in their (later) reports on the 'Deutschtum' in Australia.
42. *KZ* 10 November 1888
43. *KZ* 30 September 1888
44. Cf. Stack *Ethnic Identities*.
45. *KZ* 28 December 1888. Zöller, though, does not speculate about population increases.
46. ibid.
47. Cf. Semon *Im australischen Busch* p.535, quoted in Overlack 'Queensland' p.198

Chapter 10. Imagining an Australian nation: The German community of South Australia during the nineteenth century

1. The portfolio is today in the Mitchell Library (ML Ms 67 x), along with other memorabilia of Muecke.
2. Leslie Bodie in his article on Püttmann in the *Australian Dictionary of Biography* (*ADB*) vol.5, p. 462. See also Bodie "Herrmann Püttmann'. The biographical information is taken from the relevant volumes of the *ADB*, from Loyau *Notable South Australians* and from Harmstorf and Cigler *The Germans in Australia*.
3. On the immigration to Australia of the Forty-Eighters see the article on Australia in *Handwörterbuch f'ur das Grenz- und Auslanddeutschtum* vol.1, Breslau, 1934, p.181. Cf. also Price 'German Settlers in South Australia' and Lodewyckx *Die Deutschen in Australien*. On German immigration to South Australia generally see the work of Ian Harmstorf, particularly his collection 'Some Information on South Australian German History'.
4. Cf. Gilson and Zubrzycki *Foreign Language Press*, also quoted in Harmstorf and Cigler p.100
5. Muecke *National Schools* p.3
6. *Australische Zeitung* 16 July 1883. A copy is in ML Ms 67 x.
7. ibid.
8. ibid.
9. ibid.
10. ibid.
11. Horne *Lucky Country* p.96
12. Cf. Zainu'ddin 'Early History of the *Bulletin*'.
13. The contention of a racist attitude as part of the German-Australian concept of Australianism is largely speculative; my own readings have not yielded enough positive evidence to substantiate this thesis fully, but it seems an obvious question why the German-Australians should not have shared the racist vision that was such a central part of the Australian historical experience. Researchers in the field of German-Australian history have, to my knowledge, so far avoided tackling this problem.
14. Quoted in Harmstorf 'Some Information'
15. ibid.
16. Quoted by Borrie *Italians and Germans* p.202. Here and in what follows I am indebted to Borrie for his translations of excerpts from the German language press, although my conclusions are substantially different.
17. ibid.
18. The fact that naturalisation had been valid only in the colony where it was granted, not in the whole of Australia, was 'a constant grievance in the German Press' of Australia at the time and one of the reasons for the support for Federation among German-Australians, as R.B. Walker has shown in his 'German-Language Press and People'. However, the problem was by no means resolved with Federation.
19. Quoted by Borrie *Italians and Germans* p.204
20. ibid. p.205
21. Cf. Paul M. Kennedy's exhaustive account of the growing conflict between Britain and Germany, *The Rise of the Anglo-German Antagonism.*
22. A copy of the poem is in ML Ms 67 x.
23. Cf. Hüppauf *Literaturgeschichte zwischen Revolution und Reaktion* pp.269–70
24. Borrie *Italians and Germans* p.202
25. ibid. p.203; emphasis original
26. ibid.
27. ibid. p.206
28. ibid. p.207

29. ibid.
30. *Australische Zeitung* 26 May 1909, quoted by Borrie p.207
31. *New South Wales Tutorial Guide* 25 April 1914, quoted in Crowley *Modern Australia in Documents* p.207
32. Editorial comment in Crowley *Modern Australia* p.203
33. ibid. pp.203, 204
34. *Daily Telegraph* (Sydney) 15 January 1914, quoted in Crowley *Modern Australia* p.207
35. For a discussion of the history of the German-Australian community during World War I see my *Enemy Aliens.*

Chapter 11. The 'Vossification' of Ludwig Leichhardt

1. Turnbull *Leichhardt's Second Journey* p.57
2. Stow *Midnite* pp.85–86
3. Cf. Bunce *Travels with Dr Leichhardt.*
4. Turnbull *Leichhardt's Second Journey* p.47
5. Cf Shapcott 'Developments in the Voyager Tradition'.
6. Turnbull *Leichhardt's Second Journey* p.21
7. Cf. Carter *Road to Botany Bay*; despite Peter Porter's review ('A local habitation and a name' *TLS* 4 417, 27 November – 3 December 1987) the book is an excellent study.
8. Carter *Road to Botany Bay* p.25
9. ibid. p.74
10. ibid. p.75
11. ibid. p.182
12. ibid. p.56
13. ibid. Heising (*Die Deutschen in Australien* p. 65) reports that the president of the NSW Parliament welcomed Leichhardt back to Sydney with the following sentences stressing the scientific, economic and political importance of his recent discoveries: 'Es würde in der That schwierig sein, irgend einen Reisenden zu nennen, dessen Weg die Durchführung eines ebenso kühnen Unternehmens auf der einen Seite darbote, und auf der anderen durch die Resultate, betrachte man sie sowohl in wissenschaftlicher als auch in ökonomischer und politischer Hinsicht, gleich wichtig wäre. Wenn eine so grosse Strecke von der Oberfläche unseres Landes von einem civilisirten Manne zum ersten Male durchdrungen wird, so kann man die verschiedensten Entdeckungen erwarten, welche den wissenschaftlichen Forscher, sei es in der Geologie, der Botanik oder Zoologie im höchsten Grade interessiren ... In socialer wie in politischer Hinsicht ist es schwer, ja unmöglich, die Wichtigkeit der kürzlich gemachten Entdeckungen jener unbegränzten fruchtbaren Landstriche zu überschätzen, welche sich gegen Norden ausdehnen und bald mit unzähligen Heerden als Wohnsitz des civilisirten Menschen gesucht sein werden. In politischer Hinsicht kann der Besitz eines umfangreichen Landstriches, der zuerst entdeckt wird, um mit all den Gaben der Natur, die zum Bestehen und Gedeihen der civilisirten Gesellschaft nothwendig, erfüllt zu werden, nur als etwas Wichtiges betrachtet werden; wie auch der Besitz einer ununterbrochenen Strecke schönen und fruchtbaren Landes, welches uns mit den Küsten des indischen Ocans [sic] in Verbindung bringt, was den australischen Continent als eine Vergrösserung des indoanglikanischen Reiches von nicht geringer Bedeutung erscheinen lässt.'
14. Leichhardt *Journal of an Overland Expedition*, here quoted from Fitzpatrick *Australian Explorers* p.227. See also Leichhardt's remark (ibid. p.240): 'we had travelled along never failing, and, for the greater part, running waters: and over an excellent country, available, almost in its whole extent, for pastoral purposes.'
15. Leichhardt *Journal* p.240

16. Cf. Carter *Road to Botany Bay* pp.2, 3, 46, 49, 83, 107.
17. ibid. p.67
18. See Leichhardt *Journal* pp.217, 225, 229, 233, 243, 245.
19. Carter *Road to Botany Bay* p.58
20. ibid. pp.58–59
21. Cf. Aurousseau *Letters of F.W. Ludwig Leichhardt* vol.1, pp.276–77.
22. Cf. ibid. vol.1, pp.321, 323, 324.
23. Cf. ibid. vol.3, p.959.
24. Cf. ibid. vol.3, p.960.
25. Cf. Roderick 'New Light on Leichhardt' pp.166–90; see also Vietta *Romantik in Niedersachsen*, esp. pp.1–22; and the review article by Manning Clark, 'Ludwig Leichhardt's letters' p.406.
26. *Letters* vol.3, p.994
27. Cf. ibid. vol.2, pp.603, 714, 750.
28. ibid. vol.3, p.965
29. Cf. Leichhardt *Journal* pp.214, 225, 235–36, 249.
30. ibid. p.222
31. ibid. pp.223–24
32. ibid. p.234
33. Carter *Road to Botany Bay* p.237
34. ibid. p.243
35. *Letters* vol.3, p.955
36. ibid. vol.2, pp.764–65
37. Cf. Novalis' poem 'An Tieck' (c.1800).
38. Turnbull *Leichhardt's Second Journey* p.53
39. Cf. *Letters* vol.3, pp.894, 928, 951, 989, 1005, 1009.
40. Carter *Road to Botany* p. 80
41. Cf. Gerald H. Supple 'The Dream of Dampier: An Australian Foreshadowing— A.D. 1686 in Sladen *Australian Poets* pp.529–40.
42. Cf. John B. O'Hara 'Flinders' in Stevens *Anthology of Australian Verse* pp. 154–55.
43. Cf. Lewin 'The Story of Abel Tasman' pp.328–30.
44. Houghton *Victorian Frame of Mind* p.198
45. Cf. ibid. p.206.
46. Cf. ibid. p.309.
47. Turnbull *Leichhardt's Second Journey* pp.56–57
48. Cf. Houghton *Victorian Frame of Mind* p.207.
49. Cf. ibid. p.306.
50. Gosse 'Agony of the Victorian Age' p.295, here quoted from Houghton p. 305
51. Cf. Houghton *Victorian Frame of Mind* p.306.
52. Clark 'Heroes' pp. 57–84, 61–62
53. Cf. Houghton *Victorian Frame of Mind* p.223.
54. Eden *Australia's Heroes* Preface. See also Strang *Romance of Australia* Preface; Scott *Romance of Australian Exploring*; and Kingsley's various essays on Australian explorers in Mellick *Henry Kingsley* pp. 519–63.
55. Eden *Australia's Heroes* p.2
56. Cf. Bunce *Travels with Dr Leichhardt* note 3.
57. Eden *Australia's Heroes* p.227
58. Cf. Scott *Romance of Australian Exploring* ch. 13.
59. Kendall 'Leichhardt' in *Leaves from Australian Forests*. See also the following lines (p.192):
'In a land of dry, fierce thunder, did he ever pause and dream
Of the cool green German valley and the singing Germa stream?

When the sun was a menace, glaring from a sky of brass,
Did he ever rest, in visions, on a lap of German grass?'

60. Esson 'Terra Australis' pp. 13–16
61. Coutts 'Antiquity in Australia' p.47
62. Cf. Clark 'Heroes' p.62.
63. Cf. Horne 'Australian Explorers' pp.64–70.
64. Cf. Kendall 'Fate of the Explorers' in *Leaves from Australian Forests* p.269.
65. Cf. Clark 'Heroes' p.62.
66. Cf. R. Lynd 'Lines Addressed to the Party Proceeding on the Track of Dr. Leichhardt' *Sydney Morning Herald* 3 July 1845. In Billot *Poets and Poetasters* pp.28–29 the poem is quoted as 'Leichardt's [sic] Grave'. See also 'Nemo' 'Leichhardt' *Moreton Bay Courier* 23 December 1848, a rather pointless piece.
67. Cf. *Letters* vol. 3, p.860: 'As it had long been presumed that I had either died or been killed by the blacks, my good friend Mr Lynd had written my funeral dirge, of which I'm sending you [i.e. his brother-in-law] a copy in English. The poem is a very good one. Mr Nathan, a musician, who set Byron's *Hebrew Melodies* to music in England, wrote the music for the dirge.'
68. Kendall 'Leichardt' p.190
69. ibid. p.191
70. ibid. p.193
71. ibid.
72. L. 'On Hearing of Dr Leichhardt's [sic] Return' *Port Phillip Herald* 23 April 1846
73. Malwyn 'Leichhardt's Return' *Port Phillip Herald* 16 April 1846
74. ibid.
75. E.K.S. 'Stanzas. Written on the return of L. Leichardt [sic], Esq., from an Expedition through the unexplored regions of Australia between Moreton Bay and Port Essington' *Sydney Morning Herald* 27 March 1846
76. C.D. 'Lines: Written in Commemoration of the Successful Expedition of Dr. L. Leichardt [sic], to Port Essington, on the Northern Coast of Australia, and of his safe return to Sydney' *Australian* 27 March 1846
77. ibid.
78. Cf. A.B. Paterson "The Lost Leichhardt' in Lehmann *Comic Australian Verse* pp.81–82.
79. ibid. p.81
80. ibid.
81. ibid.
82. ibid. p.82
83. Bernard O'Dowd 'Australia' in Heseltine *Penguin Book of Australian Verse* p.95
84. Cf. Blainey *A Land Half Won.*
85. Boyd *Outbreak of Love* p.128
86. Ewers 'Identity'
87. Hope 'A Letter from Rome' in *Collected Poems* p.141
88. Tom 'This Lost Place, my home' in Eyre and Webber *Farrago Australia* p.63
89. Cf. Dame Mary Gilmore, Introduction to Dawes *Fire on Earth*. See also Howard 'Discoverers of Australia'. The poem is in three parts: 'The Discoverers of Australia', 'The Early Settlers', 'The Explorers of Australia', and celebrates all the seafarers and explorers from Dampier to Cunningham and Forrest as heroes of Australian history.
90. Stewart *Voyager Poems* pp.11–12
91. Cf. Howard 'Discoverers of Australia'.
92. Cf. Devanney 'Lost Explorers' pp.63–65.
93. Cf. M. Barnard Eldershaw 'The Man Who Knew the Truth About Leichhardt . . .' *Sydney Mail* 19 January 1938.
94. ibid.
95. Cf. Chisholm *Strange New World*; quotations are from the 1973 edn.

96. Cf. Cotton *Ludwig Leichhardt and the Great South Land.*
97. Halinbourg 'Sound the Alert. January 1941' in *New Weapons* p.25
98. Halinbourg ' "V" for Victory. July, 1941' in *New Weapons* p.26
99. Griffith 'Francis Webb's Challenge' p.454
100. Chisholm *Strange Journey* p.270; see also R.F. Brissenden's parody of White's *Voss* in Field *OZShrink Lit* p.65.
101. Cf. Francis Webb 'Leichhardt in Theatre' in *Collected Poems* pp.35–45.
102. ibid. p.44
103. Griffith 'Francis Webb's Challenge' p. 452
104. Webb 'Leichhardt in Theatre' p.44
105. Cf. Griffith 'Francis Webb's Challenge' p.457.
106. Cf. Diane Fahey 'To Francis Webb' in *Voices from the Honeycomb* Jacaranda Press, Milton, Qld. 1986, pp.22–23. There are two versions of the poem, showing considerable textual differences. The earlier version (by Diane Dodwell) is to be found in: *Seven Poets: the winning entries for the Artlook/Shell Literary Award, 1977* The Nine Club, West Perth, 1977, p.27. Quotations are from the 1986 version.
107. Fahey 'To Francis Webb' p. 22
108. ibid. p.23
109. Cf. White *Flaws in the glass* p.104.
110. Blight 'Leichhardt as Voss' p.32. See also Christesen 'Voss' p.426.
111. Cf. Noel Macainsh 'Doctor Leichhardt on Board' in *Eight by Eight: Poems by Vincent Buckley, Laurence Collinson, Alexander Craig, Max Dunn, Noel Macainsh, David Martin, R.A. Simpson, Chris Wallace-Crabbe* Jacaranda Press, Brisbane, 1963, p. 63.
112. Noel Macainsh 'Voss, Also Called Leichhardt' *Quadrant* 20, 11, 1976, p.16
113. Harrison 'Leichhardt in the Desert' p.30
114. Larry Buttrose 'The Leichhardt Heater Journey' in *Leichhardt Heater Journey* p.11

Chapter 12. Leichhardt's diaries

1. Matthews *Louisa* pp.5–6
2. ibid. p.9
3. Zuchold *Dr. Ludwig Leichhardt*
4. Cotton *Ludwig Leichhardt and the Great South Land*
5. Matthews *Louisa* p.7
6. Aurousseau *Letters of F.W. Ludwig Leichhardt*
7. Letter Book, 1917, Australian Museum, Sydney, p.70
8. ML C151, Mitchell Library
9. ML C163, Mitchell Library
10. Goethe *Torquato Tasso* Act V, Sc.5. 11.3290–93
11. ML C151
12. ibid.
13. Coe 'Portrait of the Artist' p.127
14. Webster *Whirlwinds in the Plain*

Chapter 13. Intercultural encounters: Aborigines and white explorers in fiction and non-fiction

The text references are to Patrick White *Voss* and Ludwig Leichhardt *Journal of an overland expedition*

1. Cf. White 'Prodigal Son' p.39: ' . . . the idea finally matured after reading contemporary accounts of Leichhardt's expeditions and A.H. Chisholm's *Strange New World* on returning to Australia.' Cf. also White *Flaws in the Glass* p.104: 'I saw the connection between Voss and Leichhardt. This led to research and my borrowing

details of the actual expeditions from the writings of those who found themselves
enduring the German's leadership.' Cf. Schulz *Geschichte der australischen Literatur*
p.138, who talks about Leichhardt's ordeal, but adds that White made little use of
the historical details concerning the expeditions.

2. Cf. Stein *Patrick White: 'Voss'* pp.54ff.
3. Cf. ibid. p.13. Stein considers the Aborigines indispensable to the structure of the
   novel.
4. *Journal* p.54
5. Phillips (Narrative of the First Leichhardt Expedition) confirms this impression
   when he talks about 'suspicion' (p.58) and the natives' 'importunate' behaviour
   (p.124). Cf. also Gilbert's repeated warnings, quoted by Chisholm *Strange Journey*
   p.109: 'It shows the great necessity of bushmen never forgetting that, although no
   Blacks are seen, they may be within a few yards of the camp, closely observing every
   action and only awaiting a convenient opportunity for making a systematic attack.'
6. Carter *In the Steps of the Explorers* p.78
7. For a particularly humorous example of intercultural encounters cf. *Journal* p.194,
   when Aborigines visit the camp: 'We had a long unintelligible conversation, for
   neither Brown nor Charley could make out a single word of their language. They
   were very much surprised by the different appearance of Charley's black skin and
   my own. Phillips wished to exchange his jacket for one of their opossum cloaks, so
   I desired him to put it on the ground, and then taking the cloak and placing it near
   the jacket, I pointed to Phillips and, taking both articles up, handed the cloak to
   Phillips and the jacket to our old friend, who perfectly understood my meaning.
   After some time he expressed a wish to have the cloak back and to keep the jacket,
   with which we had dressed him; but I gave him to understand that he might have
   his cloak, provided he returned the jacket; which arrangement satisfied him,
8. Cf. Stein *Patrick White* pp.45ff., who points out the crucial significance of their
   relationship to the welfare of the expedition. As to the final breakdown of communication, Stein particularly blames Voss's ignorance of the tribal structure which
   emphasises the collective at the expense of the individual.
9. Cf. *Voss* pp.218ff.
10. Cf. Carter *In the Steps of the Explorers* p.73: 'Leichhardt's journal reveals that he had
    a poor opinion of the aborigines. He was, however, a keen observer of their
    food-gathering methods.'
11. *Journal* pp.157ff. It is interesting to compare Leichhardt's version of the incident
    with that of Gilbert, quoted by Chisholm (*Strange Journey* p.146).

BIBLIOGRAPHY

Anrep-Elmpt, Reinhold Graf *Australien. Meine Reise durch den ganzen Welttheil* 3 vols, Leipzig, 1881

Aurousseau, M. *The Letters of F.W. Ludwig Leichhardt* 3 vols, Cambridge University Press, 1968

Bade, Klaus J. (ed.) *Imperialismus und Kolonialmission* 1982

Barber, Lynn *The Heyday of Natural History 1820–1870* Jonathan Cape, London, 1980

Becker, Ludwig *Men of Victoria* Melbourne, 1856

Berndt, R.M. *Djanggawul. An Aboriginal Religious Cult of North-Eastern Arnhem Land* Melbourne, Cheshire, 1952

—(ed.) *Australian Aboriginal Anthropology. Modern Studies in Social Anthropology of the Australian Aborigines* University of Western Australia Press, Perth, 1970

—'Helmut Petri' *Australian Aboriginal Studies* 1, 1987, pp.97ff.

Berndt, R.M. and C.H. Berndt *The Speaking Land. Myth and Story in Aboriginal Australia* Penguin, Ringwood, Vic., 1989

Billot, C.P. (ed.) *Poets and Poetasters of Geelong* Geelong Regional Library, Geelong, 1967

Bischoff, Charitas *Bilder aus meinem Leben* Berlin, 1931

—*Amalie Dietrich. Ein Leben* Calwer, Stuttgart, 1980

Blainey, Geoffrey *A Land Half Won* Macmillan, Melbourne, 1980

Blight, John 'Leichhardt as Voss' *Literature in North Queensland* 6, 3, 1978, pp.31–32

Blunt, Wilfred *The Art of Botanical Illustration* Collins, London, 1950

Bodie, Leslie "Herrmann Püttmann: A Forty-Eighter in Australia' in Bodie et al. *German Connection* 1985

Bodie, Leslie and S. Jeffries (eds) *The German Connection. Sesquicentenary Essays on German-Victorian Crosscurrents 1835–1985* German Department, Monash University, 1985

Boltz, H. (tr. and ed.) *Wie das Känguruh seinen Schwanz bekam. Märchen und Mythen der australischen Ureinwohner* Fischer, Frankfurt, 1982

Bonwick, James *The wild white man and the black of Victoria* Melbourne, 1863

Borrie, W.D. *Italians and Germans in Australia: A Study of Assimilation* Melbourne, 1954

Boyd, Martin *Outbreak of Love* Penguin, Ringwood, Vic., 1984 (orig. publ. 1957)

Bunce, Daniel *Travels with Dr Leichhardt* Steam Press of William Fairfax & Co., Melbourne, 1859

Buttrose, Larry *The Leichhardt Heater Journey* Friendly Street Poets, Adelaide, 1972

Cannon, Susan Faye *Science in Culture: the Early Victorian Period* New York, 1978

Carroll, Alison and John Tregenza *Eugène von Guérard's South Australia* Art Gallery, Adelaide, 1986

Carter, J. *In the Steps of the Explorers* Angus & Robertson, Sydney, 1969

Carter, Paul *The Road to Botany Bay: An Essay in Spatial History* Faber, London, 1987

Cawood, John 'The Magnetic Crusade: Science and Politics in Early Victorian Britain' *Isis* 70, 1979, pp.493–518

Chisholm, Alec H. *Strange New World: The Adventures of John Gilbert and Ludwig Leichhardt* Angus & Robertson, Sydney

Christesen, Clem 'Voss: The Epilogue' *Meanjin* 18, 4, 1959, p.426

Clark, Manning 'Ludwig Leichhardt's letters' *Meanjin* 27, 4, 1968, pp.405–8

—'Heroes' in Stephen R. Graudbard (ed.) *Australia: The Daedalus Symposium* Angus & Robertson, Sydney, 1985

Coe, Richard 'Portrait of the Artist as a young Australian' *Southerly* 41, 2, 1981

Coghlan, T.A. *Wealth and Progress of N.S.W., 1886–87* Sydney, 1887

Cotter, M. 'Fragmentation, Reconstitution and the Colonial Experience: The Aborigines in White's Fiction' in C. Tiffin (ed.) *South Pacific Images* South Pacific Association, Brisbane, 1978

Cotton, Catherine D. *Ludwig Leichhardt and the Great South Land* Angus & Robertson, Sydney, 1938

Coutts, Boyd 'Antiquity in Australia' in *Magic Casements: A Book of Poems* Percival Serle, Melbourne, 1933

Crowley, F. *Modern Australia in Documents* vol.1, Wren, Melbourne, 1973

Daniel, 'The Aborigines in Australian Fiction: Stereotype or Archetype?' *Modern Fiction Studies* 27, 1981, pp.45–60

Davison, Graeme *The Rise and Fall of Marvellous Melbourne* Melbourne University Press, 1987

Dawes, John *Fire on Earth: A Trilogy in Verse on Australian Exploration* Devonshire Press, Sydney, n.d.

Denison, Sir William *Varieties of Vice-Regal Life* London, 1870

Devanney, James 'The Lost Explorers (Leichhardt 1848)' in *Earth Kindred* Wilmot, Melbourne, 1931 pp.63–65

Dooley, J.C. 'Centenary of Melbourne-Toolangi Magnetic Observatory' *Journal of Geophysical Research* 63, 1958, pp.731–35

Eden, Charles H. *Australia's Heroes: A Slight Sketch of the Most Prominent Amongst the Band of Gallant Men Who Devoted Their Lives and Energies to the Cause of Science and the Development of the Fifth Continent* Society for Promoting Christian Knowledge, London, 1885

Elkin, A.P. 'Missionary Policy for Primitive Peoples' *Morpeth Review* 27, 1934, pp.1–15

—*The Australian Aborigines. How to understand them* Angus & Robertson, Sydney, 1938, repr. 1957

Elliott, Brian and Adrian Mitchell (eds) *Bards in the Wilderness: Australian Colonial Poetry to 1920* Nelson, Melbourne, 1970

Esson, Louis 'Terra Australis: Fragments of a Conversation' *The Heart of the Rose* 1, 1, 1907, pp.13–16

Ewers, John K. 'Identity' in *I Came Naked: A Selection of Verse 1970–1975* Conrad Bailey, Black Rock, Vic., 1976, pp.20–21

Eyre, Nigel and Rowena Webber (eds) *Farrago Australia: a collection of interviews, stories and photographs* Students' Representative Council, Melbourne University, 1986

Feeken, E., G. Feeken and O. Spate *The Discovery and Exploration of Australia* Nelson, Melbourne, 1970

Field, Michele (ed.) *OZShrink Lit: Australian Classic Literature Cut to Size* Penguin, Ringwood, Vic., 1983

Fitzpatrick, Kathleen (ed.) *Australian Explorers: A Selection from their Writings* 3rd edn, Oxford University Press, London, 1965

Fletcher, John 'Humboldt-Briefe in Australien' *Alexander von Humboldt Stiftung, Mitteilungen* 44, October 1984, pp.33–38

Gibbs, W.J. *The Origins of Australian Meteorology* AGPS, Canberra, 1975

Gilbert, J., Diary of the Leichhardt expedition, Ms 1844–45, Mitchell Library

Gilson, M. and J. Zubrzycki *The Foreign Language Press in Australia 1848–1964* ANUP, Canberra, 1967

Goodwin, Craufurd D.W. *The Image of Australia. British Perceptions of the Australian Economy from the Eighteenth to the Twentieth Century* Duke University, Durheim, NC, 1974

Gosse, Edmund 'The Agony of the Victorian Age' *Edinburgh Review* 228, 1918

Griffith, Michael 'Francis Webb's Challenge to Mid-Century Myth-making: Francis Webb and Ludwig Leichhardt' *Australian Literary Studies* 10, 4, 1982, pp.448–58

Gunson, Neil (ed.) *Australian Reminiscences and Papers of L.E. Threlkeld, Missionary to the Aborigines 1824–1859* vol. 2, Australian Aboriginal Studies No.40, Australian Institute of Aboriginal Studies, Canberra, 1974

Günther, S. 'Georg von Neumayer' in *Festschrift zur Feier des 80 Geburtstages seiner Exzellenz des Wirkl. Geheimrates Herrn Dr. Georg v. Neumayer* Bad Dürkheim, 1906

Halinbourg, Beryl *New Weapons of the Spirit* Melbourne, 1945

Hambruch, P. (ed.) *Der Tanz der Vögel. Märchen aus der Südsee* dtv München, 1964

Harmstorf, I. 'Some Information on South Australian German History' South Australian College of Advanced Education, 1985

Harmstorf, I. and M. Cigler *The Germans in Australia* Melbourne, 1985

Harrison, Keith 'Leichardt [sic] in the Desert' in *Points to a Journey* Dufour Editions, 1967

Hay, H.R. *From Ape to Angel* Methuen, London, 1958

—'Development of Scientific Knowledge of the Aborigines' in H. Sheils (ed.) *Australian Aboriginal Studies* Oxford University Press, Melbourne, 1963

—'Australasian Anthropology and ANZAAS: "Strictly Scientific and Critical"' 'in R. McCleod (ed.) *The Commonwealth of Science. ANZAAS and the Scientific Enterprise in Australasia 1888–1988* Oxford University Press, Melbourne, 1988

Hazzard, Margaret *Australia's brilliant daughter, Ellis Rowan: artist, naturalist, explorer, 1848–1922* Greenhouse

Heidke, P. 'Neumayer als Deutscher und Gelehrter' *Annalen der Hydrographie und Maritimen Meteorologie* Beilage, June 1926, pp.1–17

Heising, Albert *Die Deutschen in Australian* Verlag von Julius Albert Wohlgemuth, Berlin, 1853

Heseltine, Harry (ed.) *The Penguin Book of Australian Verse* Penguin, Ringwood, Vic., 1972

Hiatt, L.R. (ed.) *Australian Aboriginal Mythology. Essays in Honour of W.E.H. Stanner* Australian Institute of Aboriginal Studies, Canberra, 1975

Hoare, M.E. ' "The Half-Mad Bureaucrat": Robert Brough Smyth (1830–1889)' *Records of the Australian Academy of Science* 2, 4, 1973, pp.25–40

Home, R.W. 'First Physicist of Australia: Richard Threlfall at the University of Sydney, 1886–1898' *Historical Records of Australian Science* 6, 3, 1986, pp.333–57

Hope, A.D. *Collected Poems 1930–1970* 3rd edn, Angus & Robertson, Sydney, 1972

Horne, Donald *The Lucky Country* Penguin, Harmondsworth, 1964

Horne, Richard Henry 'Australian Explorers' in Elliott and Mitchell *Bards and the Wilderness*

Houghton, Walter E. *The Victorian Frame of Mind, 1830–1870* Yale University Press, New Haven and London, 1957

Howard, John 'The Discoverers of Australia' in *Nuggets from a New Mine; or, The Musings of an Australian Bard* Wheatland & Huckell, Melbourne, 1937

Humboldt, Alexander von *Kosmos* J.S. Cotta, Stuttgart, Band IV, 1858

Hüppauf, B. *Literaturgeschichte zwischen Revolution und Reaktion 1830–1870* Athenaum, Frankfurt, 1972

Jurgensen, Manfred and Alan Corkhill (eds) *The German Presence in Queensland* Queensland University Press, St Lucia, 1988

Kendall, Henry *Leaves from Australian Forests: Poetical Works of Henry Kendall* Rigby, Adelaide, 1975

Kennedy, Paul M. *The Rise of the Anglo-German Antagonism 1860–1914* Allen and Unwin, London, 1980

Keyser, Christian *Eine Papuagemeinde* Neuendettelsauer Missionsschriften Nr 65, Bärenreiter-Verlag, Kassel 1950 (orig. publ. 1929)

Klaus, D. and I.A.M. Teichmann 'Townsend, not Kosciusko: A myth dispelled?' *Journal of the Royal Australian Historical Society* 74, 1988, pp.48–58

Koch, Ludwig *Die Arachniden Australiens* Bauer and Raspe, Nürnberg, 1871

Koskinen, Aarne A. *Missionary influence as a political factor in the Pacific Islands* Helsinki, 1953

Kretzer, Hans-Jochen *Windrose und Südpol: Leben und Werk der grossen Pfälzer Wissenschaftlers Georg von Neumayer* Pollichia, Bad Dürkheim, 1984

Krieger, Ursula *Hugo Zöller. Ein deutscher Journalist als Kolonialpionier* Konrad Tritsch, Würzburg-Aumühle, 1940

Kwiet, Konrad and Olaf Reinhard 'A "Nazi" Assessment of Australian Racial Policy from 1935' *Australian Journal of Politics and History* 34, 3, 1989

Lebzelter, F.F. *Die österreichische Weltreisende Ida Pfeiffer, 1797–1858, mit besondere Berücksichtigung der naturwissenschaftlichen Ergebnisse ihrer Reisen* Vienna, 1910

Lehmann, Geoffrey (ed.) *Comic Australian Verse* Angus & Robertson, Sydney, 1972

Leichhardt, Ludwig *Journal of an Overland Expedition in Australia from Moreton Bay to Port Essington, a Distance of Upwards of 3,000 miles during the years 1844–45* Boone, London, 1847

Lendenfeld, Robert von *Report of the results of the examination of the central part of the Australian Alps* Government Reports of the Department of Mines, Sydney, 1885

—*Forschungreisen in den Australischen Alpen. Petermann's Mitteilungen* (Gotha) Erganzungsheft, 1887

—'Australia Felix' *Preussische Jahrbücher* 65, January–June 1890, pp.171–85

—*Australische Reise* Innsbruck University Press, 1892

Leonhardi, Moritz Freiherr von 'Über einige religiöse und totemistische Vorstellungen der Aranda und Loritja in Zentralaustralian' *Globus* 91, 1907, pp.285–90

Leske, Everard (ed.) *Hermannsburg. A Vision and a Mission* Lutheran Publishing House, Adelaide, 1977

Lewin, Frances Sescadorowna 'The Story of Abel Tasman' in Sladen *Australian Poets*

Lodewyckx, A. *Die Deutschen in Australien* Stuttgart, 1932

Löffler, A. (ed.) *Märchen aus Australien. Traumzeitmythen und -geschichten der australischen Aborigines* Diederichs, Düsseldorf, 1981

Lommel, Andreas 'Notes on Sexual Behaviour and Initiation. Wunambal Tribe, North-Western Australia *Oceania* 20, 2, 1949, pp.162ff.

—*Die Unambal. Ein Stamm in nordwest Australien* Museum für Völkerkunde, Hamburg, 1952

—'The Rock Art of Australia' in Hans-Georg Handi et al. *The Art of the Stone Age. Forty Thousand Years of Rock Art* Methuen, London, 1961

—*Shamanism. The Beginnings of Art* transl. Michael Bullock, McGraw-Hill, New York, Toronto, 1967

—'The Art of Oceania' in Luis Pericot-Garcia, John Galloway and Andreas Lommel *Prehistoric and Primitive Art* Thames & Hudson, London, 1969

—*Fortschritt ins Nichts. Die Modernisierung der Primitiven* Safari bei Ullstein, Frankfurt am Main, Berlin, Vienna, 1981 (orig. 1969)

—'Changes in Australian Art' in Pilling and Waterman *Diprotodon to Detribalization*

—*L'arte dei primitivi dell' Australia e dei Mari del Sud* Sansoni Editoe, Florence, 1987

Lommel, Andreas and Katharina *Die Kunst des fünften Erdteils. Australien* Staatliches Museum für Völkerkunde, Munich, 1959

Loyau, G.E. *Notable South Australians: or, Colonists—Past and Present* Adelaide, 1883

Madigan, C.T. *Central Australia* OUP, London, 1936

Manes, Alfred *Ins Land der sozialen Wunder* Berlin, 1913

Matthews, B.E. *Louisa* McPhee Gribble/Penguin, Fitzroy and Ringwood, Vic., 1988

Maynard, Lesley 'The Archeology of Australian Aboriginal Art' in Sidney M. Mead (ed.) *Exploring the Visual Art of Oceania, Australia, Melanesia, Micronesia, and Polynesia* University Press of Hawaii, Honolulu, 1979

McNally, Ward *Aborigines, Artefacts and Anguish* Lutheran Publishing House, Adelaide, 1981

Mellick, J.S.D. (ed.) *Henry Kingsley* University of Queensland Press, St Lucia, 1982

Metin, Albert *Le Socialism sans doctrines* Paris 1901

Meyer, H.A. *Erinnerungen an Dr. H.A. Meyer nach seinen eigenen Aufzeichungen* Hamburg, 1890

Micha, Franz Joseph 'Der Handel der zentralaustralischen Eingeborenen *Annali Lateranensi* 22, 1958, pp.41–228

—'Die Tauschmittel an den Märkten der zentralaustralischen Eingeborenen' *Anthropos* 54, 1959, pp.377–400

—'Eingeborene als Arbeitskräfte auf den Viehstationen der südöstlichen Kimberley, vornehmlich auf Gordon Downs Station' in *Kulturgeschichtliche Studien* Herrmann Trimborn zum 60. Geburtstag von seinen Schülern gewidmet. Limbach, Braunschweig, 1961

—'Zur Geschichte der australischen Eingeborenen *Saeculum* 16, 4, 1965, pp.317–42

—'Trade and Change in Australian Aboriginal Cultures: Australian Aboriginal Trade as an Expression of Close Culture Contact and as a Mediator of Culture Change' in Pilling and Waterman (eds) *Diprotodon to Detribalization*

Mountford, C.P. *Nomads of the Australian Desert* Rigby, Adelaide, 1976

Moyal, Ann 'Collectors and Illustrators. Women Botanists of the Nineteenth Century' in D.J. and S.M. Carr (eds) *People and Plants in Australia* Academic Press, Sydney, 1981

Muecke, Rev. Carl *National Schools for South Australia* Adelaide, 1866

Mühlmann, W.E. *Geschichte der Anthropologie* Aula, Wiesbaden, 1984, chs 7 and 11

Mulvaney, D.C. and J.H. Calaby *'So much that is new'. Baldwin Spencer 1860–1929. A Biography* Melbourne University Press, 1985

Neumayer, Georg *Results of the Magnetical, Nautical, and Meteorological Observations made and collected at the Flagstaff Observatory, Melbourne, and at Various Stations in the Colony of Victoria, March 1858 – February 1859* Melbourne, 1859

—'Description and System of Working of the Flagstaff Observatory' *Transactions of the Philosophical Institute of Victoria* 3, 1859, pp.94–103

—'On Dove's Law of the Turning of the Wind, as illustrated and supported by Observations made at the Flagstaff Meteorological and Magnetic Observatory, Melbourne' *Transactions of the Philosophical Institute of Victoria* 4, 1859, pp.102–115

—*Results of the Meteorological Observations taken in the Colony of Victoria, during the years 1859–1862; and of the Nautical Observations collected and discussed at the Flagstaff Observatory, Melbourne, during the years 1858–1862* Melbourne, 1864

—*Discussion of the Meteorological and Magnetical Observations made at the Flagstaff Observatory, Melbourne, during the years 1858–1863* Mannheim, 1867

—*Results of the Magnetic Survey of the Colony of Victoria, executed during the years 1858–1864* Mannheim, 1869

—*Auf zum Südpol* Berlin, 1901

—'Ein deutscher Seemann und die Erschliessung der Goldausbeute in Australien' in Wislicenus *Auf weiter Fahrt*

—'Bericht über die Erfolge des Berichterstatters in Beziehung auf die Erichtung eines Observatoriums für die vereinigten Zwecke der Navigation & des Terrestrischen Magnetismus in Melbourne', Deutsches Museum, Munich, photocopy in Neumayer-Archiv, Bad Dürkheim (to be published, with English translation, in *Historical Records of Australian Science,* 1991).

Nida, Eugene A. *Customs and Cultures. Anthropology for Christian Missions* Harper & Row, New York, 1954

North, Marianne *Recollections of a Happy Life* London, 1893

—*A Vision of Eden. The Life and Work of Marianne North* Webb & Bower, Exeter, 1980

O'Dowd, Bernard 'Australia' in Harry Heseltine (ed.) *The Penguin Book of Australian Verse* Penguin, Ringwood, Vic., 1972, p.95

Orel, H. 'Is Patrick White's Voss the real Leichhardt of Australia?' *Costerus* 4, 1972, pp.109–119

Overlack, Peter 'Queensland in the Journals of Reinhold Graf Anrep-Elmpt, Richard Semon and Hans von Lippa' in Jurgensen and Corkhill *The German Presence in Queensland*

Parker, K. Langloh *Australian Legendary Tales* London, 1896, now selected and ed. H. Drake-Brockman, Angus & Robertson, Sydney, 1953, repr. 1978

Paulus, A. 'Neumayer als Förderer der Schiffahrt' *Annalen der Hydrographie und Maritimen Meteorologie* Beilage, June 1926, pp.18–28

Peron, M.F. *A Voyage of Discovery to the Southern Hemisphere* London, 1809

Pescott, R.T.M. *Collections of a century. The History of the First Hundred Years of the National Museum of Victoria* Melbourne, 1954

Petri, Helmut 'Kurangara. Neue magische Kulte in nordwest Australien' *Zeitschrift für Ethnologie* 75, 1950, pp.43ff.

—*Sterbende Welt in nordwest Australien* Limbach Verlag, Braunschweig, 1954

—'Dynamik im Stammenleben Nordwest-Australiens *Paideuma* 6, 3, 1956, pp.152–68

—'Gibt es noch "unberührte" Wildbeuter im heutigen Australien?' *Baessler-Archiv* Neue Folge, 10, 35, 1963, pp.291–308

—'Kosmogonie unter farbigen Völkern der westlichen Wüste Australiens' *Anthropos* 60, 1965, pp.468–79

—'Traum und Trance bei den Australiden' *Bild der Wissenschaft* 4, April, 1965, pp.227–85

—'Gibt es eine "Historische Ethnologie" *Kölner Ethnologische Mitteilungen* 4, 1965, pp.181–95

—'Landrechte der australischen Aborigines' in R. Schenkel et al. *Biologie von Sozialstrukturen bei Tier und Mensch* Vandenboeck Ruprecht, Göttingen, 1983, pp.69–79

Petri, Helmut and Gisela Petri-Odermann 'Nativismus und Millenarismus im gegenwärtigen Australien' in Eike Haberland (ed.) *Festschrift für Ad. E. Jensen* Renner, Munich, 1964, pp.461–66

—'Stability and Change: Present-day Historic Aspects among Australian Aborigines in Berndt *Australian Aboriginal Anthropology*

Petri-Odermann, Gisela 'Das Eigentum in Nordwest-Australien *Annali Lateranensi* 21, 1957, pp.30–97

—'Heilkunde der Njangomada, Nordwest-Australien' *Paideuma* 6, 1958, pp.411–28

—'Holz- und Steinsetzungen in Australien' *Paideuma* 7, 2, 1959, pp.99–114

—'Das Meer im Leben einer nordwest-australischen Küstenbevölkerung' *Paideuma* 9, 1, 1963, pp.1–18

—'Australisches Frauenleben im Kulturkontakt' *Kölner Ethnologische Mitteilungen* 4, 1965, pp.196–204

Pfeiffer, Ida *Reise einer Wienerin in das Heilige Land* 2 vols, Jakob Dirnbock, Vienna, 1844

—*Eine Frauenfahrt um die Welt* 4 vols. Karl Gerold, Vienna, 1850 (transl. William Hazlitt, 3 vols, 1852)

—*Reise nach dem skandinavischen Norden und der Insel Island im Jahre 1845* Pest, 1855

—*Meine zweite Weltreise* 4 vols. Karl Gerolds Sohn Vienna, 1856

—*Reise nach Madagascar* (ed. O. Pfeiffer) Karl Gerolds Sohn, Vienna, 1960

Phillips, W., Narrative of the First Leichhardt Expedition, Ms 1844–45, Mitchell Library

Pilling, Arnold R. and Richard A. Waterman (eds) *Diprotodon to Detribalization.*

Studies in Change among Australian Aborigines Michigan State University Press, East Lansing, 1970

Roderick, Colin 'New Light on Leichhardt' *Journal of the Royal Australian Historical Society* 72, pt 3, 1986, pp.166–90

Ross, C. Stuart 'Our Observatory: The Story of its Establishment' *Victorian Historical Magazine* 6, 4, 1918, pp.134–44

Rowan, M. Ellis *A Flower Hunter in Queensland and New Zealand* Murray, London, 1898

Sabine, E. 'On Periodical Laws discoverable in the Mean Effects of the Larger Magnetic Disturbances' *Philosophical Transactions of the Royal Society of London* 141, 1851, pp.123–39; 142, 1852, pp.103–129

Savours, A. and A. McConnell 'The History of the Rossbank Observatory, Tasmania' *Annals of Science* 39, 1982, pp.527–64

Scherer, Philip 'Death on "The Line"' in *Yearbook of the Lutheran Church of Australia* 1974, pp.26–57

Schulz, Agnes S. *Felsbilder in Nord-Australien* Franz Steiner Verlag, Wiesbaden, 1971

Schulz, J. *Geschichte der australischen Literatur* Munich, 1960

Scott, G. Firth *The Romance of Australian Exploring* Sampson & Low, Marsden & Co., London, 1899

Seelhorst, Georg *Australien in seinen Weltausstellungsjahren, 1879–1881* Augsburg, 1882

Semon, Richard *Im australischen Busch und an den Küsten des Morallenmeeres. Reiseer lebnisse und Beobachtungen eines Naturforschers in Australien, Neu-Guinea und den Molukken* Leipzig, 1903

Shapcott, Thomas 'Developments in the Voyager Tradition of Australian Verse' in Chris Tiffin (ed.) *South Pacific Images* University of Queensland Press, St Lucia, 1978

Sladen, Douglas W.B. (ed.) *Australian Poets 1788–1888; Being a Selection of Poems Upon All Subjects Written in Australia and New Zealand During the First Century of the British Colonization, With Brief Notes on Their Authors and an Introduction by Patchett Martin* Griffith, Farran, Okeden and Welsh, London, 1888

Smith, Bernard *Art as Information. Reflections on the art from Captain Cook's voyages* Sydney University Press for the Australian Academy of the Humanities, 1979

Spencer, B. and F.J.Gillen *The Arunta. A study of a stone age people,* 1927

Spoehr, F.M. *White Falcon: the House of Godeffroy and its Commercial and Scientific Role in the Pacific* [publisher] Palo Alto, Calif., 1963

Stack, John F. (ed.) *Ethnic Identities in a Transnational World* Westport, Conn., 1981

Stanner, W.E.H. *After the Dreaming* The 1968 Boyer Lectures, ABC, Sydney, 1969

—*White man got no dreaming. Essays 1938–1973* Australian National University Press, Canberra, 1979

Stein, T. *Patrick White: "Voss"* Munich, 1983

Stevens, Bertram (ed.) *An Anthology of Australian Verse* 2nd edn. Angus & Robertson, Sydney, 1906

Stewart, Douglas *Voyager Poems* Jacaranda Press, Brisbane, 1960

Stolz, Johann Julius 'Carl Strehlow. Aranda Missionary at Hermannsburg, Finke River, Central Australia. A Life and Character Sketch' in *Auricht's Book Almanac (Australian Lutheran Almanac)* Adelaide, 1924, pp.114–19

Stormon, E.J., S.J. (tr. and ed.) *The Salvado Memoirs. Historical Memoirs of Australia and particularly of the Benedictine Mission of Nova Norcia and the Habits and Customs of the Australian Natives* University of Western Australia Press, Perth, 1977 (orig. publ. 1851)

Stow, Randolph *Midnite: The Story of a Wild Colonial Boy* Bodley Head, London, 1984

Strang, Herbert (ed.) *The Romance of Australia: Its Discovery and Colonization-Adventures of its Explorers and Settlers* Henry Frowde and Hodder & Stoughton, London, n.d.

Strehlow, Carl *Galtjintana pepa Kristianirberaka Moontale* (Teaching papers/book for Christians at Moonta) Hermannsburg, 1891

—*Testamenta Marra. Jesuni Christuni ngantjani jaura ninaia kiritjimalkana wonti dieri jaurani. J.G. Reuter, C. Strehlow, jaura jinkinietja wulana* (The New Testament. Praying to Jesus Christ, it was translated into the Dieri language by the two pastors J.G.R. and C.S.) Gedruckt für die Ev. Luth. Immanuel Synode in Australien v. G. Auricht, Tanunda, 1897

—*Galtjindinjamea-Pepa. Aranda wolambarinjaka. Nana intelelamala Carl Strehlow* (Instruction papers/book for Child Congregations) Carl Auricht, Tanunda, 1904

—'Einige Sagen des Arandastammes in Zentral-Australien' *Globus* 92, 1907, pp.123–26

—*Die Aranda- und Loritja-Stämme in Zentral-australien* (Veröffentlichungen aus dem Völker-Museum, Frankfurt am Main, herausgegeben von der Direcktion) 5 vols, Baer, Frankfurt, 1907–1920: vol. 1: *Mythen, Sagen und Märchen des Aranda-Stammes* bearbeitet von Moritz Freiherrn von Leonhardi, 1907; vol.2: *Mythen, Sagen und Märchen des Loritja-Stammes. Die totemistischen Vorstellungen und die Tjurunga der Aranda und Lortija* bearbeitet von Moritz Freiherrn von Leonhardi, 1908; vol.3: *Die totemistischen Kulte der Aranda- und Loritja-Stämme* 2 parts, 1910, 1911; vol.4: *Das soziale Leben der Aranda- und Loritja-Stämme* 2 parts, 1913, 1915; vol.5: *Die materielle Kultur der Aranda-und Loritja-Stämme. Mit einem Anhang: Erklärung der Eingeborenen-Namen* 1920

—'Einige Bemerkungen über die von Dr. Planert auf Grund der Forschungen von Missionar Wettengel veröffentlichte Aranda-Grammatik' *Zeitschrift für Ethnologie* 90, 1908, pp.698–703

—*Intalinja Nkenkalabutjika Galtjeritjika* (Papers written for teaching) Adelaide, 1920

—'Aborigines of Central Australia—Interesting Questions' *Adelaide Register* 7 December 1921

—*Pepa Araqulinja. Aranda katjirberaka. Nana intelelame Carl Strehlow, galtjindadnindanala* (Old Testament for Children written by C.S., teacher) Tanunda, 1928

Strehlow, T.G.H. *Aranda Traditions* Melbourne University Press, 1947

—*Journey to Horseshoe Bend* Angus & Robertson, Sydney, 1969

—*Songs of Central Australia* Angus & Robertson, Sydney, 1971

Sumner, Ray, 'Amalie Dietrich and the Taipan' in *New Beginnings. The Germans in New South Wales and Queensland* Stuttgart, 1983

—Amalie Dietrich in Australia, PhD thesis, University of Queensland, 1985

—'Amalie Dietrich and Queensland Botany' in *People, Place and Pageantry*, Brisbane History Group Papers No.6, 1987

—'Amalie Dietrich. A German Naturalist in Queensland' in *The German Presence in Queensland* University of Queensland Press, St. Lucia, 1988

Tampke Jürgen 'Pacesetter or Quiet Backwater? German Literature on Australia's Labour Movement and Social Policies, 1890–1914' *Labour History* 36, May 1979, pp.3–17

—(ed.) *Wunderbar Country* Hale and Iremonger, Sydney, 1982

—'Amateurs analyse Australia. Some Comments on the Reiseberichte about the Fifth Continent before 1914' in Voigt *New Beginnings* 1983

Tipping, Marjorie 'Portrait of William Buckley, attributed to Ludwig Becker' *La Trobe Library Journal* 1, 1, 1955, pp.87–91

—*Eugéne von Guérard's Australian Landscapes* Lansdowne Press, Melbourne, 1975

—'Becker's portraits of Billy and Jemmy (Tilki)' *La Trobe Library Journal* 6, 22, 1978, pp.1–7

—*Ludwig Becker, artist and naturalist with the Burke and Wills Expedition* MUP, Melbourne, 1979

—*An Artist on the Goldfields* Currey O'Neill, Melbourne, 1982

—*An Australian Song: Ludwig Becker's Protest* Greenhouse, Melbourne, 1984

Turnbull, Henry *Leichhardt's Second Journey: A First-Hand Account* Halstead Press, Sydney, 1983

Veit-Brause, I. 'German–Australian relations at the time of the Centennial International Exhibition, Melbourne, 1888' *Australian Journal of Politics and History* 32, 1986, pp.201–216

—'Australia as an "object" in nineteenth century world affairs' *Australian Journal of Politics and History* 34, 1988, pp.142–59

—*Enemy Aliens, Internment and the Homefront Experience in Australia, 1914–1920* University of Queensland Press, St Lucia, 1989

Vietta, Silvio (ed.) *Romantik in Niedersachsen: Der Beitrag des protestantischen Nordens zur Entstehung der literarischen Romantik in Deutschland* Olms, Hildesheim, 1986

Voigt, J. *New Beginnings. The Germans in New South Wales and Queensland* Stuttgart, 1983

Walker, R.B. 'German-Language Press and People in South Australia, 1848–1900' *Journal of the Royal Australian Historical Society* 58, 2, 1972, pp.121–40

Webb, Francis *Collected Poems* 2nd edn. Angus & Robertson, Sydney, 1977

Webster, E.M. *Whirlwinds in the Plain* Melbourne University Press, 1980

White, Patrick *Voss* Longman's, London, 1957

—'The Prodigal Son' *Australian Letters* 1, 2, 1958, pp. 37–40

—*Flaws in the Glass. A Self-Portrait* Jonathan Cape, London, 1981; Penguin, Ringwood, Vic., 1983

Whitelaw, Bridget *Australian Landscape Drawings 1830–1880* National Gallery, Melbourne, 1976

Wiederkehr, K.-H. 'Die Hamburgische Seefahrt und die Einführung der meteorologisch-geophysikalischen Navigation' *Zeitschrift des Vereins für Hamburgische Geschichte* 73, 1987, pp.1–26

Wiederkehr, K.-H. and W. Schröder 'Georg von Neumayers geophysikalisches Projekt in Australien und Alexander von Humboldt' *Gesnerus* 46, 1989, pp.93–115

Wislicenus, G. (ed.) *Auf weiter Fahrt* vol. 5, Leipzig, 1907

—'Georg v. Neumayers Wirken für die deutsche Marine' *Marine-Rundschau* 20, 1909, pp.840–84

Zainu'ddin, Ailsa 'The Early History of the *Bulletin*' in M. Beever and F.B. Smith (eds) *Historical Studies. Selected Articles. Second Series* MUP, Melbourne, 1967

Ziegler, O.L. *Snowy Saga* Oswald Ziegler, Sydney, 1960

Zöller, Hugo *Rund um die Erde* 2 vols, Cologne 1881

—*Deutsch-Neuguinea und meine Ersteigung des Finisterre Gebirges* Stuttgart, 1891

—*Als Jurnalist und Forscher in Deutschlands grosser Kolonialzeit* Leipzig, 1930

Zuchold, Ernst A. *Dr. Ludwig Leichhardt. Eine Biographische Skizze* Leipzig, 1956

INDEX

References to illustrations appear in italics

Abbott Peak 75, 76
Aborigines, Aboriginal vii, viii, ix, x, xi, 71, 85, 87, *91, 94 , 100, 103, 106,* 101, 158, 185, 193, 229–40, artefacts 54, 64, 96 European attitudes toward 81–2, Adelaide tribe 92, Aranda and Loritja tribes, religion and myths 110, 111, 112, 113, 114, 117, 118, 128–9 Dieri tribe and language 111, Nngarinyin tribe 140,Tati Tati tribe 90, Yarra Yarra tribe 89, Wunambal tribe 140, Kurungali and Banar, Kurungali 141, Kurangara cult 142, Kurangara magic 143, Jinimin cult 145, Tasmanian Aborigines 87, 90, 92 Aborigines' Protection Society 90, Aboriginal Police Corps 92, Victorian Parliamentary select committee on the condition of Aborigines (*1858*) 92, selling of skulls 98, religion 126–9
Adelaide 43, 93, 95, 111, 113, 138, 156, 170, 176, 177, 188, 208 University of 138, 176, 177, Adelaide German Club 185
Adelaide Deutsche Zeitung 7
Adelaide Observer 186
Adler 3
Africa 169
Agadir 5
Agassiz, Louis 86
Albert, Prince of Saxe-Coburg 40
Alice Springs ix, 109
Amsterdam 137
Anning, Mary 59
Anrep-Elmpt, Reinhold Graf 155, 158, 167
Antarctica 3, 19, 49
Arnhem Land 109, 148
Atkinson, Louisa 60
Audouin, Jean-Victor 36
Aurousseau, Marcel 23, 220
Australia, Australian, nationalism x, 179, 182, republicanism 185, colonial rivalry with Germany x, anti-Germanism vii, 65, 69, Irish in 69, Scots in 69, Australian Museum 99, 220, colonial economy 161, 163, wool production 162, Anglo-celtic working class 167, Australian Natives Association 185
Austria 67
Australische Zeitung 178

Bade, Klaus 110–11

Baden-Baden 159
Ballarat 87
Banks, Sir Joseph 81
Barkly, Sir Henry 95
Barnes, A. 114
Bartels, A.H.F. 177
Bartling 29, 30, 31
Basedow, Martin 177
Basędow, Herbert 118
Baudin, Nicolas 82
Bavaria 41, 87
Baw Baws 99
Beaumont, Elie de 36
Becker, Ludwig ix, 40, 97 , 99, 105, education of 83–6, contact with and paintings of Aboriginals 87, 89, 90, 101, gives evidence before Victorian Parliamentary Select Committee on the condition of Aborigines 92, description of Aboriginal physique 92–3, and Great Exploring Expedition 99
Becker, August 86
Becker, Ernst 86
Becquerel, Antoine-C sar 36
Beinssen, Ekkehard 136, 137–8, 139
Bendigo 87, 90
Benecke, Professor, 26
Beher, Ludwig ix
Berlin 158, 159, 223, University of 25, 31, 33, 154, 176, 184
Berndt, Catherine H. 109, 114, 119
Berndt, Ronald M 108, 109, 127
Bischoff, Charitas (née Dietrich) 55, 56, 64, biography of Amalie Dietrich, 58, 60
Biett 37
Biology, development of theories on and effect on Aborigines 82–3
Bismarck, Otto von 190, 214
Blandowski, Wilhelm 40, 96, 98–9
Bleasdale, Reverend John 98
Blight, John 216
Blumenbach, Johann Friedrich 29, 30, 31, 82, 90
Boehme, Jakob 203
Bogenhausen Observatory 42
Bois de Bologne 159
Bonn, University of 176
Bopp, Franz 25–6, 200
Boyd, Ben 199
Boyd, Martin 212

Brisbane 56, 64, 157
Brisbane, Thomas 42
Britain, British vii, 164, 179, British Association for the Advancement of Science 44, 49, 87, 92, colonialism 156, 166, British Museum 60, 68, Boer War 192, deterioration of Anglo-German relations 193–5
Broken Hill 161
Broome 138, 145
Brongniart, Adolphe 35
Brongniart, Alexandre 35
Brooke, Rupert 5
Brussels 159
Buckley, William 87
Bulloo River 102
Bunce, Daniel 197, 206, 214
Burdekin, Mrs 200
Buring, Leo 178
Buring, Thomas 177, 178
Burmeister, Hermann 22, 32
Burton, Sir Richard 5
Burke, R. O. ix, 6, 16, 45, 86, 205, 207, 215
Buttrose, Larry 217
Buvelot, Louis 107
Byron, Lord 104, 200, 205

Cadell, Captain Francis 89
Calaby, J.H. 114, 115, 116
Canberra 113, 208
Cape Catastrophe 199
Cape Flattery 199
Cape Manyfold 199
Cape Tribulation 199
Carlyle, Thomas 205
Carter, Paul 198, 200
Catholic Church, Clergy 70, and Aborigines 145, Jesuits 129, 130
Chevalier, Nicholas 95, 96, 107
Chevreul, Michel Eugène 36
Chewings, Charles 119
China, Chinese 71–2, 193
Christchurch 67
Chisholm, Alec H. 214
Clarke, Andrew 93
Clarke, W.B. 221
Clarke, W.B. Rev 221
Coghlan, T.A. 172
Columbus, Christopher 213
Cook, Captain James 81, 197, 206, 213
Cordier, Pierre-Louis 36
Cotton, Catherine D. 214, 219
Cracow 99
Curr, Edwin M. 116

Dallachy, John 11
Dampier, William 81, 204
Darling River, 96, 97, 98
Darwin 208

Darwin, Erasmus 204, 210
Dawson, James (and family) 95, 116
Denison, Lady, 87
Denison, Sir William 87
Denmark, 42
Devaney, James 214
Diderot, Denis 131
Dietrich, Amalie viii, early life 55, travels in Europe 55–6, first visit to Australia 56, work in Australia 64–5, awarded for efforts 60
Dietrich, Wilhelm 55, 56, 57, 61
Dirksen 32
Dixon Library, Sydney 219
Dove, Heinrich Wilhelm 47
Drake-Brochman, F.S. 4
Dresden, Botanical Society 62
Duffy, Charles Gavan 93
Dufrènoy 36
D''urer, Albrecht 85
Durkheim, Emil 118, 120
Dutch 137

Eades, Dr Richard 98
Eden, Charles 206
Edward viii, King of England 5
Ehrenburg, Christian Gottfried 34
Ehrlich, L. 118
Eldershaw, M. Barnard 214
Elkin, A.P. 113, 119
Ellery, R.L.J. 52
Esson, Louis 207
Ewald, Georg August 200
Ewald, Georg Heinrich 28
Ewers, John. K. 212
Eylmann, Erhard 118
Eyre, Edward 206, 215

Fahey, Diane 215
Faraday, Michael 44
Fawkner, John Pascoe 93
Fichte, Johann Gottlieb 26
Flagstaff Hill 41, 44
Flagstaff Observatory 41, 48, 50
Flinders, Matthew 204
Flinders Ranges 7
Forrest, John 18, 206
Forster, Georg 131
Fox, Douglas 138
France, French 69, 82, 154, 188, 189, 222
Franco-Prussian War 189, 190, 191
Frankfurt 112, 137, 138, 184
Frazer, James 116, 118
Freud, Sigmund 3, 118
Friedrich August II, King of Saxony 62
Friedrich, David Caspar 85
Frobenius, Leo 135, 136, 137, 142, Frobenius Expedition 135–6, 139, 148,

Frobenius Institute 135, 139, 149

Gans, Eduard 32
Garke, Christian August Friedrich 62
Gauss, Carl Friedrich 49, 50
Gay-Lussac, Joseph Louis 36
Geelong 87, 89
Gennep, A. van 117, 120
Germany, 175–6, 178, German 69 136–7, 155–6, 162 community in Australia x, 164, 'identity' and loyalty of 179–91, Australian patriotism of x, 40, 178, 180, 194, republicanism of 187–8, German Naval Observatory 41, attitudes to Aborigines 71, 82, Nazi organisations 137, colonialism 154, 156, 169, 172, national identity 165, 171, 172, 182–3, cultural superiority 167, working class 165, 171, German Club, Adelaide 175
Gilbert, John 236
Giles, Edward 205
Giles, Ernest 18
Gill, S.T. 89
Gillen, F.J. 114, 115, 117, 118, 120, 122, 123
Gippsland 102
Gladstone 56
Godeffroy, Johann Cäsar VI 44, 47, 56, 61, 63–4
Goethe, Johann Wolfgang von 85, 86, 105, 135, 179, 205, 223–4
Gordon Downs 149
Gosse, Edmund 205
Gottingen 224 University of 27, 28, 32, 49
Gould, Elizabeth 60
Gould, John 96
Grampian Mountains 12
Graz 67, 68
Gregory, A.C. 13,14, 93
Gregory, H.C 13
Griffiths A.W. , 59
Grimm, Jakob 28, 200
Guérard, Eug ne von ix, 83, 84 , 86 education of 83–5, contact with and paintings of Aborigines 87, 89, 101–2, painting of Australian landscape 101–5, *106*
Gulf of Carpentaria 199

Haddon, A.C. 122
Hamburg 42, 44, 47, 54, 155, 159, 184
Harrison, Frederic 206
Harrison, Keith 216
Hartland, E Sidney 120
Harvard University 86
Hay, H.R. 113
Hegel, Georg Wilhelm Frederich 26, 179
Henning, Rudolf 177

Herbart, Johann Friedrich 28, 29, 30–1, 38, 200
Hobart Observatory 49, 50
Hodgson, John 89, 93
Hoker, Sir William 16
Holland 56, 59
Homburg, Herman 177
Homburg, Robert 177
Hooker, Sir William 96
Hope, A.D. 212
Horne, Donald 184
Horseshoe Bend 113
Howard, John 213
Howitt, Alfred 102
Hughes, William Morris 194
Humbolt, Alexander von 22, 23, 43, 47, 51, 60, 82, 83, 86, 87, 96, 179
Hunter Valley 22, 35
Huxley, Thomas 92

India 49
Indonesia, Dutch East India 137
Innsbruck, University of 68
International Trade Exhibitions 160
Italy, Italian 69, 222
Isaacs, F. 200

Jena, University of 176
Jensen, Dr 137
Jugoslavia 67
Jung, Carl Gustav 3, 6, Jungian philosophy 26
Jussieu, Adrien Laurent Henri de 35

Kanaks 193
Kangatong 95
Kant, Immanuel 26, 85, 179
Kaup, Johann Jakob 83, 96
Kelly, Ned 158
Kemp, H. 111
Kendall, Henry 206–7, 208–10
Keysser, Christian 129–32
Kew Gardens 16
Kiel, University of 61
Kimberleys 4, 135, 139, 149
Kingsley, Mary 5–6
Kleist, Gerta 139
Koch, Joseph Anton 85, 104
Kölner Zeitung 177
Kölnische Zeitung 154, 155, 156, 164
Königliches-kaiserliches Hof-Naturalien-Kabinett 60
Kooliatto Creek 102
Kosciusko,Thaddeus 73, 77
Koskinen, Aarne 111
Krefft, Gerard 40, 96, 220

Lachmann, Karl 27

Lake Albina 75–7
Lake Bonney 95
Lake Disappointment 199
Lake Elphington 56
Lake Eyre 111
Lake Salvator 199
Lake Torrens 7, 93
Lake Victoria 95
Lalor, Peter 93
Lamarck, Jean Bapiste 82
Lamont, Johann von 42, 43, 50, 51
Lang, Andrew 114, 115, 116, 117, 120, 122, 123, 124
Langloh-Parker, Katherine 109, 116, 117
La Trobe, C.J. 11
Lawson, Henry 218
Lawson, Louisa 218
Ledenfeld, Robert Ignaz Lendlmayr von viii, early life and career 67–8, views on Australia 69, lectures in Australia 70, account of Australian wildlife 70–1, view of Aborigines and Chinese 71–2, surveys Snowy Mountains region 73–6
Lee, John 44
Leichhardt, Christian 223–4
Leichhardt, Dorchen 223–4
Leichhardt, Ludwig vii, viii, 4, 6, 7, 16, 17, 51, 65, 85, 86, 196, 198–9, *Journal of an Overland Expedition* xi, 201–3, 228, 230–7, 239–40, early education of 23–5, influence of philosophy on 24, 26–7, university education 25–3, 220, studies botany/natural sciences 29, 30, 31, 35, 36, medicine 33–5, attends classes in London and Paris 35–8, 40, and Aborigines 92, 93, 229–40, conception of God 203, and German Reich 213–5, diaries of 220–7, travels in Europe 222–4
Leonhardi, Moritz Freiherr von 112, 114, 115, 117, 121, 123, 124
Leske, Everard 110
Leunis, Johannes 62
Lewin, Mrs 204
Lichtenstein, 31, 57
Liebig, Justus von 43
Linnaeus, Carolus 82
Linger, Carl 177, 178
List, Friedrich 42
Löhe, Johann Wilhelm 129
Lommel, Andreas 139, and Aborigines 140–2, Aboriginal culture and art 142–3, 146–8, 149–50
Lommel, Katharina 146
London 159, 184, Royal Society of 46, 49
Ludwig III, Grand Duke of Hesse-Darmstadt 86
Lumholtz, Carl 65

Lutheran Church 111, Lutherans in Australia 25, 85, 109–10, 111, 121, 131–3, 170, 178, 181, Betshesda Station ix, 111, Hermannsburg mission station ix, 109, 110, 112, 113, 118, 123, Hermannsburg Mission Seminary, Lower Saxony, Germany 111
Lynd, R 200, 208
Lynd River 200

Macadam, Dr John 93, 98, 102
Macainish, Noel 216
Macarthur, James 77
Mackay 56
Mackenzie, Sir Evan 199
Magdeburg 176
Magnus, Heinrich Gustav, 32
Malinowski, B. 118
Mann, John F. 30
Mathew, J. 117
Mathews, R.H. 117
Maury, Mathew Fontaine 44, 47
Maximilian II, King of Bavaria 43
Maynard, Lesley 148
McCarthy, F.D. 114
McCoy, Frederick 44, 96, 98
McLeod, Don 146
McNally, Ward 110
Meggit, M.J. 114
Melanesia 137
Melbourne x, 17, 43, 44, 47, 50, 52, 67, 69, 72, 89, 90, 95, 96, 99, 154, 157, 159, 164, 166, 208, Melbourne observatory 87, Philosophical Institute 96, 99, University 98, 114
Meredith, Louisa 60
Merian, Maria Sibylla 59
Meyer, Heinrich Adolf 61
Micha, Franz Joseph 149
Mitchell, David Scott 221
Mitchell Major Thomas 4, 90, 204, 214, 220
Mitchell Library, Sydney 30, 219, 220, 221
Mitscherlich, Eilhardt 32
Molloy, Georgina 60
Mörlin, Charles 52
Moreton Bay 22, 43, 221
Moroka River 102
Mountford, Charles P. 108, 124,
Mount Clarke 75
Mount Bogong 71
Mount Buller 11
Mount Deception 199
Mount Despair 220
Mount Desperation 220
Mount Gambier 12
Mount Hope 199
Mount Hopeless 220
Mount Kosciusko ix, 73, 75 -77

Mount Lofty Ranges 7
Mount McConnel 200
Mount Nicholson 199
Mount Townsend ix, 73–7, 74 ,75
Muecke, Carl Wilhelm Ludwig x, 170, 175,
    early life and education 176, and educa-
    tional reform 178, and Australian national-
    ism 179–81, German consciousness and
    Australian nationalism 179–91, attitudes
    towards aborigines 185
Mühlmann, W.E. 119
Müller, Carl Ottfried 28
Müller, Ferdinand Jakob Heinrich von vii,
    7,19, 40, 41, 57, 72, 96, 170, and illness
    8, family and early life 8–10, education
    9–10, moves to Australia 10, early explora-
    tion 12, and Leichhardt 13, 16–8, with
    A.C Gregory's Northern Expedition 14–5,
    Knighthood and Copley medal 19, influ-
    ence on Ludwig Becker 99
Müller, Johannes 34
Müller, Karl August Friedrich Wilhelm 58,
    62
Müller, Max 117
Müller's Peak 73, 74. 75. 76
Multiculturalism 172
Mulvaney D.J. 114
Mulvaney, John 112, 114, 115, 116, 117,
    119, 123
Munich 184, University of 42
Murray River 43, 89, 90, 96, 97, 98,102
Murphy, James 220
Murphy, John 220
Museum Godeffroy 54, 61, 65

Naples 36, 38
Nelle, Cordel 55
Neumayer, Georg Balthasar von viii, 40, 44,
    87, 96, 99–101, 102, 105, 155, early life
    and education 41–3, and German national-
    ism 42, and Deutscher Verin of Melbourne
    (German immigrant society) 46
New Guinea 18, 129, 136, 138, 157, 167
New Hebrides 138
New South Wales 95, 157, 199, 206 Govern-
    ment 70, 73, 77, 81, 172, State Library of
    221
New Zealand 67–8, 104, 162
Nicholson, Charles 199
Nicholson, John 24
Nicholson, Lucy 226
Nicholson, William 24, 29, 31–4, 37, 38, 85,
    200, 222, 226
Nida, Eugene A. 125
North America 162
North, Marianne 59
Northern Territory 109, 112
Novotny, Fritz 104

O'Dowd, Bernard 211
O'Hara John B. 204
Ohm, Georg Simon 31
Omeo 99
Oodnadatta 113
Owen, Richard 96

Paris 158, 159, Ethnographical Society 92,
Parramatta Observatory 42
Paterson, A.B. 211
Peake Range 36
Péron, François 82
Perugino (Vannucci, Pietro) 85
Petri, Helmut 138, 139, and Aboriginal cul-
    ture 143–6
Petri-Oldermann, Gisela 145–6
Pfeiffer, Ida 60–1
Pilker, J. 117
Plains of Promise 199
Point Danger 199
Point Upright 199
Port Augusta 208
Port Essington 4, 22, 220, 221
Port Fairy 90, 95
Port Phillip 87, 92, 206, 209
Port Stephens 36
Poznan 99
Prague 68
Pre-Raphaelites 85
Presbyterian, Clergy 70
Prévost, Constant 36
Prince Regent River 138
Prussia, Prussian 188, 197, 200, 206
Püttmann, Carl 177

Queensland 25, 36, 43, 59, 157, 162, 167,
    170, 171
Queen Victoria 5, 17, 40, 236

Raphael (Santi, Raffaello) 85
Regnier, Edmé de 82
Reichenbach, Heinrich Gottlieb Ludwig 62–3
Reichenbach, Heinrich Gustav 63
Reindl, Karl Joseph 42
Retreat Well 199
Reuter, JG 111
Revolutions, 1848 ix. x, 83, 86, 176, 188
    French 181
Rhotert, Dr. 136, 137
River Oder 223
Robinson, JP 200
Rockhampton 64
Roheim, Geza 118
Rome, German artists in 85
Ross, James Clark 49, 50
Royal Geographic Society 17, 19
Rowan, Kingsley 123
Rowan, Marian Ellis 59

Rümker, Christian Carl 42, 47, 52
Russia 162,

Sabine, Edward 44, 49
St Helena 49
Saint-Hilaire, Isidore 36
Salvado, Dom Rosendo 125
San Francisco 158
Scott, G. Firth 206
Scott, Robert Falcon 5
Schiller, Johann Christoph Friedrich von
    24–5, 85, 96, 200, 201, 205
Schleswig-Holstein 42, 44
Schmalfuss, Carl 201
Schmidt, Wilhelm 117–8
Schomburgk, Richard 177, 178
Schopenhauer, Arthur 26
Schulze, Agnes 139, 148
Schulze, L.G. 111
Schwartz, F.W. 111
Seelhorst, Georg 155, 165, 167
Shelley, Percy 205
Singapore 49
Smith, Bernard 125
Smyth, Robert Brough 44, 45, 52, 116
Snowy Mountains 12, 72
South Africa 4, 192
South America 82, 87, 129
South Australia 43, 93, 95, 109, 111, 123,
    157, 170, 175, 176, 177, 182, 183, 189,
    Museum of 138
Spain, Spainish 154
Spencer, Baldwin ix, 73, 110, 113, 114–5,
    116, 117, 118, 120, 121, 122, 123, 124,
    125, critique of Carl Strehlow 126–7, 128,
    133, 136, 137
Spengler, Oswald 135
Stanhope, Lady Hester 5
Stanner, W.E.H. 126–7
Stawell, Sir William 93
Steffens, Henrik 26
Stewart, Douglas 213
Stolz, Johannes 109, 111
Stow, Randolph x, 196–7, 211
Strauss, David Friedrich 31
Strehlow, Carl ix, 109, 110, 112, 115, 117,
    119, 120, 121, 122, 126, 133, early life
    and education 111, work in Australia
    111–2, influence on other scholars 118
Strehlow, Frieda (née Keysser) 111, 113
Strehlow, T.G.H. 108–9 110, 120–1,
Strutt, William 92, 93, 95, 107
Strzelzski, Graf Paul de ix, 40, 73
Süd Australische Zeitung 178
Stuart, McDouall 205
Sturt, Charles 204, 205, 215, 220
Supple, Gerald. H. 204
Switzerland 222

Sydney x, 69, 70, 72, 157, 158, 159, 208,
    Sydney Museum 67

Tanunda 177
Tanunda Deutsche Zeitung 178, 186
Tasman, Abel 204, 206, 213
Tasmania 87, 90, 93, 95, Royal Society of 87
Thiers, Adolphe 190
Thirsty Sound 199
Tholuck, 31
Thomas, N.W. 117, 120, 122, 123
Threlkeld, LE. 121
Threlfall, Richard 52
Toronto 49
Tower Hill 95
Trade Unions 167
Trbatsch 223, 244
Turnbull, Henry 196, 197, 203, 205, 208,
    214

United States of America 166, 186

Valenciennes 36
Velpeau, Alfred-Armand 37–8
Verlag, Eugen Diederichs 109
Verreaux, Jules 96
Victoria 44, 45, 50, 71, 73, 89, 92, 95, 98,
    157, 158, 159, 161, 162, 177, 204,
    National Gallery of 93, 105, Museum of
    114, 123, Royal Society of 45–6, 101

Wallfahrt, Pauline (Paula) 55
Warburton, Major 16
Webb, Francis 214–5
Weber, Ernst Heinrich 29, 30
Weber, Wilhelm 49, 50
Wentworth, William Charles 210
Western Australia 109 139
White, Patrick viii, xi, 6, 197–8, 215–6,
    228–9, 230–2, 237–40
Wiesbaden 159
Wilhelm I, Emperor of Germany 188
Willkomm, Heinrich Moritz 58, 62
Wills, W. J., ix, 6, 16, 45, 207, 215
Wilson, William Parkinson 44
Worms, A.E. 114, 127
Worsley, Frank 213
Wurm, S.A. 114

Yarra River 89

Zuchold, Ernst 219
Zöller, Hugo x, early life and education 154,
    and German colonialism 154, 156, views
    on Australia 160–5, anglophilia 164, na-
    tionalism, 165, 168, 171, benefits of Aus-
    tralian 'liberty' 165–6, German andEnglish
    culture 167–70, German contributions to
    Australia 170

NOTES ON THE CONTRIBUTORS

Irmline Veit-Brause is Associate Professor in the School of Humanities at Deakin University. Her main areas of interest are history, theory of history and historiography, epistemology in the humanities, national elites, and Australian-German relations.

Gerhard Fischer teaches German Studies at the University of New South Wales. His study *Enemy Aliens: Internment and the Homefront Experience in Australia 1914–1920* was published in 1989. The present contribution is part of larger research project on the 'Forty-Eighter' immigrants and their role within the 19th century German Australian community.

Silke Beinssen-Hesse is a senior lecturer in German Studies at Monash University. Her current research interests include modern German literature and society, German women's writing and women's studies.

R. W. Home has been Professor of History and Philosophy of Science at the University of Melbourne since 1975. He has published extensively on the history of eighteenth-century physics and, more recently, on the history of science in Australia. He is editor of *Historical Records of Australian Science* and is currently preparing a history of the Australian physics community.

Edward Kynaston wrote extensively for the *Nation Revew*. He is the author of the most recent von Müller biogrpahy.

Horst Priessnitz, *Professor für Anglistik*, Bergische Universität, Wuppertal, is an eminent authority on Australian literature, a field in which he has published extensively. He is also the editor of the newsletter *Arbeitsgemeinschaft Australien,* an inter-disciplinary association of scholars, institutions, teachers and students interested in Australia.

Volker Raddatz is a lecturer at the *Anglistische Institute* of the Free University, Berlin. Dr Raddatz, who was tutor at Sydney Universtiy during the early 1980s, is an expert on Australian literature and geography and has published widely in both fields.

Colin Roderick, Emeritus Professor of English at the James Cook University, Townsville, is the author of numerous books on Australian literature. His latest book is the comprehensive Leichhardt biography, *The Dauntless Explorer.*

David Sandeman is Professor of Zoology at the University of New South Wales. He is a neurobiologist, bush walker, scuba diver and friend and colleague of von Lendenfeld's great grandson.

Ray Sumner has written extensively on aspects of Australian history including architecture and the history of science and technology. Her research into Amalie Dietrich was begun as Science/ Humanities scholar at the (then) National Museum of Victoria.

Marjorie Tipping is the author/editor of twelve books, including two major works on Ludwig Becker and two on Eugene von Guérard. Her latest book is the monumental *Convicts Unbound.*

Walter Veit is Associate Professor at Monash University in the Department of German Studies. His teaching, research and publications are in the fields of German literature, general and comparative literary criticism, art history and cognitive theory.